Be a Better Leader

A Situational Guide

By Col (R) Bill Sprayberry

& LTC (R) David Mc Dowell

THE AUTHORS

COL (R) Bill Sprayberry

holds a Bachelor's degree from Carson-Newman University and Master’s degrees from Central Michigan University and Air University respectively. He has over 40 years of leadership experience with more than 28 years Leadership in the United States Army, 10 Years Leadership in the Defense Contracting Industry and 4 years Leadership in Academia. Additionally, he has considerable experience providing volunteer leadership in a wide array of organizations.

LTC (R) David McDowell

holds a Bachelor’s degree from The United States Military Academy at West Point and a Master’s degree from The Ohio State University Fisher College of Business. He has over 30 years of leadership experience with over 21 years Leadership in the United States Army and 10 years Leadership in the Corporate Sector. Additionally, he has extensive experience leading volunteers in a broad range of groups and organizations

FOREWARD

Through the course of researching and writing this book we have had the privilege and pleasure to sit down with and interview leaders of many disciplines. They willingly gave their time because they understand the importance of leadership at all levels in order to achieve enduring results and real success. Some key insights and perspectives from these invaluable interviews are here. You will find other comments and observations sprinkled throughout the book. The concepts they discuss are featured prominently as main themes, lending even more credibility to the need for quality leadership from the top to the bottom of all types and sizes of organizations. Full interviews, along with short biographies of these inspirational people are in Chapter 14 - "What insights can we gain from leaders across different specialties?" Our sincere thanks to each of you!

"Leadership starts with People."

- *Mr. George Simms*

"Leadership is also about ownership of the good and bad."

- *Mr. George Simms*

"Leadership means inspiring people to perform at their very best, bringing all of the technical skills and knowledge to bear."

- *Mayor George McGill*

When choosing advisors and the members of the team closest to you, look at the person's "motive for serving."

- *Mayor George McGill*

"The Leader needs to establish a vision and effectively communicate that to the organization and its employees."

- *Mr. Christopher Kane*

"At a minimum, the leader must deliver results."

- *Mr. Christopher Kane*

"Leadership is ensuring you have built a team culturally aligned with, and emotionally connected to, the vision you have established for your organization and inspiring them to meet the vision."

- *Mr. Ryan Gehrig*

"As you grow to leading larger organizations you have to grow a circle of trust."

- *Mr. Ryan Gehrig*

"It is impossible to achieve true success unless you can inspire others to follow."

- *Dr. Patti Conard*

"Most importantly, Leaders look to cultivate the best in others and this truly inspires others."

- *Dr. Patti Conard*

"A leader must understand their strengths and weaknesses."

- *Dr. Beau Sparkman*

"Good leaders listen more than they speak."

- *Dr. Beau Sparkman*

Contents

Introduction

We choose to go to the moon in this decade and do the other things, not because they are easy, but because they are hard, because that goal will serve to organize and measure the best of our energies and skills, because that challenge is one that we are willing to accept, one we are unwilling to postpone, and one which we intend to win, and the others, too. - *September 12, 1962, speech by United States President John F. Kennedy at Rice University*

Leadership is not about perfection but about authenticity and genuine connection to people. Everyone, without exception, will find themselves leading at some point during their life, regardless of their desire (or lack of) to be there. It doesn't matter if you want to or not. It doesn't matter if you feel qualified or not. It will happen. We are not simply implying you are telling other people what to do. Most people don't want to be told what to do (have you ever seen the TV show "Survivor"?). People are looking to you for inspiration, motivation, connection, energy, skill and vision.

Medal of Honor Recipient Sammy L. Davis was a Private First Class on November 18th, 1967, and at the ripe old age of 19, was violently thrust into leadership.

Disregarding a withering hail of enemy fire directed against his position, he aimed and fired the howitzer which rolled backward, knocking Sgt. Davis violently to the ground. Undaunted, he returned to the weapon to fire again when an enemy mortar round exploded within 20 meters of his position, injuring him painfully. Nevertheless, Sgt. Davis loaded the artillery piece, aimed, and fired.

Read his inspirational story here:
https://www.cmohs.org/recipients/sammy-l-davis

Would you be ready? The organization you lead may be large or small. You may simply be leading yourself. Perhaps, you may find yourself in a place where many are looking to you for guidance and direction. What are you going to do? Leaders are inherently people of ***action***. Most people can solve a problem; however, the greatest difficulty is defining the problem. Many times, that problem is a lack of leadership. This book can be your guide to fixing the lack of leadership. We don't want you to start with a blank page. Use what follows and adapt it to your specific situation or need.

We are offering the Start point! A firm foundation (think of a house built on a rock) empowering you with tools and examples to apply in all circumstances or situations. Our definition of Leadership is transferable to any situation and any size organization. You need to be a practitioner of leadership, not just a student of leadership or a consumer of leadership. If you can't define it, how do you expect to do it?

Over the course of many years, we have read multiple books on the topic of "Leadership". The vast majority of those books come in two general formats:

Some offer a list of qualities, traits or characteristics of a good leader. There is an introduction listing these traits or characteristics along with a brief description and, sometimes, mentioning a famous person or two who may have displayed one of these traits. This is followed by a group of chapters discussing each of the individual traits or characteristics in some detail. Each chapter will explain how this trait is 'relevant' to being a good leader. Former British Prime Minister Margaret Thatcher once said, "Being relevant is like being a Lady. If someone has to tell you, you are; you're not!" The chapter may even detail several famous, or seemingly successful, people who've displayed this trait. This is then followed by a conclusion chapter explaining how if you want to be the best leader, you need all of these traits. However, rarely is there a real example of a single person possessing mastery of all these qualities, traits or characteristics.

The second general format provides a list of people who have experienced success in a leadership position. These may include military people, elected officials, sports figures or others. The first chapter provides a brief introduction to each person and a short description of their success. Notice we used the term "success" not 'Leadership'. It is possible to be successful without being a leader. It happens more often than you think. In this format, the following chapters will zero in on each person mentioned in the introduction and there is much detail about who, what, when, where and how the person achieved success or notoriety. The final chapter concludes with some form of 'compare and contrast' of the people used as examples. We don't find a common thread for the successes of the individuals being discussed. This is because each one is different, with a wide array of experiences, educational backgrounds, religious backgrounds, childhoods, socio-economic backgrounds, et al. It's also possible that they have gained success in different career fields. Remember, we are talking about "Success" and not "Leadership." Achieving success is different for an athlete, politician, student, soldier, etc. Conversely, leadership will often have similarities across disciplines.

Most leadership books and explanations we have encountered use the base terms Leadership, Management and Administration interchangeably or try to change the affixes of these words to make them seem synonymous. Either way, they are simultaneously attempting to make the terms Responsibility and Authority synonymous. They are not!

Below you will find this work's foundational definitions and graphical depictions to help you visualize how these definitions interact.

The first table outlines the definition of Leadership and shows the differences between Leadership, Management and Administration. This same table also provides the differences between Responsibility and Authority. To baseline these concepts, we applied standard dictionary definitions for these words (found in the bibliography near the back of this book) and discovered two things: The word itself is used in its own definition. We felt this was a circular error that must be eliminated. This led us to the definitions in the table. Second, we found these terms were used interchangeably. Again, a circular error requiring elimination if you are going to truly understand 'Leadership'. We want to provide definitions applicable across a Full Spectrum of situations applicable to any size organization or group from self, to an entire country, in the case of the United States today a population of more than 334 million.[1]

Definitions		
Leadership	**Management**	**Administration**
Leadership = Motivating & Positively Influencing **People**	Management = Directing & Influencing **Stuff (Resources)**	Administration = Implementing & Influencing **Function / Process**
President John F. Kennedy Set a vision to motivate and inspire **PEOPLE** in an entire nation to go to the moon.	Johnnie Bryan Hunt Influenced how **Stuff** and **Resources** move within an entire nation.	Steven Paul Jobs produced tools to Influence how **Functions** and **Processes** work around the world.

[1] Census Researchers. " Measuring America's People, Places, and Economy." United States Census Bureau. November 17th, 2023. https://www.census.gov/ - November 17th, 2023.

Leadership is the ability to foster an environment in which people motivate themselves to achieve beyond their own perceived capabilities, and face problems for which there appear to be no simple solutions.	**Management** is bringing the right resources together at the right place and time to achieve the leaders and organizations goals and objectives.	**Administration** is applying stream-lined functions / processes to an organization which facilitate the accomplishment of the leaders and organizations goals and objectives.
Responsibility is the acceptance of blame for all things good, bad or indifferent in the organization.	Responsibility for the entire organization. It doesn't matter if you were present. It doesn't matter if you knew it was happening. It doesn't matter whether you are awake or asleep.	Final **responsibility** can only be held by one person. The leader!
Authority is being empowered with the ability to make decisions based on the responsibility held by the overall leader!	This is a subset of a larger organization. Think of this as specialized sets of an organization (examples may include: Logistics / Human Resources / Communications)	Authority can only be delegated / granted by the overall leader.

- ***Table 1 (Definitions): These are definitions derived by the authors during years of experience. Dictionary definitions are located in the bibliography.***

We also have a graphic showing the relationship between a Leader, Manager and Administrator and exhibits where Responsibility actually resides and how Authority is applied.

Leadership is at the top of the diagram. Simply sitting in the leadership position does NOT make a person a leader! ***You are not a leader if you cannot motivate yourself and / or others.*** Referring to our definition of leadership, there are many examples that can be called upon–even by you–of people who have occupied the formal leadership position; however, they couldn't motivate a thirsty man wandering in the desert to a canteen of water. Later in this book we will discuss weak leaders; they are not leaders at all. They are in a leadership position without a clue.

In Graphic 1, note how Leadership overlaps with Management and Administration. This illustrates two things. First, the Leader needs information from and trust in the Manager and Administrator in order to make cogent decisions. Second, the Manager and Administrator need Authority and some level of autonomy from the Leader in order to be effective. Without this inter-relational trust the Leader will become overwhelmed and the Manager and Administrator will never grow to become the Leader. Tom Peters, author of 'In Search of Excellence'

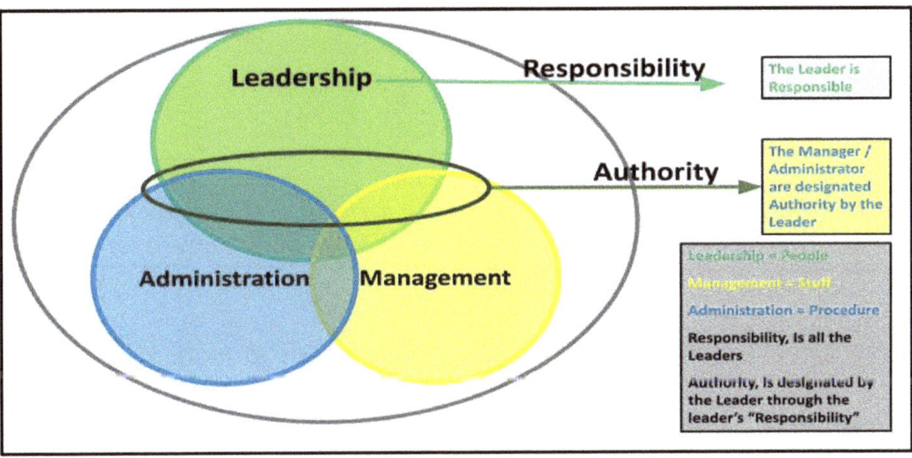

said, "Leaders do not create followers, they create more leaders." The person who aspires to Leadership, that is not everyone, should aspire to be a Leader of Leaders!

- ***Graphic 1 (Venn Diagram): This is a graphic depiction of the relationship between Leadership, Management and Administration, and the Responsibility and Authority for decision making.***

Next, we have a graphic portraying the relationship between Leadership, Management, and Administration and how Responsibility and Authority are applied. As in the previous illustration, Leadership is at the pinnacle since leaders are the driving force. Authority flows to Management and

Administration in order to enable action for the organization. This Authority facilitates decision making on behalf of the Leader and also serves as an opportunity for the Leader to grow more leaders from the Management and Administration ranks of the organization. The Leader may also use stand-alone events or projects to provide this experience and development. As this cycle progresses, the Manager and Administrator gain experience to become Responsible and, ultimately transcend into becoming the Leader. This is a Leader growing Leaders.

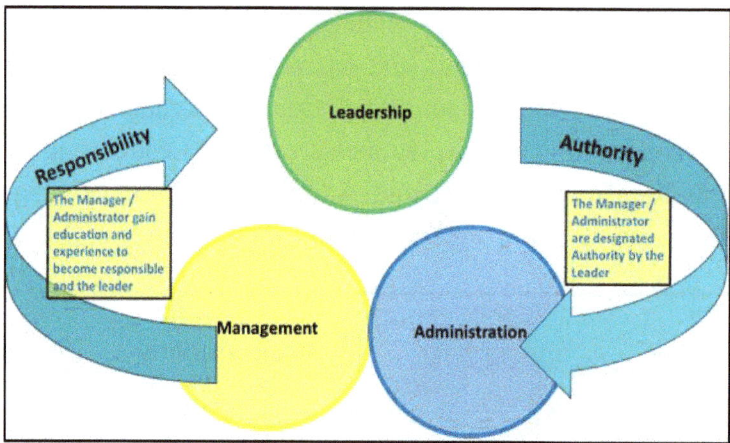

- ***Graphic 2 (Diagram): This is a graphic depiction of the relationship between Responsibility and Authority moving from the holder of one to the other.***

Here, a graphic exhibiting the phases of Leadership growth.

Phase One is Self Leadership. This requires individual personal discipline. In most, if not all situations of self-leadership, there is no one looking over your shoulder to make certain the work is correct or completed in a timely fashion. You are responsible for yourself. This may be a foreign concept to many as you often see people trying to blame others. There is a scene in the movie "The Blues Brothers" (Released by Universal Pictures on June 20th, 1980) in which the character played by the late John Belushi frantically exclaims:

> ***"I ran out of gas, I had a flat tire, I didn't have enough money for cab fare, my Tux didn't come back from the cleaners, an old friend came in from out of town, someone***

stole my car, there was an earthquake, a terrible flood, locusts, IT WASN'T MY FAULT…I SWEAR TO GOD."

When you are the leader, everything is your fault! You are (or should be) responsible for everything that happens or fails to happen.

Phase Two is Tactical Leadership - leading others. This usually starts out in a small setting. It will likely start in a small group of coworkers for a specific effort, students for a group project, or internal to the family. You are accepting responsibility for others. This is also an opportunity to "test" various leadership styles in a smaller group setting. As you gain more confidence and success in your leadership capabilities, the scale of your responsibility may also grow into leading larger, more complex groups.

Phase Three is Operational Leadership - leading leaders at scale. This requires vision and long-term goals and objectives. In this phase you need to be able to match people and skills to teams for the long-term effectiveness of the organization.

Phase Four is Strategic Leadership - mentoring leaders. At this point, your decisions touch every level of the organization. You are not thinking about tomorrow, next week, next month or even next year. Your attention and focus is 5 to 10 years down the road.

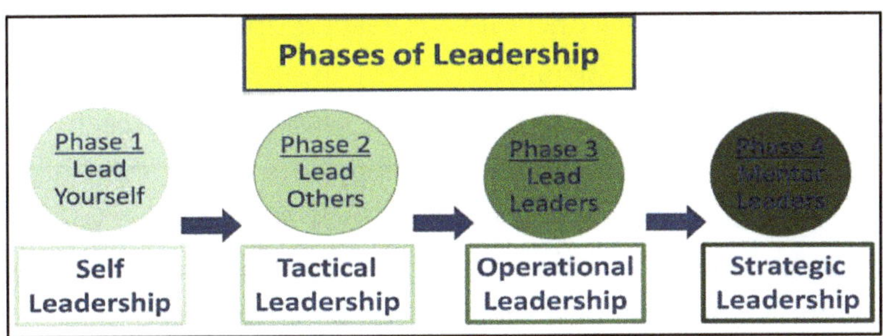

- ***Graphic 3 (Diagram): The Phases of Growing Leaders and Leadership.***

Finally, a graphic to highlight where the vast majority of leaders will spend their leadership time. This is a position where we are a leader and we are simultaneously expected to be followers. The reality is, if we can't follow, how do we lead? I have often heard this adage, "Lead the way you want to be led and follow the way you want to be followed."

This strongly implies several key relational requirements with both our Leader and with those whom we lead. With our leader:

First, get to know your leader! Don't let them surprise you. It's easier to get to know some leaders; however, part of your responsibility is to know that person as well as you can.

Next, once your leader makes a decision and communicates it to you, carry it out as though the decision was yours, even if you don't agree. Those you lead need to have confidence in the actions they are directed to take. If you want to question your leader's decision, do it with your leader one-on-one. Don't question or disagree with your leader in an open forum; would you want those you lead to do this? Also, proactively communicate with your leader. Don't wait for the leader to ask you questions or seek information. Today, this should be easy: text, email, phone call, video chat, teams, etc. Communications can be near instantaneous. Remember: "Bad news doesn't get better with time." Never compromise your integrity, the truth is ***always*** the right answer!

Even a glance at Graphic 4 clearly indicates peer leaders. You need to know your peers and what to expect from them. These peer leaders, like you, achieved their positions with hard work, technical competence and displays of increased potential. Your leader will recognize and appreciate your effort to work with your peers toward common goals and objectives. Don't be inconsistent with the people you lead. They should generally know what to expect and how you will react. I once heard this analogy: If you call a new puppy to you and swat it on the nose every time it comes, it will either stop coming or bite you (I will use this later). Don't risk being bitten by those you lead. If you want people to follow you, you must set an example in followership.

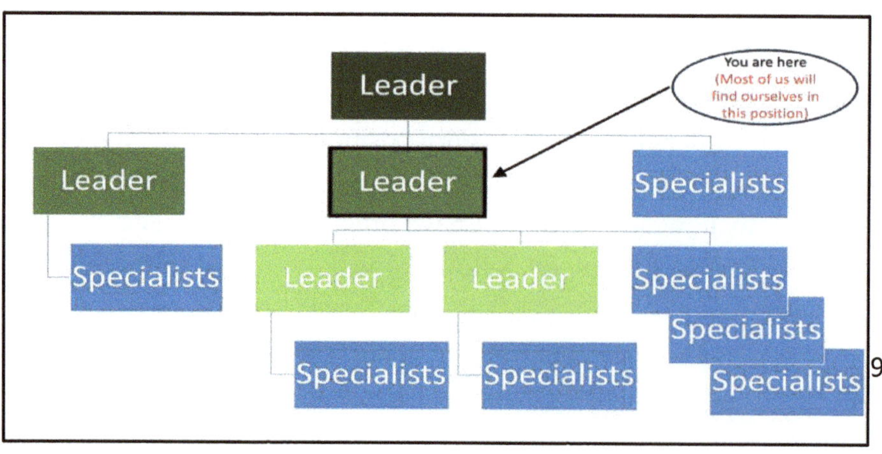

- ***Graphic 4 (Diagram): The vast majority of us will be in a position with a Leader while simultaneously Leading Leaders. Also note, laterally there are peer leaders.***

We know we are not perfect. We are sure there are some who know us and are thinking 'they know nothing.' Yep, we're human. We are certain there are flaws and / or omissions in what follows. As in every situation, there is always someone bigger, stronger, faster, smarter. However, we pose these questions: Are you a "Leader"? Do you want to be a "Better Leader"? Read on!

Chapter 1 - <u>How to progress through the Phases of Leadership?</u>

People don't simply happen upon their positions. You don't pull someone off the street and make them a Company Chief Executive Officer (CEO) or General in the military. They are cultivated over time. They progress through the four basic phases of leadership from "Self Leadership" through "Strategic Leadership". This requires desire, experience, discipline, opportunity, education, learning and some luck.

Chapter 2 - <u>Overview of the Leadership, Management, Administration (LMA) Model.</u>

These terms are used in various environments in how we perceive a person's leadership or management capabilities. One person's definition of a good leader is not necessarily the same as another's. When we discuss leaders or managers, we don't ask, "What specifically about this person makes them a good leader?" While we may not consciously tally those attributes that attract us to a leader, we do remember how a person (leader) made us feel. This is the human connection a leader makes with a "follower"--a sense of positive attributes the leader has imparted upon those he/she has interacted with. That elusive goal of being thought of as a leader steers some into believing that mastering management or administration translates into being a leader. The failure to transition from being a manager or administrator into a leader is often the reason why organizations don't succeed.

Chapter 3 - <u>Responsibility vs Authority.</u>

All authority flows from the leader. When you look at the definitions of these two words, they are clear. In order to accept the mantle of leadership you accept the blame for the good, the bad and the ugly. If you lead an organization that succeeds, you have succeeded. If you lead an organization that fails, you have failed. If you lead a defeated organization, you are defeated as both your responsibility and authority are gone.

Chapter 4 - Self Leadership "If you can't lead yourself, how can you lead others?"

This goes directly to the cornerstone of leadership. This is all about you leading, motivating and taking responsibility for yourself. Phase One of Leadership actually starts with the individual (self-leadership). It is an organization of one! Remember our definition of Leadership = *the ability to foster an environment in which people motivate themselves to achieve beyond their own perceived capabilities, and face (and solve) problems for which there appear to be no simple solutions.* You must lead yourself because you are "Responsible" for you.

Chapter 5 - Communication "Do leaders really communicate or just tell people what to do?" - Learning to communicate with others.

Remember the children's game you might have played at parties? Everyone sits in a circle and the first person whispers a message into the second person's ear. Then the second whispers to the third and so on until the message is whispered to the last person. That last person then says the message out loud as everyone laughs because it is nothing like the original message. Talk about poor communication! It is our experience that positive, cogent communication is one of the key foundational building blocks to leadership and, by extension, problem solving. The most effective leaders know how to and when to communicate.

Chapter 6 - How to Build Trust and to Trust in Others.

Trust doesn't happen overnight. It builds gradually, so don't be pushy or do anything out of the ordinary for your personality in an attempt to build immediate trust. This could have the opposite impact and create distrust. Trust is learned and earned in tough times and maintained in good times. Leadership is about authenticity and genuine connection to people. This is making certain others know your words and actions are not contrived, letting them know you deserve their trust.

Chapter 7 - <u>Leading Others - When is the First Time We Lead Someone Other than Ourselves?</u>

Phases Two and Three (Tactical and Operational Leadership) focuses on leading others and leading leaders. After Self Leadership, chances are the next place to practice your leadership is in a small group setting. Likely among a group of friends, fellow students, sports team, group of volunteers, coworkers or within your family. This is Tactical Leadership. Transitioning to Phase Three of Leadership means you are looking at the systems used by your organization and making certain they are the most effective and efficient for organizational success.

Chapter 8 - <u>"Influential Leadership … It Doesn't Need a Title" (Phase 4)</u>

Leading without a title is, arguably, more challenging than leading in the traditional sense. There is a level of leadership and influence where there may or may not be a title. There is likely no official efficiency report. Think about it, who would write an efficiency report for The President of the United States? There are other forms of evaluation for that position: public opinion, elections, the 25th Amendment, Articles of Impeachment or veto-proof legislation. If you think about it, you can come up with others who don't have a title, yet they exert influence or leadership in an impactful way. These are most often considered the upper tier of the Strategic Level of Leadership; however, you don't need name recognition to be a Strategic Leader. You do need vision and the ability to mentor leaders.

Chapter 9 - <u>"Volunteer Leadership"</u>

Leaders are inherently people of action. This is especially true in volunteerism, where volunteers seek role models to inspire them. Volunteering and the leaders in volunteer situations create unique circumstances and challenges, including rewards and satisfaction. Many believe the volunteer environment is the most difficult and demanding place to lead.

- If you are the leader of volunteers: show respect, give recognition and be humble. The quickest way to stifle volunteerism and lose dedicated people is to be the "my way or the highway" or the "I know better than you" type leader.
- If you are the volunteer, do what you signed up for: be present, be on-time, dress appropriately and be nice (follow the rules, avoid profanity, integrity beyond reproach). No one will want you around, regardless of your good intentions if you can't do these things.

Chapter 10 - <u>Military Leadership</u>

"A man does not have himself killed for a half-pence a day or for a petty distinction. You must speak to the soul in order to electrify him." – Napoleon Bonaparte

The mission of the United States Military is woven into the very fabric of the nation. Article 1, Section 8 of the Constitution instructs the Legislative Branch to "*provide for the common defense*."

Leading in any situation can be challenging. Leading in combat requires enhanced leadership. These leaders embody two distinct roles: one as a member of the "Chain of Command" and the other is "Rank", which is displayed on each servicemember's uniform. The Leaders in the Chain of Command are ultimately responsible for everything that happens or fails to happen within their organization. The Rank of Military Officers–confirmed and commissioned by the US Senate–provides enhanced authority for military leaders. While the military provides a clear line of responsibility and authority, inspiring soldiers to *achieve beyond their own perceived capabilities* becomes challenging when decisions involve life and death. The focus of the military leader becomes how well they develop their subordinate leaders to execute independently.

Chapter 11 - <u>"Does Your Title Make You a Leader?"</u>

Most organizations advance people into leadership positions because they have demonstrated potential for additional responsibility. Remember, being promoted only means your title will change but it doesn't automatically make you a leader. They also fail to realize the responsibility they posses. Some people have been leaders–or in leadership positions–for so long they act infallible.

Chapter 12 - Corporate Leadership, "How Leadership and Management is applied in for-profit organizations."

Nearly 7 in 10 of US employees work in private for-profit organizations.[2]

Regardless of company size, their main goal is to maximize profits and grow company value. "Corporate" leadership requires the ability to set a vision, understand how to apply resources and inspire employees to perform their best–often without that unifying "North Star" we find in the military. But the same traits that make effective leaders in other areas apply in this setting. Becoming a genuine and authentic leader starts with self-development and understanding how to apply your skills for the betterment of your employees and the organization.

Chapter 13 - Leadership Fears: Crippling!!!

Most people are perfectly content to let someone else lead. There are many reasons for this, all of which start with fear, self-doubt or a lack of confidence. In this chapter, we discuss some common fears associated with leadership and why many people shy away from "stepping up" and provide some of the ways to overcome those fears and LEAD!

Chapter 14 - What insights can we gain from leaders across different specialties?

Interviews with Leaders from multiple disciplines revealed key themes:

- ➢ Trust is a must.

[2] Claire McAnaw Gallagher. U.S. Bureau of Labor and Statistics. Spotlight on Statistics. October 2023. https://www.bls.gov/spotlight/2023/for-profit-nonprofit-and-government-sector-jobs-in-2022/ - July 27,2024

- ➢ Creating and communicating vision to the team generates success.
- ➢ Listen to those closest to the work.
- ➢ Know that you don't know everything. You have subject matter experts on your team.
- ➢ Be available and be on time. This is a show of respect to those whom you lead.
- ➢ Lifelong learning is your responsibility to yourself.

Chapter 15 - Summary & Takeaways.

We are all going to lead, even if you're only leading yourself. If we think we're smarter than the people we are leading, don't respect the people we're leading, or are threatened by the people we are leading, we are headed for trouble.

Chapter 1
How do we progress through the Phases of Leadership?

"Great leaders are almost always great simplifiers who can cut through argument, debate and doubt to offer a solution everybody can understand." —Gen. Colin Powell

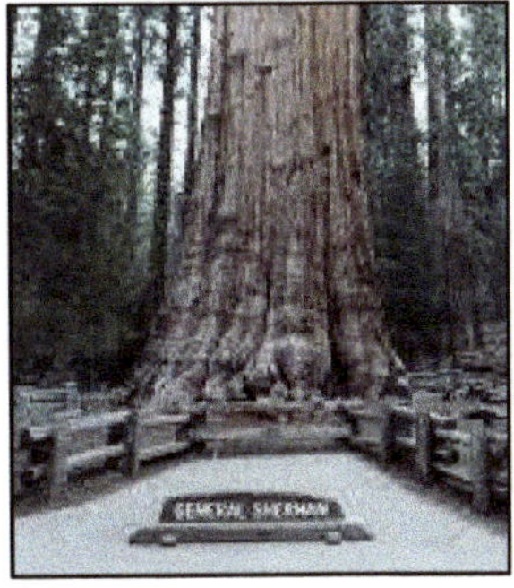

Imagine visiting Sequoia & Kings Canyon National Parks to see the "General Sherman Tree", which is estimated to be around 2,200 years old.[3] To be around for over 2 millennia requires some nutrients, care and even some luck. This tree did not just appear overnight. It needed time to grow.

The same holds true for senior leaders (Strategic Leaders). Some people are born with a healthy propensity to lead. However, these people never reach their full potential without nurturing leadership tendencies (the same for entertainment, science, athleticism, et al).

There are other trees in the world estimated to be even older than the "General Sherman Tree". You can't simply transplant one of those trees to the Sequoia & Kings Canyon National Parks and put a sign in front of it and call it "General Sherman." Just because the other tree is older, doesn't mean it can be considered the same or better suited than the original tree.

---

[3] Sequoia & Kings Canyon National Parks. "General Sherman Tree." December 6, 2023. https://www.nps.gov/places/000/general-sherman-tree.htm - January 19th, 2024.

Also consider the Fortune 500 Company Chief Executive Officers (CEO) whose average age is 57.[4] Think about military Generals or Admirals,[5] averaging over 51 years old.[6] You would have a hard time finding someone on the street of the correct average age, put them in the position, or put a uniform on them, and announce they're now the CEO or the General. These individuals didn't simply happen upon their positions; they were cultivated over time. They progressed through the four basic phases of leadership from "**Self Leadership**" and culminating in "**Strategic Leadership**".This requires desire, experience, discipline, education, learning and yes, some luck.

- ***Graphic 3 (Diagram): The Phases of Growing Leaders and Leadership.***

In the movie "A Bug's Life", Hopper said, "The first rule of leadership: everything is your fault." (Release date: November 14, 1998, Distributed by: Walt Disney Pictures, Walt Disney Studios Motion Pictures). Mayor George McGill of Fort Smith, Arkansas said, "The leader is the one who "carries the weight" (See Chapter 14 - What insights can we gain from leaders across different specialties?). Put another way, the leader is responsible for everything that happens or fails to happen.

Phase One is **Self Leadership**. In this organization of one, you are responsible for ***everything***; Leading, Managing and Administering. This

[4] Walter Loeb. "Fortune 500 Company Chief Executive Officer." January 19th, 2024. https://www.forbes.com/sites/walterloeb/2023/10/20 - January 19th, 2024.

[5] Time Staff. "Army & Navy: The Admirals." © 2019 TIME USA, LLC. https://content.time.com/time/subscriber/article/0,33009,850782,00.html - January 19th, 2024.

[6] U.S. Naval Institute Staff. Department of Defense 2022 Demographic Profile. U.S. Naval Institute News. November 29, 2023. https://news.usni.org/2023/11/29/department-of-defense-2022-demographic-profile - August 26, 2024

requires individual personal discipline and the desire to succeed. You are responsible for yourself. You must hold yourself to the standard you have set. It is important to ensure the standard is not so low that it implies failure; however, you must also ensure it is not so high that the goal becomes unachievable. In this phase, there is room to "fail" and time for "discovery learning" from mistakes. In order to reach Phase Two (Tactical Leadership) and to lead others you must first develop the capability to successfully lead yourself.

The Self Leadership phase demands individual personal discipline. As a self-leader, you're solely responsible for your actions and decisions. You are leading yourself and *fostering an environment where you motivate yourself to achieve beyond your perceived capabilities.* Mastery of self-leadership is a prerequisite for advancing to the next phase. In this leadership phase, you can determine your strengths and weaknesses. This, in turn, sets the stage for you to plan and focus your learning efforts to both overcome or minimize your weaknesses and solidify your strengths. Dave Ramsey said: "The way I see it, you stop growing the moment you stop learning." During the self-discovery phase, your core values are also emerging: what is important to you; what motivates you; what will your work ethic look like; what learning methodologies work best for you. During this phase, you have time to build self-confidence and be not only a leader but also a great team member and contributor. You will also have time to embrace both personal responsibility and the responsibility that comes with the mantle of leadership.

Everyone goes through the Self Leadership phase. There is no set start time or duration for us this phase. It can be very short while some aspects of Self Leadership last a lifetime. Heisman Trophy winner and National Football League great Herschel Walker, was cut from his Junior High School Football team because he was in poor physical condition from a sedentary lifestyle. His classmates also ostracized him because of a speech impediment. To overcome these, even at an early age, he led himself. First, "he began a regimen of push-ups and sit-ups. He did chin-ups while hanging from a tree in his backyard." Second, "each day, he sat in front of a mirror and read aloud to himself, determined to defeat the stutter others picked on him for." "When he returned to school the next year for ninth grade, he was the fastest kid in his class. He became the football team's star, leading the school to a state championship in his senior year. He also became the class valedictorian."[7] In order to overcome adversity and become highly successful, Herschel first practiced Self Leadership. There is also some luck involved. A physical injury could have easily derailed his athletic ambitions causing a different outcome. Self Leadership is a skill he–and you–will use for the rest of your life. Chapter 4 (Self Leadership "If you can't lead yourself, how can you lead others?" goes into more detail about Self Leadership.

Phase Two is **Tactical Leadership** - leading others. The keys to this phase of leadership are being present, engaging in effective one-on-one communication and receiving and implementing vision and guidance from the next level leader. This usually starts out in a small setting, examples include: youth sports; a small group of coworkers for a specific effort; students for a group project; internal to the family; or a team part of a larger organization. If you are a Tactical Leader, you are in routine direct contact with those you lead. This phase builds on the skills and personal development from Phase One. Most organizations promote based on successful prior performance and a display of potential for additional responsibility. Moving to Phase Three (Operational Leadership) means you have "mastered" the concepts presented in Tactical Leadership.

In this phase you are advancing from being an individual contributor to leading others by leveraging their skills for the good of the group or organization. You establish roles and responsibilities for individual team members and give feedback regarding their performance and

---

[7] Drew Brooks. "Herschel Walker shares his story with Bragg troops." The Fayetteville Observer. Feb. 20th, 2018. https://www.fayobserver.com/story/news/military/2018/02/21/herschel-walker-shares-his-story-with-bragg-troops/14159338007/ - January 19th, 2024.

development. You should also build trust (Chapter 6 - How to Build Trust and Trust in Others.) with your team and your direct leaders. You are gaining experience with responsibility for day-to-day actions and requirements while also assessing and making recommendations about the future of the organization.

Advancing to Tactical Leadership means you are ready and willing to accept the responsibility for others' performance and, in many cases, their training and well being. You are taking the vision and guidance of Operational / Strategic Leadership and putting it into action with an expectation of success. You should gain confidence in your ability to coach, teach and mentor your team while establishing a stronger professional relationship with each member. You should also be increasing your knowledge and skills as a communicator while concurrently learning what works best for you and working to improve your development areas. In our interview with Mr. Ryan Gehrig (See Chapter 14 - What insights can we gain from leaders across different specialties?) he noted "Most leaders want better oratory skills."

During all phases you should continue to proactively be a *Lifelong learner*. This includes taking advantage of formalized training generated by the organization and community. A more detailed look and examples of formalized training and education will be part of the discussion related to Phase Three. (Chapter 7 - "Leading Others - When is the First Time We Lead Someone Other than Ourselves?" has more information about leading small groups.)

Phase Three is **Operational Leadership** - leading leaders at scale. This requires vision and the identification and establishment of long term goals and objectives. In this phase you must be able to match teams to goals, objectives and strategies for the long term effectiveness of the organization. You are able to identify subordinate leaders to whom you can delegate and have a high assurance for success. You are now at the level where you establish and enforce priorities for the application of resources. You are providing guidance and direction to subordinate leaders and teams. In order to accomplish this, you must be able to effectively employ multiple forms of communication (See Chapter 5 - Communication "Do leaders really communicate or just tell people what to do?" - Learning to communicate with others.). You should be determining the needs of your organization. You should hire and cultivate the right people to meet those needs. Operational Leaders are responsible for obtaining and maintaining organizational results (see Mr. Christopher Kane's interview in Chapter 14 - What insights can we gain from leaders across different specialties?). At this leadership level, you are looking at the systems used by your organization and making certain they are the most effective and efficient for success.

You are focused on the future by ensuring your vision is nested within the vision of the Strategic Leader. For your organization to remain competitive and effective, change is required. The Greek philosopher Heraclitus is credited with the idea that change is the only constant in life.

Remember the "Blockbuster" video rental stores? In the late 1980s and 1990s, this company brand was a household word. The first of those stores opened in 1985. 14 years later, there were 6,000 Blockbuster stores nationwide. At their height in 2004, they had nearly 9,000 stores but a new competitor was also on the rise. Netflix entered the market with a different model that challenged Blockbuster's dominance. In 2010 Blockbuster filed for bankruptcy. They failed to embrace emerging video technology and did not change quickly enough.[8] Having a clear vision with the ability to drive and implement the vision can generate positive change and ensure the health and success of your organization far into the future.

Ford Motor Company was founded in 1903 by Henry Ford and 11 associate investors. They've been around ever since. Mr. Ford established a strong and enduring company

ckbuster: The rise and Fall." https://www.businessinsider.com/rise-and-fall-of-blockbuster - January 20th, 2024.

vision of improving the customer's driving experience. This vision would be tested as 200 car manufacturers existed in 1920.[9] To remain competitive (and in business), Ford lowered costs by implementing interchangeable parts and expanding operations into international markets. These actions, along with improving the company's internal processes under the leadership of Henry Ford's grandson Edsel Ford III required innovation, forward thinking and adaptation to a changing world. These steps have enabled them to remain a market leader one century later–especially when compared to similar companies no longer in operation (Pontiac, Mercury, Plymouth, Studebaker, and hundreds of defunct car manufacturers).

Leader Development and Professional Training:

In Phase One (Self Leadership), you learn to become a lifelong learner. Your leader development and training are most often self-generated. If you are part of a larger organization, there may be some formal development and training opportunities. In Phases Two (Tactical Leadership) and Three (Operational Leadership), most organizations offer or even require formal professional development and training. If you are a leader in Phase Three you will likely have some input into those requirements and, if you are a leader in Phase Four you will not only have input into formal professional training requirements but also be directing leader development.

Trades:

Most trades and professions have formal educational and training programs. My wife had a 30+ year career as a Registered Nurse and her profession also had routine educational and professional development requirements. Today we have information at our fingertips. You can quickly and easily research the needs and requirements in your trade or profession. Remember, leadership and leading leaders don't happen overnight. Leaders are grown with experience and education. If you are a tradesperson (examples include: carpenter, electrician, plumber, etc.)

---

[9] Tefi Alonso. "How Ford Adapted To The Changing Automobile Market." February 9, 2023. https://www.cascade.app/studies/ford-strategy-study - March 6, 2024.

there are progressive levels including apprentice, journeyman, master craftsperson.

Apprentice –
An apprenticeship is an arrangement in which you get hands-on training, technical instruction, and a paycheck—all at the same time. Apprentices work for a sponsor, such as an individual employer or a business-union partnership, who pays their wages and provides training. Formal apprenticeship programs usually last about 4 years, depending on the employer or occupation, although they may take as little as 12 months or as many as 6 years. Many of these programs are registered with the U.S. Department of Labor (DOL). At the end of a registered apprenticeship program, apprentices get a nationally recognized certificate of completion as proof of their skills.[10] Once the apprenticeship ends, you should be technically proficient and have a good sense of your strengths and development areas.

Journeyman –
After you complete an apprenticeship, you can become a journeyman. This usually requires 8,000 hours of On-The-Job-Training (OJT) and formal classroom training. Journeymen typically report to a master tradesperson like a master craftsperson. Journeymen possess required licenses and skills needed to perform their job well. Journeymen often diagnose issues and identify problems within the equipment they're working on, so they must possess strong problem-solving skills. Journeymen often need a strong attention to detail, since many journeymen's duties require working with precise measurements or dangerous equipment. Journeymen typically work on a team with other journeymen within their trade, so it's important that they possess excellent communication skills. Journeymen train to use specialized equipment while working, so it's important that they have strong

[10] Elka Torpey. Apprenticeships: Occupations and outlook. U.S. Bureau of Labor and Statistics.
https://www.bls.gov/careeroutlook/2017/article/apprenticeships_occupations-and-outlook.htm - January 20th, 2024

technical skills that allow them to handle the equipment safely and effectively.[11]

Perfect Practice Makes Perfect.
In order to become the "best" in a certain field or industry, the amount of practice and development matters. One often cited example is how a relatively unknown and obscure musical band grew to become one of the most influential bands of all time, The Beatles. After forming in 1962 in Liverpool, England the band failed to gain traction in the local music scene. They decided to move to Germany and played in small clubs and bars–honing their creativity, writing songs, and working closely as a team for years. With over 1,200 performances and more than 10,000 hours of rehearsals, practices, sound checks, writing and live shows, The Beatles became Master Craftsmen in their profession and are one of the most recognizable and well known bands of the 20th century.[12]

Master Craftsperson –
A journeyman transitions into a master craftsperson after gaining extensive experience and applying their skills consistently. Masters supervise journeymen to ensure they are completing their work in an efficient and safe manner. You can qualify for a master exam after you've logged 4,000 hours of working experience in your trade.

Public Schools, for example, have Novice Teacher Programs, for new and probationary teachers, lasting two - three years including formal instruction, self-paced on-line requirements and classroom observation with written feedback by experienced teachers. Every state has some form of ongoing annual educational requirement. One state actually requires 180 hours per year of continuing education contact hours for educators. Many school districts provide formal continuing education

[11] Indeed Editorial Team. What is a Journeyman? Indeed. August 8th, 2022. https://www.indeed.com/career-advice/career-development/what-is-a-journeyman - January 20th, 2024
[12] Jennifer Seeley and Cam Beard. 10,000 Hours & The Beatles. Athletes Lab Articles. Feb 4th, 2022. https://www.athleteslab.org/articles-by-a-lab/10000-hours-the-beatles - March 5th, 2024

opportunities. In many areas of the country, multiple school districts are members of centralized "Educational Service Cooperatives" providing formal opportunities for educators that are state approved and encouraged by school and district administrators. Technology allows states to provide an online cafeteria style lineup of opportunities to meet the teacher's educational requirements. It should be recognized that in most school districts and states, teachers are not paid for the time they spend meeting these annual continuing education requirements. Yes, we shamelessly and positively recognize teachers for what routinely goes unnoticed. Many public schools also conduct Professional Learning Communities (PLCs). These are teams of educators who share ideas to enhance their teaching practice and create a learning environment where all students can reach their fullest potential (*fostering an environment where people motivate themselves to achieve beyond their perceived capabilities*). Most PLCs operate within a school building, across a district or along the lines of the subject (Math, Science, Social Studies, English).

Corporate Training Programs:
Many companies offer both employee (individual) and leadership / management training, often using a mix of instructor led, virtual, and self-paced instruction. In many cases, formalized leadership training is not offered until you become a manager.

For individual contributors, training is designed to ensure the individual can perform their job more effectively. Individual skills development often includes understanding the business, organizational processes and tip to improve your ability to support the business. This training upskills the individual to being more productive. In addition, self-development opportunities are available to sharpen your own skills, set your career path and improve other administrative tasks. Like the education and military industries, many companies offer professional certificates (technical, college, advanced degrees) and may even cover associated costs.

For managers and leaders, companies create dedicated programs to train them–regardless of experience level–with access to a suite of learnings The training ranges from self-leadership to strategic leadership. Training development for leaders and managers is predominantly focused on Administration and Management. Most topics covered are team building, talent development, coaching for impact, driving performance, empower the team, foster feedback, guide careers, and set clear direction. As we've noted before, growing into a Strategic Leader requires a desire to expand your capabilities by being a Lifelong Learner–enhancing what your company or organization offers.

Companies also offer generalized training to help individuals and managers with personal development goals. In addition, they are designed to improve your daily productivity. These include interpersonal skills, effective use of technology, and presentation skills.

Military Development Programs:

The military has extensive formal education and training programs for Officer and Non-Commissioned Officers (NCOs) designed to enhance leadership throughout the career of military members and strengthens our entire force regardless of the term of service, 4-years or 30-years, of individual members. In addition to the technical skills (e.g. Infantry, Field Artillery, Quartermaster, etc) each Officer and NCO receives, military development programs are a career-long study of leadership. This introduces the concept of "Leadership as a profession" or the continual commitment to improving each individual's ability to lead and develop others.

Each service (Army, Navy, Air Force, Marine Corps) has a formal development program. For enlisted soldiers, the Army calls it the Non-Commissioned Officers (NCO) Professional Development System, which provides lifelong learning and development.[13] This includes chronologically:

Basic Leaders Course (BLC) - a branch or specialty immaterial course providing basic leadership training. BLC provides soldiers an opportunity to acquire the leadership skills, knowledge, and experience needed to lead a team-sized unit (Tactical Leadership).

Advanced Leaders Course (ALC) - a branch or specialty-specific course providing soldiers selected for promotion to Staff Sergeant (E-6) an opportunity to enhance leadership, technical skill, tactical expertise and experience needed to lead squad-size units (Tactical Leadership).

Seniors Leaders Course (SLC) - a branch or specialty specific course providing an opportunity for soldiers selected for promotion to Sergeant First Class (E-7) to acquire the leader, technical, and tactical skills, knowledge, and experience needed to lead platoon-size units. This course represents a transition from Tactical to Operational level leadership and focuses on leading leaders of small teams or squads.

Master Leaders Course (MLC) - a branch immaterial or speciality course providing an opportunity for soldiers selected for promotion to Master Sergeant (E-8) to acquire the leader skills required for success at both troop and staff assignments throughout the defense establishment (Operational Leadership).

Sergeants Major Course (SMC) - the capstone of enlisted training. Master Sergeants are prepared for both troop and staff assignments throughout the defense establishment. The SMC is task based and performance oriented. Areas of study include leadership, combat operations, sustainment operations, team building, communication skills, training management, and professional development electives (Operational to Strategic level leadership).

---

[13] United States Army Human Resources Command. December 11, 2023. https://www.hrc.army.mil - January 22nd, 2024.

Along with this formal structure and self development throughout Lifelong Learning, there are many other training opportunities and experiences along the military leadership path.

The Active Duty Officer Career Timeline for the Army is also very structured and includes:

Basic Officer Leaders Course (BOLC) - The attendees are Second and First Lieutenants (O-1 /O-2). The length of this course varies by specialty but is generally divided into two major blocks of instruction: Common Core and Branch or Specialty specific training. Common Core (1-3 weeks) is a general overview and refresher course of basic Army knowledge and skills that all Lieutenants learned from their commissioning sources. Branch or Specialty specific training (4-18 weeks) consists of formal classroom training, practical exercises and field training focused on the specifics of the branch or specialty (Self and Tactical leadership). After this formal training, officers are assigned to the force for several years and gain valuable technical, hands-on, and leadership experience. They also have opportunities for other, shorter duration, formal training opportunities.

Captains Career Course (CCC) - The attendees are predominantly Captains (O-3). The length of this course varies by specialty. Like BOLC, the course is divided into two major blocks of instruction: Common Core and Branch or Specialty specific training. Again, the Common Core (1-3 weeks) is a general overview and refresher course of basic Army knowledge and skills. Branch or Specialty specific training (4-18 weeks) consisting of formal classroom training, practical exercises and field training focused on the specifics of the branch or specialty (Tactical and Operational leadership). After this formal training, officers are again assigned to the force for several years and gain valuable technical, hands-on, and leadership experience. They also have opportunities for other, shorter duration, formal training opportunities.

Army Intermediate Level Education (ILE) - broadly describes the US Army's formal education system for field-grade, mid-career Army officers preparing to serve in staff and command roles. It is the Army's formal education program for senior Captains and Majors. ILE consists of a common core (16 weeks) of operational instruction offered to all Officers and additional education opportunities are tied to the requirements of the Officer's branch or functional Area. The Army determines eligibility to attend resident ILE common core and the 24 week Advanced Operations and Warfighting Course (AOWC) (crosses the spectrum of Tactical, Operational and Strategic leadership). After this formal training, Officers are again assigned to the force for several years where they gain valuable technical, hands-on and leadership experience. They also have opportunities for other, shorter duration, formal training opportunities.

Senior Service College (SSC) - Representatives from all Services and selected government agencies are centrally chosen for attendance in the 10+ month long school. The military students are Colonels, Lieutenant Colonels, or Navy Captains and Commanders with 17 to 23 years' service. They operate at the Operational and Strategic levels of leadership. This course is focused on national security, strategic thought and Strategic Leadership. Graduates are assigned to senior positions in the military and governmental defense agencies.

Phase Four is **Strategic Leadership** - mentoring leaders. At this point, your decisions touch every level of your organization. You are not thinking about tomorrow, next week, next month or even next year. Your attention is focused on 5 to 10 years down the road. You must be able to take a panoptic view of your organization and understand its relationship with other organizations. Your decisions can influence both internally and externally. You mentor others to eventually grow into being strategic leaders. “The difference between a good leader and a great leader is one who learns to anticipate rather than react.” - Craig Groeschel, founder of Life Church. At this phase of leadership your vision predicts and drives the need for change.

Accountability, "the ability, willingness or obligation to take responsibility of one's (or your group's) action"[14] is one of the most powerful motivators for change you can imagine. This is similar to the Leader being responsible for everything that happens or fails to happen in the organization they lead. In the book of Proverbs, Solomon challenged his readers to build accountability into their lives (plans fail when there is no counsel, but with abundant advisors they are established - Proverbs 15:22 ESV). When you reach Strategic Leadership you are responsible for the change in your organization ensuring a successful future. There are many situations with the potential to drive change. Some examples include: technology, political climate, population, and the environment. There are others, of course, but these can be some of the most impactful situations.

Technology - There are inventions you can't deny have changed the world: Printing Press, Wheel, Automobile, Compass, Lightbulb, we can go on.[15] Today, technological advances happen everyday and at a more rapid pace. The most recent concepts are "Artificial Intelligence" and "Machine Learning" (AI/ML). If you are a Strategic Leader you should have already thought about how AI will impact your business or organization, regardless of size. At a minimum, take the time to familiarize yourself with new technology and how it may impact your company's core mission, the marketplace, and your position in the marketplace. If it will have an impact–it most likely will–you are now implementing change to accommodate or take advantage of it. You are looking at and beyond the horizon to see what's coming.

The political climate in the United States and the world is as fluid as the ocean tides. All you have to do is look at the news headlines. Some of those include wars fought along religious or ideological boundaries and not some line on a political map; United States Supreme Court decisions;

---

[14] Merriam-Webster. Accountability. https://www.merriam-webster.com/dictionary/accountability - April 28th, 2024.

[15] Jessica Leggett, Natalie Wolchover. "20 inventions that changed the world." July 19, 2023. https://www.livescience.com/33749-top-10-inventions-changed-world.html - January 23rd, 2024.

climate concerns; whether to legalize or not and many others. How will these impact your workforce, clients, supply chain, or product? How important are these issues to your employees and how do they bring themselves to work? If you are a Strategic Leader, you anticipate issues and make change happen now to survive and thrive.

Population shifts are all in the news today, both internally in the United States and internationally. The fluctuating push / pull factors[16] causing movement of people, forces Strategic Leaders to think about transportation, food, housing, employment, facilities and schools, among other things and how to pay for it all. Does your business, organization, or institution have a stake in these? Strategic leaders are making changes now and taking action.

John Emerich Edward Dalberg-Acton

Environment is not simply the weather or climate. It also includes the prevailing public opinion trend or other aspects of public life.[17] Ask Anheuser-Busch Inbev if they saw it coming.[18] Strategic Leaders who don't embrace change management are likely doomed for failure.

As we look at Strategic Leadership we must also be cognizant of the greatest pitfall. 19th century British politician Lord Acton is credited with saying: "Power tends to corrupt, and absolute power corrupts absolutely." While working on my second Masters Degree I was told by a college professor that "being educated only makes you educated, it doesn't make you smart." We can apply the same rationale to leadership. Being successful only makes you successful, it doesn't make you a leader. Being elected only makes you

[16] Mario Bruzzone. "Understanding Migration: Why "Push Factors" and "Pull Factors" Do Not Explain Very Much." https://refugees.org/wp-content/uploads/2020/12/7.27.20-Policy-Brief.pdf - January 23rd, 2024.

[17] Cambridge University. Cambridge University Press & Assessment 2024. https://dictionary.cambridge.org/ - January 23rd, 2024.

[18] The Associated Press. Bud Light brewer is still reeling from trans promotion backlash as U.S. revenue tumbled 13%. October 31st, 2023. https://fortune.com/2023/10/31/bud-light-earnings-dylan-mulvaney-transgender-promotion-backlash/ - 28 April 2024.

elected, it doesn’t make you a leader. Being promoted to the highest position only makes you promoted, it doesn’t make you a leader.

We regularly see instances where successful people submit to their hubris, making them think they are leaders or more important than others. A recent story highlighted how an entertainer charged outrageous prices for tickets to their show and then arrived at the performance several hours late. My point is success doesn't make you a leader. It is not unusual to find some person who has fame from sports or entertainment using name recognition to seek high-level public office with no other credentials. Winning the election puts them in the position but they must still prove they are leaders.

Some leaders allow their position and time in it to cloud their own self-worth. We’ve all seen it and many of us have fallen into the trap. I once reported to a Major General (2-Star) who was on a rant with his staff in the room and stated: “Don’t even try to keep up with me. You’ll never be able to think as fast as I can!” As I looked around the room at the other Colonels and the Brigadier General (1-Star) seated there, it was clear he was no longer leading. It was the professionalism of those in the room keeping everyone poised. This should never happen. The higher your position and the more success you experience, the more selfless you should be. This reiterates the first sentence of this book, “It’s about authenticity and genuine connection to people you are responsible for.” Show respect for yourself and for those you lead. “For if anyone thinks he is something, when he is nothing, he deceives himself.” Galatians 6:3 ESV.

Many people are fortunate enough to start with a propensity, a knack, for music, math, science, athleticism, etc. Yet they still study, learn, practice, gain experience and work to become more proficient. Others have a lesser start point and yet still are able to grow to tremendous expertise and succeed in these areas. Leadership is no different. Leaders are grown, they don’t happen by accident. Everyone will lead at some point. Some people start with more natural abilities than others. However, they all need a road map, a plan and experience to reach their full potential. What are you doing to maximize your potential?

- Become a Lifelong Learner
- Gain Experience
- Discover your Strengths and Weaknesses
- Determine your Motivation / North Star
- Establish and follow a Work-Ethic; embrace Discipline
- Build and sustain Self-Confidence
- Be Present, both Physically and Mentally
- Develop effective one-on-one communication skills
- Receive and Implement guidance and vision
- Build Trust within yourself and among others

Chapter 2
Overview of Leadership, Management, Administration (L, M, A)

> "A leader is best when people barely know he exists. When his work is done, his aim fulfilled, they will say: we did it ourselves."
>
> - Lao Tzu, Chinese philosopher

We have seen many leadership books, dictionaries and even well respected scholarly articles interchangeably use the terms "Leadership", "Management" and "Administration" or indicate in some way they are synonymous. They are not! No amount of changing affixes will make this true. They are all separate and distinct functions but complement each other when we think about an effective leader.

These terms are used in various environments in how we **perceive** a person's leadership or management capabilities. One person's definition of a good leader is not necessarily the same as another's. When we discuss leaders or managers, we don't ask, "What specifically about this person makes them a good leader?" We don't consciously tally those attributes that attract us to a leader but we do remember how a person (leader) made us feel. This is the human connection a leader makes with a "follower"; a sense of positive attributes the leader has imparted upon those he/she has interacted with. That elusive goal of being considered a "leader" leads some to believe that mastering management translates into being a leader. The failure to transition from being a manager into a leader is often the reason why organizations don't succeed.

Some of the common mistakes in using these terms interchangeably are:

- Not understanding the difference between the two and how they fit into driving organizations and leading people.

- Assuming leadership is only at the top of the organization and that all subordinate levels are only managers and administrators.
- Leadership is based on personality or charisma.[19]

Becoming a leader requires work, dedication, and a desire to connect with people at all levels. It is harder than being a manager. As one gains a greater understanding of the work environment, how things are done, how things can be improved and learning to be comfortable with the administration of an organization, the effective manager emerges. Confidence grows in the manager as they can dispatch problems that arise. They have historical context on the organization's previous problems and know the right people in the organization to achieve results. The organization becomes more efficient as the manager's capabilities improve. But there is a ceiling or cap in a manager's effectiveness. They need to grow past management and administration to become a leader.

Our leader emerges when most of their time is focused on inspiring and motivating others to excel and perform. They think about what is approaching for their organization and empower managers and administrators to focus on the now. The table below shows the clear distinction among Leadership, Management and Administration.

Leadership	**Management**	**Administration**
Leadership = Motivating & Influencing **People**	Management = Directing & Influencing **Stuff (Resources)**	Administration = Implementing & Influencing **Function / Process**

- ***Table 2 (Functions): Functions of Leadership, Management and Administration***

[19] John P. Kotter. Management Is (Still) Not Leadership. Harvard Business review. January 9th, 2013. https://hbr.org/2013/01/management-is-still-not-leadership, - May 27th, 2024

Each of these functions is important, and being proficient in all of them is crucial to effective leadership. We create a system or process through Administration and align resources against the system or processes. Each element requires competency, skill and committed people working in each of these areas to guarantee the health and success of an organization. As you read on, discussions and graphic depictions help you visualize how these definitions interact. These terms are further refined and distilled into the essence of each.

Definitions		
Leadership	**Management**	**Administration**
Leadership is the ability to foster an environment in which people motivate themselves to achieve beyond their own perceived capabilities, and face problems for which there appear to be no simple solutions.	**Management** is bringing the right resources together at the right place and time to achieve the leaders and organizations goals and objectives.	**Administration** is applying stream-lined functions / processes to an organization which facilitate the accomplishment of the leaders and organizations goals and objectives.

- ***Table 3 (Definitions): Refined definitions of Leadership, Management and Administration***

The Leader:

Leadership is the ability to *inspire people* to be productive within their function or process. This distinction of 'inspiring people' is how leadership differs from management. Inspiration is a verb–an active effort to connect with people and generate the best out of them. An effective manager has aligned the resources available to the work being performed. Leaders should have a strong grasp of management and administration but delegate those tasks to others. This allows space and time for the Leader to focus on organizational goals, strategic vision, and people. In most cases, the Leader is managing change or managing through change. They are less focused on organizing people to get work done and more on finding ways to align and influence them.[20]

In his book, “On Becoming a Better Leader”, Warren Bennis lays out clear distinctions between the Leader and the Manager:

- The manager administers; the leader innovates.
- The manager maintains; the leader develops.
- The manager relies on control; the leader inspires trust.
- The manager asks how and when; the leader asks what and why.
- The manager does things right; the leader does the right thing.[21]

Set and Communicate Vision:
As we noted before, the distinction between a leader and a manager is the leader’s ability to set the organization’s direction and to effectively communicate that vision to managers, administrators and employees. In addition to communicating a vision–via a town hall (for example), statement of annual goals or objectives or some other method–is to involve your team. Put another way, empower your team to execute your vision. Seek their input or insights. Not only does this help ensure they understand your vision, it allows them to apply their own set of solutions to a problem or goal and provide them a sense of ownership. Use these quick reference tips to help set and communicate your vision.

- Communicate your vision
- Involve your team
- Align your resources (management)
- Overcome resistance to your vision
- Be open to change based on feedback or new guidance

[20] Matt Gavin. Leadership vs. Management: What’s the Difference? Harvard Business School Online. October 31 st, 2019. https://online.hbs.edu/blog/post/leadership-vs-management - June 8th, 2024
[21] Warren Bennis, On Becoming A Leader, Basic Books, 2009 (pg 42)

- Inspire and trust others to internalize and execute the vision

Understand your people and their capabilities:
Investing in becoming proficient in an organizations' processes and procedures improves your management and administrative skills. Investing in your people will proportionally improve your ability to meet company objectives with an inspired and engaged workforce. Confidence grows from acclimating to and thriving in a new environment. Decisions come easier with a firmer grasp of the overall problems and issues.

Empower Leaders, Managers and Administrators:
Months before our deployment to Iraq in early 2003, we deployed on a training and certification mission to White Sands, New Mexico–in preparation for a combat deployment to Iraq. We also received the latest Multiple Launch Rocket Systems (MLRS) version, M270A1.[22] Some of the enhancements were faster shooting time, greater accuracy, and improved crew survivability. When a unit receives new equipment, they have to demonstrate their ability to effectively operate and maintain unfamiliar lethal equipment. We were evaluated for several factors, including our ability to move 18 MLRS launchers and the hundreds of soldiers and accompanying equipment from home station to a training (or combat site), set up for firing operations, and efficiently engaging targets.

One of the tests was a synchronized exercise to provide suppressive fires against an enemy. A Suppression of Enemy Air Defenses (SEAD) mission involves a Field Artillery unit firing missiles or projectiles, temporarily stopping incoming fire. As the suppressive fires from artillery cease, rotary-wing aircraft then enter the battlespace–through a designated air corridor–to engage and neutralize selected targets. Once the aviation assets complete their mission, they return back through that corridor and Field Artillery lays down another round of suppressive fires.

---

22 Lockheed Martin Staff. Copyright 2024. Multiple Launch Rocket System (M270). https://www.lockheedmartin.com/en-us/products/m270.html, June 10th, 2024.

This complex operation requires integration of ground, air, radar, and command assets to execute effectively.
To prepare for the graded evaluation for the SEAD mission, we rehearsed, practiced, and refined our approach over the course of several days. We conducted Rehearsal of Concept (ROC) drills, which included a full mockup of the area of operation. We would physically walk through each phase of the exercise-scenario until the Leader felt we adequately understood our tasks and responsibilities. The next day, we transitioned from practicing drills to the graded exercise.

Even though we rehearsed, practiced, and collaborated on this exercise extensively, we failed to correctly sync our artillery fires to provide a safe air corridor for our air assets. There were timing mismanagement issues, inconsistent communication, and an overall lack of focus throughout the entire unit.

Clearly frustrated with our performance, the Battalion Commander (COL Sprayberry) called his four subordinate Commanders, accompanying First Sergeants, and his primary staff for an emergency meeting. He gathered us around two body bags. They represented the pilots of the aircraft for which we were supposed to provide suppressive fires. He reminded us of the "why" by remarking, "Those pilots don't care if you had a bad day, got a 'Dear John' letter, had no sleep, are suffering from diarrhea or are having any other problems. They trust we will do our job and be ready to provide support regardless of our excuses for not performing. The price for our **failure** is their life. I have already done your job and I'm not interested in doing yours again." Soon thereafter, we successfully completed our SEAD mission with top marks.

In this case, the Leader conveyed trust in his organization by not taking over and undermining his subordinate leaders. He trusted that his direct leaders would execute his intent and vision without having to micro-manage but needed to re-focus his leadership team to focus on providing results. This also provides the space for those emerging leaders to observe how leaders inspire in difficult situations. Trust is the vehicle to empower others. Managers and administrators generally respect leaders who allow them to perform their job–even if that means providing constructive feedback. Another leader, faced with an imminent combat deployment, may want to take control of all of the unit's decisions, which will eventually erode the effectiveness of that organization.

The Manager:

Most managers are generalists not specialists; however, they usually begin their careers in administrative or specialty roles. For a manager to gain the highest levels of success, they must learn details of the business by doing, gaining experience by working in lower levels of the business, and discovering how the parts of the organization work together. This is being technically and tactically proficient. Good managers have figured out what is common in the business and uses that knowledge to help the business successfully move forward and to improve performance. While working as a defense contractor, we had a Sector Vice President with 31 years of company experience. This person started as an apprentice and worked their way up through multiple levels of management and leadership to become the Sector VP with a multi-million dollar annual salary. This leader grew from the roots of the company and successfully applied his acquired management and administration skills to become an effective manager.

Risk:

It is the Leader's responsibility to consider, assume, and mitigate risk. Managers and subordinate leaders should be providing leaders with reasonable courses of action for attaining the desired end results. This should always include a risk assessment and strategies for risk mitigation.

Planning:

Good managers also develop plans to support and augment the overall leadership vision. The planning phase requires developing goals which fully support the leader's intent and organizational goals. It is imperative the manager keeps the leader informed regarding any portion of the intent that they may not be able to support or understand. Set clear guidance and give employees the space to ask for clarity.

Depending on the task and urgency, the leader should always seek insights or ideas from their managers and employees. This also helps to build trust, leading towards a consistently collaborative environment.

Successful planning means aligning the management goals with the overall desired endstate, taking into account any aspects potentially impacting operations internally and externally, and setting a reasonable timeline while considering all resources.

There are three levels of planning:

Strategic:
Characterized by identifying the long-term or overall aims and interests and understanding the means of achieving them; designed, planned, or conceived to serve a particular purpose or achieve a particular objective.[23]

Operational:
A detailed roadmap based on a strategic plan. The operational plan aligns timelines, action items and key milestones. In this way, an operational plan outlines the organization's key objectives and goals and clarifies how the organization will achieve them.[24]

Tactical:
A daily, weekly, and / or monthly list of requirements related to higher level plans. This details actionable steps including tasks and deadlines to help meet key milestones from the Strategic / Operational plans. This provides the detail of your day-to-day operations, outlining who, what, when, where, why and, many times, how each task or requirement will be accomplished.

Organizing:

---

[23] Oxford English Dictionary. https://www.oed.com/dictionary/strategic_adj?tab=meaning_and_use#1209062450 - April 12th, 2024

[24] ibid

Good managers will employ previously developed plans, including learning from past experiences and applying successful solutions to current problems. This is the process of assigning work. This can be to individuals, teams, departments, or sectors. This will also help identify potential personnel or other resource shortfalls and demonstrate the critical path to success. Organizing should also set responsibility and authority levels for every subordinate leader, manager and administrator involved.

Some of the derivatives of organizing include having an operational structure, displaying potential points of friction and points requiring coordination and collaboration between groups. We discuss being an effective communicator in Chapter 5 (Communication "Do leaders really communicate or just tell people what to do?" - Learning to communicate with others) which also highlights key points of communication. The manager should also seek the leader's intent to prioritize tasks and resources.

Resourcing:
Ensures the availability of all the materials, money, staff, tools, and other assets necessary for effective operation. Remember, operations drive resourcing and logistics. Not the other way around. A good manager will be able to explain any resourcing constraints to the leader and have a risk mitigation strategy for the leader to consider. Those are the types of decisions under the leader's purview.

Budgeting:
Creating estimates for the cost of all materials, staff, tools, facilities and other assets for the duration of the operation. All budgets and spending should be monitored tightly. Any sign of a project or operation running over predetermined levels should be brought to the leader immediately, and root causes should be identified, as well as remediation steps. 25 years ago there was a TV commercial whose punch line was, "Are you suggesting I build a catapult and throw money at the problem?" Having funding is great; however, effective budgeting is better.

Staffing:

Similar to budget management, a good manager will break-down the human capital requirements. This includes skills (and skill levels) and the number of people required for each skill and task. You can't build a house with only carpenters. You also need plumbers, electricians, masons, et al. Failing to identify human capital requirements can also negatively impact the budget (recruitment, on-boarding, training).

Supplies:

Each member of the staff or team for a project will require tools and supplies associated with their particular skill. Having the correct set of tools can make or break success. Not every problem requires a hammer and a nail. As with every aspect of the project, failure to properly identify supplies can negatively impact budget and stop a project before it begins.

"The secret to my success is that we have gone to exceptional lengths to hire the best people in the world."
Steve Jobs

Scheduling:

This is another byproduct of the planning process. No one can plan for everything. A phrase often stated in military circles is "the enemy always has a vote." We also can't forget Murphy's Law, "Anything that can go wrong will go wrong." However, having a schedule with as much detail as possible will help to assuage many negative issues, permit correct monitoring (see below), and allow both leaders and managers to make informed decisions.

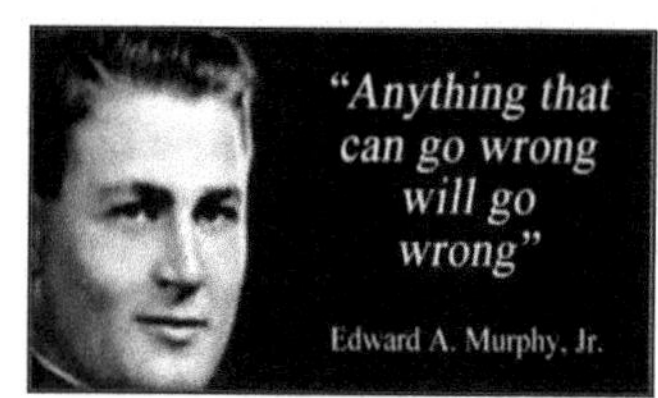

Monitoring:

Proper monitoring ensures quality performance and timely progress while identifying points and times for adjustment. Good managers are also monitoring resources and budgets. Most managers will have the authority–from the leader–to proactively make some adjustments and take corrective actions on their own. The best managers will know when it is time to take decisions to the leaders.

Reporting:
Routinely updating the leader on progress or lack of progress. Depending on criticality, length or type of work or project this can happen on any interval. As a battalion commander in Iraq, I received one daily update from my subordinate commanders and staff, which was conducted over secure radio communication. I also had a set of criteria known as "Commander's Critical Information Requirements" (CCIR) that, if met, would require an immediate (anytime of the day or night) report directly to me. These reports allow the leader to make decisions, update directives or even alter goals. Good managers understand their boundaries, where their authority ends, and where the leader's responsibility begins.

Remember, the most effective managers are the ones capable of taking the leader's guidance and intent (vision), then plan, organize, resource, schedule, monitor and report with a focus on organizational success. This will leave the leaders mental capital free to think forward and have branches and sequels in the event of required changes or new information.

The Administrator:

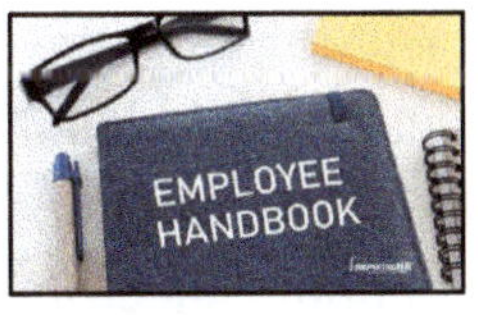

Understanding the role of the administrator is critical for leaders. The administrator oversees functions implemented as a set of rules for making decisions regarding key functions. These rules are objective and usually written to ensure consistency and fairness. A perfect example of a set of administrative procedures are the rules, policies and procedures outlined in a typical employee handbook or manual. This handbook will outline employee-related processes for requests such as vacation time, sick leave, dress code, company holidays, and grievance procedures.[25] There will usually be a set of administrative

[25] Inspiring HR. "Employee Handbooks – The Best Ones are Never Done." © Copyright 2012-2024, Inspiring HR, LLC. https://inspiringhr.com/why-the-best-small-business-employee-handbooks-are-never-done/ - April 12, 2024

rules for the sole use of management, such as procedures governing hiring, firing, promotion, and budgeting, to name a few. A key thing to remember regarding administration is there is an "exception to every rule." It is often difficult to convince people who work in this arena to be very flexible. This is where the leader gets involved to make a final decision. Even the Constitution of the United States, as great a document as it is, was written in 1787 by people and people are fallible. Due to human fallibility, the document has been amended 27 times. Our constitution was only four years old the first time it was amended with the Bill of Rights in 1791 (The first 10 amendments). So, don't believe the document you have is perfect, there will be exceptions and changes. If you are the leader, be ready.

Administrative departments and operations are important and play a key role in the smooth functioning of the organization at all levels. They keep us from missing steps that could hinder operations, delay resources and force missed opportunities. The department is key in the functions for a variety of tasks ensuring the efficient running of the company, including, but not limited to:

Facilities administration:
In many organizations the administrator or administration department makes certain the organization's facilities are well-maintained and ensures a safe and healthy working environment for all employees. This includes the cleanliness and functionality of actual structures along with the associated infrastructure, such as heating and cooling systems, plumbing, electrical systems, and Wi-Fi / Internet and intranet.

Office administration:

The administration department is also responsible for day-to-day operations of the office. This includes things such as office supplies (pens, pencils, paper, et al), maintaining office equipment (printers, copiers, phones, computers, maybe even the coffee pot) and making certain the office is clean and organized with procedures for routine functions like mail delivery and custodial activities.

Human resources:
The administrator is usually tasked with the paperwork and procedures associated with hiring and firing, establishment and function of employee training programs,
the operation of employee benefits like compensation, leave programs, insurance and retirement plans, and the maintenance and servicing of employee records.

Legal compliance:
In larger organizations, the administration team establishes policy and procedure to make certain relevant laws and regulations, including labor laws, health and safety regulations, and environmental regulations are followed.

Finance:
Administrators are also involved in organizational finances, including budget preparation, monitoring routine expenditures and conducting payroll operations.

Information Technology (IT):
In most organizations, the information technology functions fall under the administrator. They maintain the associated hardware and software, ensure cyber security, and make certain all systems and programming are up-to-date and operating correctly and efficiently.[26]

A good administrator and administrative team provide leadership with the freedom necessary to focus on other aspects of the organization's mission. These functional or domain experts are also learners and take their administrative duties and tasks very seriously. Administrators take functional-specific training or gain certifications to become the domain expert, many to be renewed annually.

---

[26] Wicky David. "Understanding The Role of Administration Department in Corporate." LinkedIn Corporation © 2024. March 19th, 2023

Many administrators doggedly hold on to policies and procedures. Let's remember, these documents are written by people who are fallible (we're all human!). Also, be certain, there is an exception to every rule, policy, or procedure. This exception is where the leader makes an impact by making a decision. While leading a team in defense contracting, one of my responsibilities was recruiting and hiring talent. It is not uncommon for the customer to write the position descriptions into the contract. In one particular case, we published the job requisition using the kludged customer and company requirements, accepted applications, performed interviews and asked our Human Resources department to extend an offer. They balked because we had not interviewed a female candidate. No female candidates had applied. Partly because the customer stipulated a very specific requirement - graduate from a very specialized school. We discovered there were only four qualified female candidates in the United States. Of those four, three were serving on Active Duty in the U.S. Army, and the fourth was a member of the Army National Guard. Our explanation fell on deaf ears in the Human Resources Department. They would not budge from the policy. In the end, it required the Sector Vice President to advance the hiring process. In many instances, leadership can still make impacts past the point of execution.

- **Management** is about resources.
  - Risk mitigation
  - Planning
  - Organizing
  - Scheduling
  - Monitoring
  - Reporting

- **Administration** is about function and process. Examples include:
  - Facilities
  - Office Administration
  - Human Resources
  - Legal Compliance

- Finance
- Information Technology

Chapter 3
Responsibility vs Authority

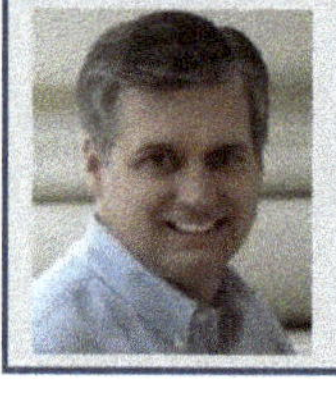

"Leadership is intentional influence."
– Michael McKinney

Responsibility vs Authority:
Both managers and administrators have authority based on the leader's responsibility. If they want to eventually lead, they must prove themselves, which is accomplished with the decision-making authority they receive.

As we mentioned in the introduction, we have found "**responsibility**" and "**authority**" used synonymously. This could not be further from the truth. There can only be one responsible person, ***The Leader***! All authority flows from the leader. When you look at the definitions it is clear. In order to accept the mantle of leadership you accept the blame for the good, the bad and the ugly. If you lead an organization that succeeds - you have succeeded. If you lead an organization that fails, you have failed. If you lead an organization that is defeated - you are defeated - your responsibility and authority are gone.

Responsibility & Authority Defined		
Responsibility is the acceptance of blame for all things good, bad or indifferent in the organization.	For the entire organization: It doesn't matter if you were present. It doesn't matter if you knew it was happening. It doesn't matter whether you are awake or asleep.	Final **responsibility** can only only be held by one person. The leader!

Authority is being empowered with the ability to make decisions based on the responsibility held by the overall leader!	This is for a subset of a larger organization. Think of this as specialized sets of an organization (examples may include: Logistics / Human Resources / Communications)	Authority can only be delegated or granted by the overall leader.

- ***Table 4 (Definitions): Refined definitions of Responsibility and Authority***

There is a well-known story in the Bible commonly referred to as the "Parable of the Talents", in Matthew 25:14–30. It tells of a wealthy man who was taking a trip. Before departing he gave some money to his servants. One servant was given five talents, the second was given two talents, and the third was given one talent. A talent was considered a large amount of money. When the wealthy man returns from his trip, the man asks his three servants for a rundown of the money. The first and the second servants explain they each invested the money and doubled what they were given and were rewarded. "His master said to him, 'Well done, good and faithful servant. You have been faithful over a little; I will set you over much. Enter into the joy of your master." The third servant hid his talent. His master punished him, "He also who had received the one talent came forward, saying, 'Master, I knew you to be a hard man, reaping where you did not sow, and gathering where you scattered no seed, so I was afraid, and I went and hid your talent in the ground. Here, you have what is yours.' But his master answered him, 'You wicked and slothful servant! You knew that I reap where I have not sown and gather where I scattered no seed? Then you ought to have invested my money with the bankers, and at my coming I should have received what was my own with interest. So, take the talent from him and give it to him who has the ten talents. For to everyone who has will more be given, and he will have an abundance. But from the one who has not, even what he has will be taken away. And cast the worthless servant into the outer darkness. In that place there will be weeping and gnashing of teeth.'

If you aspire to become a leader, you can't be timid. You must be able to make reasonable and cogent decisions with the best information available and know when to assume risk and how much risk to assume. I once knew a Major General (2-Star) managing the Army Budget Office. He was talking about the beginning of his presentation to the Chief of Staff and Vice Chief of Staff of the Army. It started like this, "Sir, we have money for anything you want. We don't have money for everything you want!" This clearly shows that the leader is responsible for prioritizing resources and requirements. Sometimes it seems our "elected" officials don't realize this. Of course, like the parable, you can always play it safe by hiding the resources or finding an interest bearing account.

Note, there can only be one "responsible", the Leader.

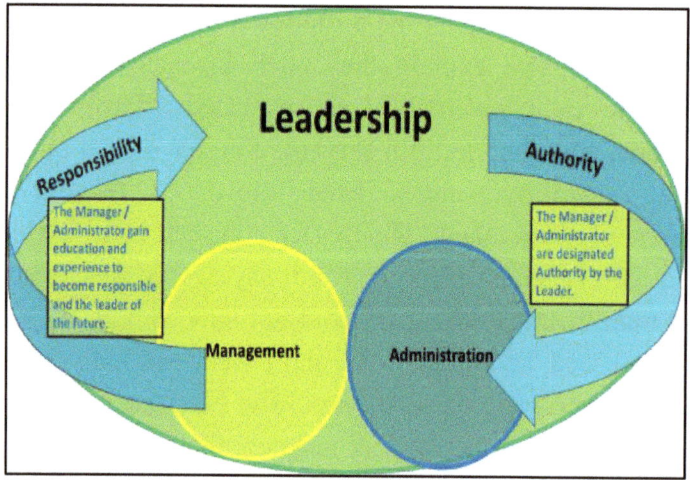

- ***Graphic 5 (Diagram): This is a graphic depiction of the relationship between Leadership, Management and Administration.***

Notice in the graphic EVERYTHING falls under the purview of the leader. The leader is the one with the responsibility, the one granting and delegating decision making authority. I have heard it said, "We take bows together." In other words, the leader stands alone to take the blame for failures and shortcomings but stands with the team and top performers for the accolades.

Graphic 6 (below) shows how responsibility increases as a person progresses up the hierarchy of leadership while the authority associated with that level of leadership widens at the base.

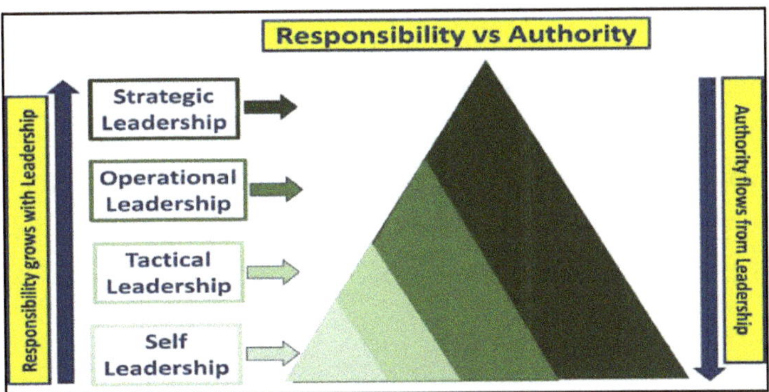

- *Graphic 6: The hierarchy of Leadership compared to Responsibility and Authority.*

Responsibility:
Rests squarely on the shoulders of the leader.

- President Harry Truman said: "The buck stops here."
- An Anonymous quote … "Responsibility is accepting that you are the cause and the solution of the matter."
- British Prime Minister Winston Churchill opined: "The price of greatness is Responsibility."
- President Franklin D. Roosevelt stated: "Great Power involves great Responsibility."

Everyone must eventually take responsibility, even if it is at the lowest level of leadership, Self-Leadership (taking responsibility for yourself). You can cultivate responsibility as part of Lifelong learning. Here we will provide some examples and later in the book go into greater depth on several of the ideas and concepts:

Recognize your strengths and weaknesses.
Once you have done this, you can begin to capitalize on your strengths and look for solutions to overcome (or at least minimize) your weaknesses. To accomplish this, you need to be honest with yourself and do a candid self assessment. You can also seek feedback from people in your life whom you trust. There's always room to improve.

Establish goals and make a plan for improvement
(See Chapter 4 - Self- Leadership "If you can't lead yourself, how can you lead others?"). If you are able to set individual goals, establish a plan to reach them and then maintain focus on that goal until you achieve it. This will help your confidence as you expand this process to groups and organizations. Ask yourself, "Where do I want to be next year, 5 years from now, or 10 years from now?" Then, lay out a path to get there.

Learn from your mistakes.
We are all going to make mistakes. I have heard it said that most people learn more from a mistake than getting a situation or an answer 100% right. This means doing a blunt personal assessment of the mistake and determining what it will take to get it right the next time. What is most important is how you deal with mistakes.

Do what you say you are going to do.
This is a key point of the discussion in Chapter 9 ("Volunteer Leadership"). The moment you make the commitment, someone else is counting on you. This requires follow through, meeting deadlines–applying your self-leadership skills and possessing self-awareness. It also proves to others and, more importantly, yourself that you can be trusted and that you have integrity.

Strive to continuously improve your communications skills
(See Chapter 5 - Communication "Do leaders really communicate or just tell people what to do/" - Learning to communicate with others.). Good communication can overcome many problems and issues. A person with

efficient and effective communication skills can make more meaningful connections with people and may even influence their decisions.[27]

As the leader, everything, including failure is yours. When I assumed command of my first battery, my leader told me, "You are responsible for everything that happens or fails to happen". Throughout our military career, most officers get this advice but don't internalize or understand the gravity of that statement until that guidon is handed to them. This becomes a solemn responsibility to ensure you exercise the best version of your leadership capabilities throughout your entire command! The pressure of being responsible for the lives of 94 other men and women can lead some leaders to shoulder every task– to retain control of their environment.

Authority:

Formal authority is delegated downwards based on the responsibility level of the leader. It flows from the top to the bottom of the organization. It comes from the highest level of leadership to their subordinate leader and, in turn, from the subordinate to another leader working under them and so on. Authority is often given to Managers and Administrators for the purpose of making sure certain organizational goals are met. Authority routinely resides with positions, not in specific people.[28]

Delegated Authority:

I recall a time when a junior ranking Sergeant (E-5) exercised his delegated authority. During the 1990s, after the breakup of the Soviet Union, Yugoslavia fell into ethnic conflict and a portion of the former country–Bosnia-Herzegovina–fell into civil war. After nearly four years of fighting, the Dayton Peace Agreement was eventually negotiated in

[27] Indeed Editorial Team. Personal responsibility: importance, attributes and benefits. Indeed Career Development. December 1st, 2022. https://uk.indeed.com/career-advice/career-development/personal-responsibility - May 6th, 2024.

[28] Renu Lamba. Authority, Responsibility and Its Delegation. Slide Share. May 29th, 2023. https://www.slideshare.net/slideshow/authority-responsibilitypptx-258115372/258115372 - May 3rd, 2024

1995.[29] The United States and several other countries committed nearly 60,000 soldiers to help enforce the peace agreement. At the time, I was assigned as a Lieutenant to a Field Artillery unit stationed in Germany. We received deployment orders in early 1997, as part of NATOs Stabilization Force (SFOR). The Battalion Commander decided to split the deployment of his unit in three phases: 1) advance party of senior leaders and key personnel 2) the main body–the bulk of the 300+ soldiers and 3) the trail party, those needing to transition work and responsibilities to a Rear Detachment unit (those not deploying). I was in the first group to deploy. Due to the proximity between Germany and Bosnia, the advance party–predominately senior military officers and their non-commissioned officers–drove the 14 hours in a chartered bus into the general area and arrived at the first staging base before entering the "Theater of Operations". We would stay in this encampment for a few days before moving to our final deployment location. Before disembarking the bus, a young Sergeant (E-5) came on the bus to give us an orientation and camp rules of engagement. He was outranked by 90% of the people on the bus and in a normal situation, he would have a hard time giving orders to many of them. He began his briefing with, "Do not confuse your rank with my authority". The Leader empowered him–the Base or Ground Commander–whereby authority was delegated to him to carry out and execute the Leader's vision and guidance.

Once you delegate, you have to empower that person with the authority (still your responsibility) to make decisions on your behalf to get the job done and achieve organizational goals. This includes working outside the organization if / when necessary. If you let the best and brightest of your team stretch their leadership legs, you run the risk of them being poached by another organization. Even so, delegating and checking on the work with cogent feedback helps them become better leaders who can contribute more to your organization. Don't forget to challenge employees and provide actionable feedback!

Authority by Influencing:

[29] Organization for Security and Co-operation in Europe. Dayton Peace Agreement. December 14th, 1995. https://www.osce.org/bih/126173, May 11th, 2024.

Sometimes it is possible to earn authority from below. In fact, people can influence others and gain cooperation when they don't have formal authority. Authority is not simply a derivative of the size of your team or budget. Here are some ways to gain influence even without formal authority:

Skill:
The skill with which you handle your work can influence your level of authority. Others will take note of your acumen and will naturally seek you out in situations where you have demonstrated skill.

Performance:
Success breeds success. Top performers earn the most respect in an organization, whether it is athletics, business or the military. People naturally look to the person best in their area of endeavor.

Expertise/Ethos:
As a Battalion Commander, I often used phrases such as "know and do your job." If you don't know your job, how can you do it? Now it requires others to work twice as hard because they must accomplish both their job and yours. The better you know your job and stay on top of developments in your field, the more quickly other people will follow your lead.

Comportment:
If you carry and portray yourself in a professional and confident manner it can greatly influence the behavior of others. Ask yourself some questions:

- Do you act in a way naturally allowing people to accept your authority?
- Are you positive and upbeat, even in what others might consider tough situations?
- Do you introduce new ideas or ways of doing things as opportunities for success, not obstacles?

Trust:
We spend an entire chapter (Chapter 6 - How to Build Trust and Trust in Others.) discussing trust. If you earn and maintain trust, others will come to you on a regular basis and your authority will grow.[30]
Using these forms of influence can cultivate the sway (or ethos) you carry in many situations even without formal authority. As a public school teacher, I was "responsible" for several things within my classroom: providing a safe environment, maintaining discipline, providing learning opportunities, evaluating student progress and making adjustments, among others. The school principal delegated "authority" to me outside the classroom to ensure safety and discipline. However, over time, employing the factors above, I became a trusted source of support in other areas. I am proud to say the students under my care raised their reading levels each year. Our principal even brought outside guests to my class to discuss literacy and would ask me to provide the guest with copies of packets I had made for the students to use to improve reading comprehension. I gained some respect and with it some modicum of authority.

Lead Up:
Most people will spend the majority of their time in positions where they are being led and have people they are leading. It is important to lead in two directions. In other words, there are situations when you have to be able to lead your leader and teach them something. As a leader you have to be open to this or you will lose a valuable asset. I have been fortunate to have had many great subordinate leaders over the years. There are two very specific situations that come to mind when I was taught by the subordinate leader, a Sergeant. The first came during a training exercise in Thailand. I sustained an injury and was transported to a Thai Army medical facility. That was all well and good except...I didn't speak Thai and no one there spoke English. About two hours after I arrived at the hospital, my Sergeant showed up with a translator

---

[30] American Management Association Staff. Factors That Determine a Manager's Level of Authority. American Management Association. May 20, 2020. https://www.amanet.org/articles/factors-determine-managers-authority/ - May 6th, 2024.

from the local U.S. Consulate. He said, “Every soldier in the Army has a Sergeant to take care of them and I am your Sergeant!” A great lesson.

Later in my career, I was assigned to a position where for the first time I was leading female soldiers. My senior sergeant was a Master Sergeant and I scheduled time for an “initial counseling”, something all leaders should do with their subordinates. I walked in the morning of the event, closed the door, and sat down. She walked over and opened the door. I had asked, “What are you doing?” She told me she reviewed my records and knew this was the first position where I had female soldiers under my leadership. She said, “The moment you close that door I can say anything I want about what happened here and everyone will believe me and no one will believe you!” This was my first lesson. What an eye opener from a great leader. We solved the issue by having a disinterested third party sit in. Leaders are lifelong learners, so be open to the lessons when they come.

There is only one responsible person, the **Leader!** There are “leaders” at all levels. We’ve laid out the foundational definitions of Responsibility and Authority. Each is distinct and plays an important role in becoming an effective leader.

- **Responsibility** increases with the hierarchy of leadership achieved.
  Cultivate your ability to accept responsibility by: recognize your strengths and weaknesses, make a plan for improving on your weaknesses, learn from mistakes, do what you say you are going to do, and improve your communications skills.

- **Authority** is delegated downward based on the responsibility level of the leader.
  Expand your authority by: being skillful, demonstrate superior performance, display expertise and ethos with professional comportment, earn and maintain trust.

Chapter 4
Self Leadership If you can't lead yourself how can you lead others?

> ***Before you become a leader, success is all about growing yourself. When you become a leader, success is all about growing others.***
>
> ***- Jack Welch***

Phase One of leadership starts with self (Self Leadership). It is an organization of one! Remember our definition of **Leadership** = *the ability to foster an environment in which people motivate themselves to achieve beyond their perceived capabilities, and face (and solve) problems for which there appear to be no simple solutions.* You must lead yourself because you are "Responsible" for you (**Responsible** = *the acceptance of blame for all things good, bad or indifferent in the organization*).

One great instance of self leadership I witnessed was a young soldier exemplifying the definition of "Moral Courage". It came when I was sitting on a battalion level promotion board for soldiers seeking to be promoted to Sergeant (E-5). We didn't have a Sergeant Major, and consequently, as a Field Grade officer, I sat in to complete the board. A group of senior non-commissioned officers (NCOs) was asking a young soldier questions. The soldier was doing a great job of responding. Out of respect, the Senior NCOs asked if I would like to pose a question. To their shock I did. I asked, "What is your definition of moral courage?" After a pause of 30 to 45 seconds, he looked at me and said, "Sir, it's what you do when you're alone." This soldier was practicing full-on Self Leadership. And, per our definition, was "motivating" himself to do the right thing, even if no one else would know.

US Navy Admiral, William H. McRaven, delivered a speech about the importance of doing the little things like making your bed, embracing the fears of life, and changing the world for generations to come.[31] This is self-leading, motivating yourself and having moral courage because no one else is going to do it for you and you are responsible for you. No matter what you do, it requires you to lead yourself in three actions. First, you must decide you are going to do something! You should do it without hesitation; no backing down; no making excuses; no procrastination. Second, you must be consistent! You need: a plan; a schedule; resources; milestones; and a goal or desired end state. Third, you must recognize the specific actions for the thing you have decided to do! Think of this as leading, motivating, and inspiring yourself towards achieving a New Year's resolution you will actually attain. According to the New York Post, the average American abandons their resolution in the first 30 days. Most lack a plan to help get them there–no wonder they didn't succeed!

- ***Decide you are going to do it!***
- ***Be consistent in your actions!***
- ***Recognize the action specific requirements!***

Let's look at examples of how this would work and apply individual personal discipline.

You have decided you want to become more physically healthy and set a goal of losing 50 pounds.

First, you MUST decide you are going to do it and not let anything get in the way. This means you are going to start now. Make a plan to change your eating habits like: avoiding sugary drinks, alcohol, candy, cookies, fried and fast foods, eat reasonable portions or increase your water intake. The late comedian Rodney Dangerfield once joked, "I

[31] You Tube. Navy Seal William McRaven: If You Want To Change The World, Make Your Bed! https://www.youtube.com/watch?v=3sK3wJAxGfs - November 11th, 2023

went on a diet to lose weight. I am only eating salad but I am eating 12 pounds of salad a day." Make a plan to exercise for at least 30 minutes a day (going for a walk, riding a bike, or doing push-ups). Establish intermediate goals, including losing one pound per week or six pounds a month, walking a mile every day for the first month and then increasing distance).

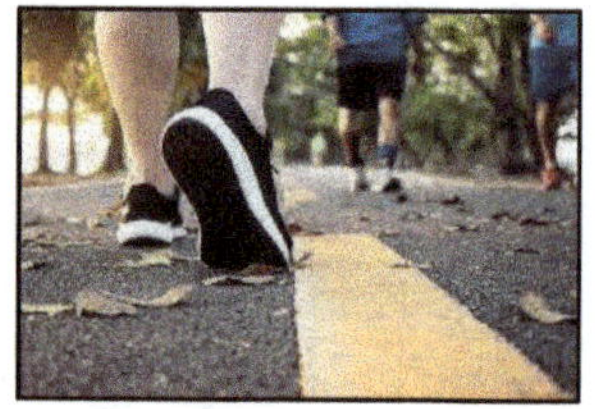

Second, you MUST be consistent in your actions! This means sticking to the plan. Nothing is going to happen overnight. If you want real lasting results, you must lead and motivate yourself to achieve beyond your *perceived capabilities.* If you are unable to lead yourself, how do you expect to lead others? You can't stop at the fast food drive-thru window on your way home from work because no one will know. You can't rationalize having an afternoon of beer and pizza while watching the game. You can't try to justify to yourself that dinner out with your spouse doesn't count, so order the "Chocolate Lover's Dream" for dessert. You can't convince yourself that sleeping for 30 more minutes is healthier than going for a brisk morning walk. You have to be able to lead and motivate yourself to success. No one else will.

Finally, recognize the action specific requirements! In this case, losing weight for your health, there is only one way to do it. You must burn more calories than you eat. This is a hard core truth of weight loss and it doesn't matter who you are. When you meet or see someone that has noticeably lost weight, your first question is, "How did you do that?" The response might be anything: I had lap band surgery; I did the KETO diet; or, I did one of those plans you see advertised on TV. IT DOES NOT MATTER! In the end they burned more calories than they consumed. Everything here is doable. We all know people who've accomplished this. Be strong.

Let's look at another popular New Year's resolution as an example of motivating and leading yourself–that organization of one! Remember to apply individual personal discipline, if you can't lead yourself, how will you ever lead others?

You have decided to motivate and lead yourself to become "debt-free". Like other goals or end states, this is not going to happen with the flip of a switch. A genie is not going to come out of a lamp and grant your wish. You MUST apply moral courage because no one is going to be there 24 hours a day to watch you, except you!

First, you MUST decide you are going to do it and not let anything get in the way. This means you are going to start now. Make a plan to change your financial habits (What were you expecting us to say?). Dave Ramsey, CEO of Ramsey Solutions, eight-time national bestselling author, personal finance expert and host of The Ramsey Show says you must "act your wage."[32] While it may seem harsh, it is important to heed Ramsey's advice by not spending more than your wages allows you to afford. Decide what you "NEED". Starting now you will not eat out 7 nights a week, have more shoes than Imelda Marcos, drive a car with a payment, have 250 channels on your TV while paying for 4 other streaming services, carry five credit cards in your pocket or, collect Beanie Babies (Whatever the latest fad is). What specifically in your life can you jettison? You get the idea!

Second, you MUST be consistent in your actions! This means sticking to the plan. Nothing is going to happen overnight (What were you expecting us to say?). If you want lasting results, you must lead and *motivate yourself to achieve beyond your perceived capabilities.* You shouldn't go on to your "shopping app" out of boredom, looking for a trendy new pair of shoes. You can't rationalize flying to Grandma's house when it's cheaper to drive. You don't justify to yourself that your next door neighbor has a boat and you don't. You can't convince yourself that an 85 inch Smart TV will make the game more enjoyable. You should start a savings account (see Dave Ramsey) for emergencies. You have to be able to lead and motivate yourself to success. No one else will.

---

[32] Dave Ramsey Staff. Ramsey. 2023 Lampo Licensing, LLC. https://www.ramseysolutions.com/dave-ramsey - November 15th 2023

Finally, recognize the action specific requirements! In this case, becoming debt free, there is only one way to do it: you must spend less money than you earn–"Act your wage". The truth is painful; however, if you are consistent, you'll establish good habits becoming "debt free" allowing you to do far more than you ever dreamed. To accomplish this, you don't have to be rich, win the lottery or get an inheritance from a distant relative. All that's required is leading yourself.

Let's look at one other common resolution as an example of motivating and leading yourself–that organization of one! Again, remember to apply the individual personal discipline mantra: if you can't lead yourself, how will you ever lead others?

You have decided to motivate and lead yourself to acquire an education. This can range from finishing high school or earning your General Equivalency Diploma (GED), attending a trade school, earning a new certification, or getting an Advanced Degree. Again, like other goals, this is not going to happen overnight. You MUST apply moral courage because no one is going to be there 24 hours a day to watch you–except you! There is a compelling reason to achieve this objective. Even a cursory review of the information in Table 5 (below) provides a clear difference in the lifetime earning power of those earning education degrees past high school. In addition, education also sets the stage for Lifelong learning, empowering yourself with a feeling of self-assurance and an appreciation of your own capabilities, a foundational element of confidence and setting the stage towards leading others.

Education Levels and Earning - The United States in 2021			
Education Level	**% of U.S. Population**	**Median Earnings**	**Comparison of Earnings**
Less than Highschool	8.9%	$20,200	
Highschool / GED	27.9%	$30,700	35% > Non-Highschool Grad
Some College, No Degree	14.9%	$39,000	22% > Highschool / GED
Associate Degree	10.5%	$41,400	6% > Some College
Bachelor's Degree	23.5%	$61,600	33% > Associate's Degree
Master's Degree or Higher	14.4%	$74,600	21 % > Bachelor's degree
https://www.census.gov/newsroom/press-releases/2022/educational-attainment.html - November 27th, 2023		https://nces.ed.gov/programs/coe/indicator/cba/annual-earnings - November 27th, 2023	

- ***Table 5 (Earnings vs. Education): A comparison of education to earnings in the United States.***

Pursuing additional education still requires you to have a plan.
First, you MUST decide you are going to do it and not let anything get in the way by applying individual personal discipline. You should start as quickly as feasible–procrastinating will not help you realize your goal. Make a plan by choosing an area of study. Be real with yourself, a degree in "Underwater Basket Weaving", even from an Ivy League school, might be fun; however, is going to be worthless! Former soccer star, Megan Rapinoe, remarked that playing for the United States Women's National Soccer Team was the "worst job in the world".[33] So, choose something that you truly value and like! Something you are willing to do for the majority of your working life (Teacher, Nurse, Auto Mechanic, Carpenter). Do a time management plan giving yourself time to study, write papers, read, complete practical exercises (IE: Do the work). Remember, not EVERYTHING is done "online".

I knew a woman who was motivated to achieve a better life. She started that journey by working towards a college degree. This was in the days you were actually expected to show up for class; before you sat at home on a computer, rarely interacting with your classmates, only seeing a picture of your professor on some obscure weblink and were whining about repaying student loans (lack of self-responsibility). I watched her toil for eight years, going to school at night and working full-time. The commencement ceremony was a real live, in person, event held at the college. The night of graduation, sitting in the crowd, I was bursting with pride for my mother. The next day she went to work at the same place she'd been in retail sales for eight years, greeted by cheers from her co-workers. Many of them had personally witnessed her years long struggle and, unrealized by them, they'd been led by "*being motivated to achieve beyond their own perceived capabilities.*" That day, she was promoted and received a $3,000 annual pay raise (a big deal then). This

---

[33] Katie Jerkovich. Megan Rapinoe Calls Playing For U.S. Team 'Worst Job In The World'. The Daily Wire. Dec 14th 2023. https://www.dailywire.com/news/megan-rapinoe-calls-playing-for-u-s-team-worst-job-in-the-world - December 15, 2023

tangible outcome was inspired by motivation and self leadership. Cancer took my mother a few short years later. However, she is still leading! This story is "motivating" others; perhaps, one of those motivated may be you.

Second, you MUST be consistent in your actions! Stick to the plan. Take on an attitude of not letting ANYTHING get in your way. Nothing is going to happen overnight (yeah, the same comment!). If you want real lasting results, you must lead and *motivate yourself to achieve beyond your perceived capabilities.* There are some immutable facts about gaining an education or skill. Osmosis is not a method for success in learning. Procrastination accomplishes nothing except creating a pile of work that will not get done. Cramming for tests and exams the night prior may allow you to squeak by but you'll likely not retain anything of value. Plagiarism is not "moral courage" and is generally considered a violation of honor or ethics codes and can result in disciplinary action from a person's school or workplace. The best time to study is not at midnight but rather after a good night's sleep when you are fresh. Most colleges and universities have published guides and white papers validating the benefits of positive study habits. Find one that suits your situation and stick to it.

Finally, recognize the action specific requirements! Show up and do your best to be on time! Do the work yourself! Again, this is achievable for anyone; we all probably know someone who has accomplished this goal. The opportunities for continuing education seem endless.

There will be "naysayers" making excuses as to why they can't do the things we have discussed here. I will highlight several examples of individuals who have achieved great success despite facing significant challenges:

- Oprah Winfrey, John Goodman, Al Roker, Drew Carey and Mo'Nique are all examples of celebrities who have lost significant weight. A study of more than 6,000 everyday people reveals that you can keep it off. "The two main pieces of advice for maintaining weight loss from people who have successfully done it were *perseverance in the face of setbacks* and *conditioning to track food intake*, the study found."[34] (i.e., Lead yourself)

- Halle Berry once lived in a homeless shelter. Steve Harvey lived in his car. He once joked that if he ever had to live in his car again, he'd make sure it was a Rolls Royce! Jim Carrey lived in a tent as a teenager (remember, he's from Canada). "Dr. Phil" McGraw lived in a box on the streets of Kansas City while growing up.[35]

- Albert Einstein, George Washington, Leonardo Da Vinci, Pablo Picasso and Tom Cruise all suffer(ed) from dyslexia.[36]

- Stephen Hawkings suffered from amyotrophic lateral sclerosis (ALS). President Franklin Delano Roosevelt suffered from

- polio. Stevie Wonder is blind. Helen Keller was the first deaf and blind person to earn a Bachelor of Arts degree.[37]

Ask yourself, "What excuse am I going to make?" The late Zig Ziglar used to say, "If you aim at nothing, you'll hit it every time." YOU must decide you will do it, be consistent in your actions, and recognize the specific action requirements! (*Motivate yourself to achieve beyond your own perceived capabilities*).

---

[34] A. Pawlowski. 'Don't ever give up': Long-term weight-loss maintainers share tips for success. Today. March 10th, 2022. https://www.today.com/health/diet-fitness/weight-loss-maintenance-long-term-tips-rcna19358 - December 3, 2023

[35] Backpack Bed for Homeless. Dignity is a human right. Famous Actors Who Were Homeless. https://backpackbed.org/us/famous-actors-who-were-homeless/ - December 3rd, 2023

[36] Meredith Cicerchia. Famous people with dyslexia. Touch-type Read & Spell. https://www.readandspell.com/us/famous-people-with-dyslexia - December 3rd, 2023

[37] AAAPlay. 11 Outstanding People Living With Disability. https://www.aaaplay.org.au/news/2019/11-outstanding-people-living-disability - December 3rd, 2023

Start leading yourself NOW. Set a goal.

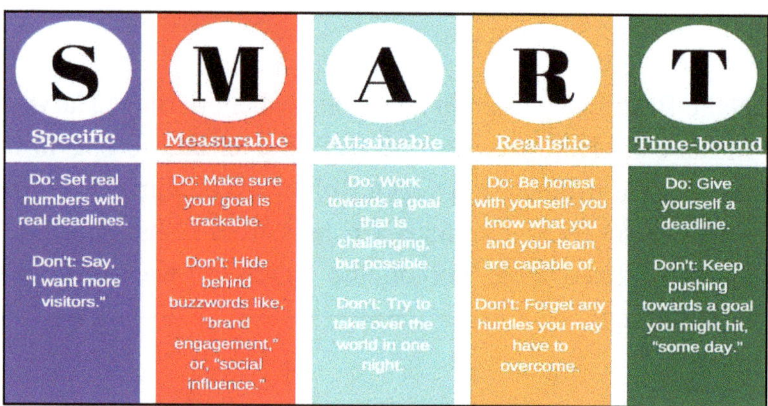

Apply these three steps:

- ***Decide you are going to do it!***
- ***Be consistent in your actions!***
- ***Recognize the action specific requirements!***

You can lead yourself to success, gaining confidence in your leadership abilities along the way. Decide your needs and wants. This is setting and visualizing your ultimate goal. It may be one of the examples explored above or it may be something else like: writing a book, completing a marathon, hiking Hadrian's Wall, tobacco cessation, creating a better relationship with a friend or loved one, having a deeper understanding of your faith, changing your environment and being around positive people. "You have time for what you choose to have time for." - Pastor Craig Groeschel, Life Church.

We all want to be better: Better parents, better spouses, better friends, better leaders; however, it can be tough to know where to start. Leading yourself will last your entire life. Learn how!

---

[38] Madison Merrihew. The Importance of Setting SMART Goals. Hydrate. https://www.hydratemarketing.com/blog/the-importance-of-setting-smart-goals - December 8th, 2023

These are common themes throughout this book and may seem obvious but they are so important to self-development, they are worth mentioning here

Set Goals:
We just mentioned this. Establishing your own self-development includes setting goals. The goals should be achievable but should also include some rigor and stretch your current capabilities. An outcome of self-development is growth. Decide what you want to accomplish both personally and professionally. Make a plan and make it happen.

Identify Your Strengths and Weaknesses:
In most interviews, you will get the popular question, "Tell me your strengths and weaknesses". If you've done your self-inventory, this should be relatively simple. Strengths are those things we tend to do well or have little trouble with. Weaknesses, sometimes called "development areas" are those things we tend to avoid or don't use often. Knowing your primary traits is just as important as the "Elevator Pitch"--that brief overview of who you are and your capabilities.

Knowing your baseline capabilities is important. As you develop along the spectrum of leadership, identifying the things you can do well and the areas you need some development will shape how you lead. There are several ways to learn about your strengths and weaknesses:

- Ask your professional and personal networks, "What do you think I do well?" and "What do you think I could improve upon?" Ideally, your network should know you well enough to provide candid and actionable insights.
- Take an assessment. While we don't endorse a specific tool, most offer a range of aptitude and cognitive results and provide specific recommendations to fortify your strengths while offering tips to uplift your development areas.

- Learn from others. Look at how effective leaders approach their goals and try to incorporate some of these techniques into your leadership.[39]

Acquire New Skills:
Any self-development plan should include acquiring new skills and capabilities. This can include skills to strengthen a known or perceived weakness or simply something you want to do. I am the head of the safety team at my place of worship. I recently attended an eight-hour training class focused specifically on church safety. I have been able to share my newly acquired skills with other members of our team. So, take a class, participate in a workshop, read books (like this one) or articles. There are many ways to facilitate your self-development.

Self-Care:
We talk about taking care of yourself as a common thread in this book. Again, this is common sense. Make time for meaningful rest to recharge your batteries. Eat healthy, exercise, take a mental break, or make time for things you enjoy. What's the cliche? "All work and no play makes Jack a dull boy."

Be around Positive People:
The environment you choose will impact who you are. If you hang out with bad people, it's likely it will rub off on you. Conversely, if you surround yourself with good people, you will be better for it.

Embrace Change:
Change will happen! It's inescapable. So, grow with it. William S. Burroughs said, "When you stop growing, you start dying." Being open to change will present new opportunities; be receptive to them, you have no idea where they may lead.

---

[39] Muslim Ameer. How To Identify Your Personal Strengths And Weaknesses. April 21, 2023. https://www.linkedin.com/pulse/how-identify-your-personal-strengths-weaknesses-muslim-ameer/ - July 27, 2024

Finding your Passion - Your North Star:

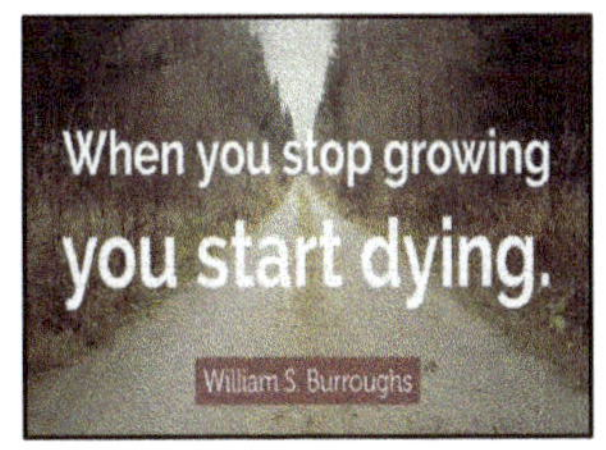

During my second year as a West Point Cadet, we "deployed" to a training center for the summer. Camp Buckner is a 16,000 acre area just 3 miles from the gates of West Point's northern entrance. This mini boot camp is designed to provide Cadets with hands-on exposure to the various military branches (and ultimately career field) offered. Throughout the camp, we learned about the primary Army branches–almost like a recruiting pitch to entice young impressionable minds to become a Tanker or Ranger or Redleg. We gained a better understanding of our possible branch choices but focused on small unit leadership tactics. Our small squad of eight to ten 19 and 20 years olds were fanned out in the woods, walking towards their next objective. We were overseen by an Army Major–who had a chest full of medals and badges. He taught us how to maneuver–as a team–through wooded terrain. In addition to gaining basic military skills, the exercise also instilled teamwork. As we patrolled, each of us made mistakes, causing our trainer to give pointed feedback and instructions on how to do better next time. Once we got to our objective, he sat us down and explained the importance of passion and dedication. "If this doesn't "turn your crank', I suggest you find another line of work!" This means finding what you love and leverage your strengths and capabilities.

Everything You Do Matters:

Life is filled with small and large decisions. We often don't realize the impact of those decisions until later or when we've had time for self-reflection. At West Point, the same held true. The Academy evaluates and "grades" you throughout your entire cadet experience. From Reception Day–the first day a cadet candidate walks into campus to the day a "Firstie" (senior) throws their hat up into the air during graduation–you are being evaluated and assessed. The Academy ranks each Cadet among three main metrics or pillars: academic, military, and physical. Each test, homework assignment, annual evaluation, or physical fitness test counts towards the cadet's class rank. That ranking often impacts the direction of a person's career. This also determines which branch you can select for your career and your first duty assignment/location. In my case, I was fortunate enough to select Field Artillery as my "career" path and Germany as my first duty location. Personally, I met (and later married) my wife. Professionally, I was able to develop my tactical leadership skills in a multinational location which I later applied to my leadership style when commanding soldiers in combat. Thinking back, had I not pushed a little harder on my fitness test or failed to study for a test, my ability to select my own path would have been severely impacted.

Be realistic:

If you are 63 years old and 5 foot 8 inches tall, you probably won't become an NBA all-star–no matter how well you embrace self-leadership. Most of us will not become professional athletes, but we can still lead ourselves to greatness in other professions or fields.

Self-development is a journey, not a destination, so be patient and enjoy the process.[40]

True leaders are Lifelong learners. Learning comes from those we interact with on a daily basis (small traits or characteristics of effective people). We learn by understanding our development areas and take active steps to improve via professional development (workshops, training, formal courses, etc.). Like the instructions flight attendants give passengers, "In the event of an emergency, oxygen masks will drop down. Please firmly secure your mask first before helping others." You can't lead or help others if you can't help yourself.

➢ Set a goal by following these three simple steps.

---

[40] Syed Wajih. The Five Steps to Self-Development: A Journey to Personal Growth. Linkedin. March 2nd, 2023. https://www.linkedin.com/pulse/five-steps-self-development-journey-personal-growth-ul-hassan/ - May 13th, 2024

- ***Decide you are going to do it!***
- ***Be consistent in your actions!***
- ***Recognize the action specific requirements!***

- Identify Your Strengths and Weaknesses - know who you are.
- Acquire New Skills - continuously.
- Practice Self-Care - you'll make better decisions if you are healthy.
- Be positive around other people - they will be positive back.
- Embrace change - don't let it embrace you.
- Find your passion - it'll make things more fun.

Chapter 5
"Do Leaders really communicate or just tell people what to do? "Learning to Communicate with others.

"Communication is the real work of leadership." – Nitin Nohria

In the book's introduction we stated a blinding flash of the obvious, "Most people can solve a problem but the greatest difficulty is **defining the problem**. Many times, that problem is a lack of leadership." Remember the children's game you might have played at parties? Everyone sits in a circle and the first person whispers a message into the second person's ear. Then the second whispers to the third and so on until the message is whispered to the last person. That last person then says the message out loud as everyone laughs because it is nothing like the original message. Talk about poor communications. It is our experience that positive, cogent communication is a key foundational building block to leadership and, by extension, problem-solving. In fact, Nitin Nohria (the10th Dean of Harvard Business School) says it is "impossible to over-communicate."

Types of Communications: Here we will discuss the four primary forms of communication: Verbal, Non-Verbal, Visual, and Written.[41] Following the original study by Mehrabian and Wiener, Albert

---

[41] Hanne Keiling. 4 Types of Communication and How To Improve Them. Indeed. July 31st, 2023. *https://www.indeed.com/career-advice/career-development/types-of-communication* and
Mehrabian, A., & Wiener, M. Decoding of inconsistent communications. APA PsycArticles. 1967. https://psycnet.apa.org/doiLanding?doi=10.1037%2Fh0024532 - March 10th, 2024

Mehrabian–a behavioral psychologist–later developed the 7-38-55 Communications Model "Based on research, Albert Mehrabian has concluded that only 7% of feelings and attitudes takes place through the words we use in spoken communications, while 38% takes place through tone and voice and the remaining 55% take place through body language."[42]

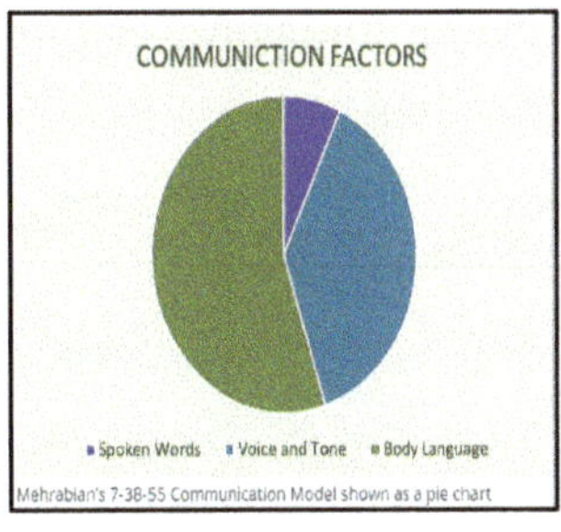

Mehrabian's 7-38-55 Communication Model shown as a pie chart

Verbal –

Verbal communication is the use of language to transfer information through speaking or sign language. It is the most common type of communication, often used during presentations, video conferences / phone calls, meetings and one-on-one conversations. Verbal communication is important because it is efficient. It's helpful to support verbal communication with both nonverbal and written communication. This form of communication allows for the real-time exchange of information and ideas. We can look back at history and the speeches leading *people to motivate themselves to achieve beyond their own perceived capabilities*. Just a few examples: In 1987 President Ronald Reagan said, "Tear down this wall." He was leading and motivating the world. In 1963 Dr. Martin Luther King said "I have a dream." He motivated a country and a movement. In 1941 President Franklin D. Roosevelt said, "Yesterday, December 7, 1941—a date which will live in infamy." This propelled the country into what became known as 'World War II'. In 1863 President Abraham Lincoln delivered the short, 271 word, Gettysburg Address, rousing a nation. In 1851 Sojourner Truth delivered her famous "Ain't I a Woman" speech at the Women's Convention in Akron, Ohio. This still strikes a chord today, nearly 175 years later. When used correctly, verbal

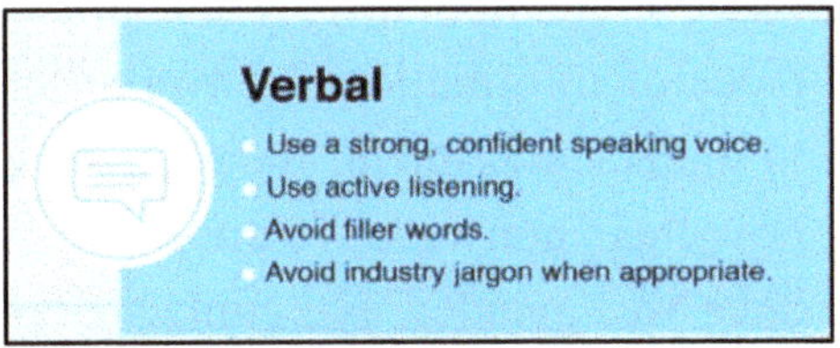

[42] World of Work Project.Mehrabian's 7-38-55 Communication Model: It's More Than Words. https://worldofwork.io/2019/07/mehrabians-7-38-55-communication-model/ - May 6th, 2024.

communication can be the most effective form of communication when leading.

Non-verbal –

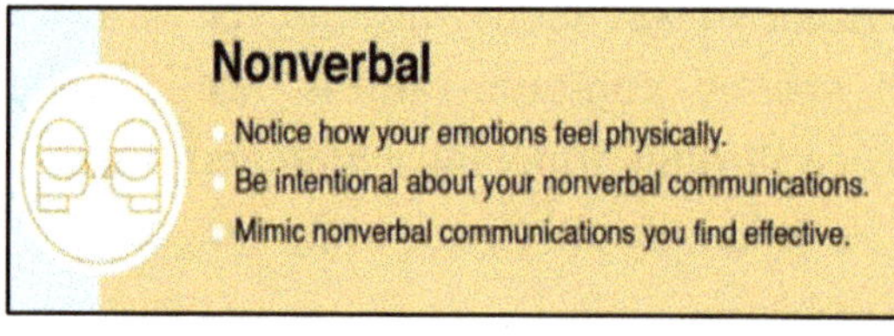

Nonverbal communication is the use of body language, gestures and facial expressions to convey information to others. It can be used both intentionally and unintentionally. For example, you might smile unintentionally when you hear a pleasing or enjoyable idea or piece of information. Nonverbal communication is helpful when trying to understand others' thoughts and feelings. Many people don't realize how their non-verbal's are being received by others. How many times have we: avoided eye contact, looked at our watch or cellphone while speaking to someone, slouched in our seat or witnessed others do these things? As leaders, we need to be cognizant of the fact that these actions are seen by those we lead. What we are communicating may not be what we intended.

Visual–

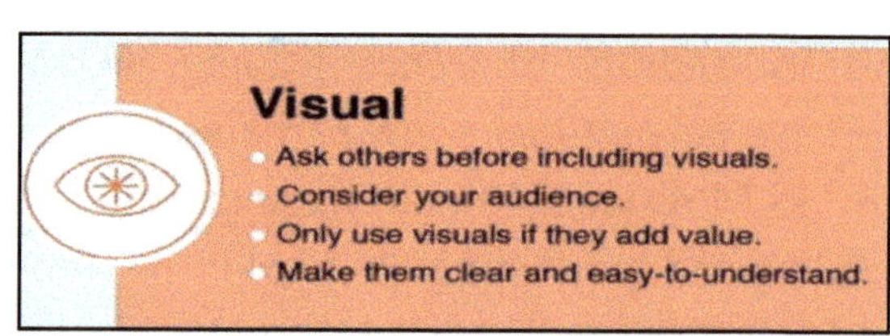

Visual communication is the use of photographs, art, drawings, sketches, charts and graphs to convey information. Visuals are often used as an aid during presentations to provide helpful context alongside written and/or verbal communication. Because people have different learning styles, visual communication might be more helpful for some in consuming ideas and information. Think of the adage, "A picture is worth a thousand words." Most of us have seen the iconic image of "Uncle Sam". It is a perfect example of visual, simple and effective communications. Nearly all of us have been in or seen a class, briefing, news cast or movie theater where some form of chart, picture or short video is employed to strengthen the communications. I spent several years as a public school teacher and regularly utilized these forms of visual aides to supplement the day's

lesson. We even use graphics in this book to help emphasize and further clarify our information. Even in great events in United States history, like the Lewis and Clark Expedition, drawings of flora and fauna were put into diaries to enhance written descriptions and explanations. Today is no different. We simply have more technology to capture the scene. In today's world it is normal for people to stop and pull out their mobile device and start recording…we've all seen it. Pew research polls indicate that approximately 70% of the United States population follow some sports team. Can you imagine, NO INSTANT REPLAY! Oh, the pain…

Written –

Written communication is exactly what you might think, such as writing, typing, or printing symbols like letters and numbers to convey information. It is helpful because it provides a record of information for reference. Writing is commonly used to share information through books, pamphlets, blogs, letters, memos and more. Emails and chats are common forms of written communication in the workplace. Reading and writing allow people to take the time to consider the communication because words have meaning and impact.

According to Forbes.com (in 2024), 23 ***billion*** texts are sent worldwide each day! It is a wildly popular form of communication. It is also very informal. My children are more likely to respond to a text than answer the phone. As an educator, I can tell you from first hand experience that texting is not helping our youth learn how to read and write. Several years ago I had an 8th grade student dictate a U.S. History paper to their computer and print it for submission without proofreading. Since I graded for spelling, punctuation, affix usage, and subject verb agreement, they did not have a passing grade.

Written communications can also be one of the most frustrating forms of communication. Recall when you had to draft an important email or letter. You spent considerable time choosing every word very carefully, double- and triple-checking, and even having a trusted friend or loved one proofread it. Then one of the following happens: The recipient doesn't understand your message. You never get a response. The response comes from someone other than the intended recipient, meaning the intended recipient probably never saw it. I've also seen managers respond to emails admonishing employees for not writing "professional" enough. Or, the response is a form letter that is only tacitly related to the topic you wrote about. Try writing an actual letter to your House of Representatives or Senate member.

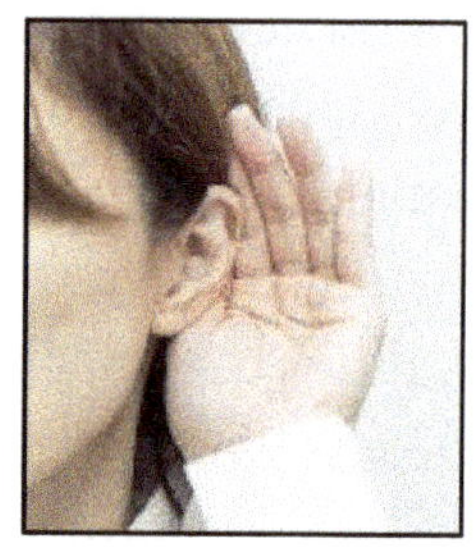

The 1st Amendment to the Constitution guarantees us five rights. One of those is the right to petition our government. Based on this, I recently sent such letters to 11 elected officials via registered mail regarding a court case I felt was not adjudicated fairly. I received replies, actual letters in the mail, from three of the elected officials' offices (I doubt the actual person ever saw the correspondence). Two of those responses basically said, "Not my problem" and the third directed me to a lower level elected official who never responded. However, if it is read with the intended level of detail, written language can be a very powerful tool. With time and a very expensive attorney, I was able to get the case in front of a higher level court and the lower level decision was nullified. Not one of the elected officials I contacted did a thing to assist. Being elected only makes you elected, it doesn't make you a leader. If you are a leader, respond, even if it is simply to say I received your correspondence.

As a leader, never underestimate the power of a handwritten (not typed) note or letter to someone you lead as a pat-on-the-back for a job well done, to say "thank you" for going above-&-beyond or to provide a "congratulations" for an achievement - talk about motivating people!

Multiple types of communication can be used simultaneously and often are. Mastering how to effectively communicate will increase your impact as a leader. It enables you to more readily *motivate people to achieve beyond their own perceived capabilities.* James 1:19 ESV states, "My dear brothers and sisters, take note of this: Everyone should be quick to listen, slow to speak and slow to become angry." By being patient and attentive listeners, we can better understand the needs and concerns of others, then respond (communicate) more thoughtfully and effectively. (IE: *motivate people to achieve beyond their own perceived capabilities, and face problems for which there appear to be no simple solutions.*)

Communication Traps to Avoid:
We introduced you to Dave Ramsey in Chapter 1 (How do we progress through the Phases of Leadership?) He is the CEO of Ramsey Solutions, eight-time national bestselling author, personal finance expert and host of The Ramsey Show.[43] If you dig deeper into the information, he shares examples of "toxic communications traps" that must be avoided.

Hoarding information.
It has been said by many that "information is power". However, today the "application of knowledge is power". Think about it, an iPhone 15 has 1 million times more computing power than the computers aboard Apollo 11 that took the first humans to the moon in July 1969.[44] Most of us carry a smartphone as a vestibule appendage with immediate access to the internet. So, a lot of information is readily available. Remember, not everything on the internet is true or accurate. You need to filter so you get what you need and are using reputable sites. How we apply the information we access is the key.

---

[43] Dave Ramsey. Toxic Communications. Ramsey. https://www.ramseysolutions.com/dave-ramsey - Nov 15th, 2023

[44] The Independent Staff. The Independent. https://www.independent.co.uk/ - Jan 3rd, 2024

In many organizations there is organizational information that becomes the key to success. If the people in leadership positions do not share the organizational information or dole it out in small bits or, worse yet, distort the information they do share, it can become toxic. Dave Ramsey calls this "mushroom communication", keeping people in the dark and feeding them manure. Some in leadership positions believe this allows them to maintain their pedestal position, however, eventually it stifles the initiative of those being led and produces a harmful environment where success is nearly impossible. Information travels in all directions, so you must always ask yourself, "***Who else needs to know?***"

There is a short scene in the movie "Dances with Wolves" (Released November 21, 1990, by Orion Pictures) in which Lieutenant John Dunbar is being sent to Fort Sedgwick by Major Fambrough. LT Dunbar asks Major Fambrough "How will I be getting there?" The Major angrily states "You think I don't know!". LT Dunbar replies "No sir, It's just that I don't know!"

If you are the leader, you must be able to communicate necessary information and be receptive to inquiry. Ask reasonable, prudent and cogent questions. Irish Playwright, George Bernard Shaw once quipped: "England and America are two nations divided by a common language." This comment highlights the problems you can face when you assume things are the same, but in reality, are similar!

Who Else Needs to Know? (The Impacts of not sharing information with your team)

When I managed a set of market facing categories as a Sourcing and Procurement Manager, I was responsible for setting the company procurement strategy and negotiated the pricing and terms of contracts with third party suppliers. Due to the complexity and time needed to negotiate a global agreement, we normally plan for the next significant sourcing event 1-2 years out. There was one category where an incumbent supplier had been performing these services for years but also had recent performance issues which affected our operations. We had an opportunity to negotiate lower pricing or consider an alternative supplier. I did my research, learned about the current market conditions, and consulted our business leaders for their needs in this category. In addition, I presented my strategy–of offering a tiered pricing model to save $4M annually–to management and received approvals to proceed. Simultaneously, the same leadership team were having alternative discussions with business operations about performing these services internally–a tented project. As the negotiation window closed, I eventually learned about the secret project and was told to wait for a go/no-go decision. Once the contract term nearly expired, our negotiating strength was lost and we had to accept month-to-month pricing until the final deal was approved. In the end, we paid 3% MORE for the next multi-year contract! During my annual evaluation, my manager noted, "You were unable to effectively manage your category and renew the contract before term expiration." I wrote a two page rebuttal in my recorded evaluation arguing that effective communication up and down the management chain may have prevented this outcome. However, my evaluation was submitted without any changes.

Gossip –
talking negatively about someone or something to anyone who is not one of your leaders. We have heard the term "Scuttlebutt". In seafaring, scuttle means drill and 'butt' refers to a fresh drinking cask on the ship. When crew would gather around for a drink, sailors would exchange rumors of the voyage and those rumors could potentially "scuttle" the ship. In fact, the one sure-fire way to bring an organization to ruin is to allow gossip to go unchecked. Leaders must promote an environment where the members of the organization know if they have a problem, they need to take it to their leader and no one else. Mark Twain said, "Two people can keep a secret if one of them is dead."

Avoiding Tough Conversations –

If you are having an issue with a person you lead, it needs to be handled as soon as possible. If you are peers, do it with the next higher level leader present. "Bad news doesn't get better with time." As the leader, you owe it to the people you lead and the entire organization to give people an honest assessment of their performance. Promotions in the military are based on potential. Promotions in the corporate world are based on prior performance, an indicator of future potential. If you have ever attended a military promotion ceremony, you have heard these words "their *demonstrated leadership potential* and dedicated service" when the order is read. I have been fortunate to be promoted in the military several times. Usually, the night before the official notification of the promotion list being released, I would receive a call from my boss congratulating me so I would know the next morning. Likewise, those who are eligible for promotion, but not selected, would also get a call to tell them they were not selected. A tough conversation has to take place. The military employs what is commonly referred to as an 'up-or-out' system. A tenure or partnership system dictates when a leader must be promoted in a hierarchical organization. Suppose a leader is not determined to be ready for promotion, and does not achieve a certain rank within a certain period of time. In that case, they eventually retire or separate from military service.[45]

Not Sharing Your Vision –
Having a vision is the difference between a JOB and a Profession. Treating people professionally and sharing your vision is motivating. Otherwise, it's the monotony of 9 to 5 that will quickly erode employee and organizational initiative.

Failing to Repeat Your Vision –
Most people learn from repetition. Pastor Andy Stanley says you have to cast your vision 21 times before anyone hears it.

---

[45] J. Connor Stull. Is "Up or Out" Holding Us Back? Army - June 22nd, 2021. https://www.army.mil/article/247749/is_up_or_out_holding_us_back - January 4th, 2024

To illustrate the importance of a vision and philosophy and, repeating it on a routine basis, we have the "**The 3 Bullets**".

Many U.S. Army officers spend the first 15 to 20 years of their careers striving to be selected as a Battalion Commander. It is not for everyone and not everyone is selected. However, once selected (and most likely even prior) many spend a lot of mental energy developing their own "Command Philosophy". Most end up writing a "Command Philosophy" paper and distributing it to the entire organization. I know one newly minted Commander who wrote a Command Philosophy 17 pages long! I doubt those under his command took the time to read and internalize the entire document. It is more likely that some failed to read the document or that others read it and then set it aside. Consequently, I didn't write one! In fact, I didn't write anything. I was, and still am, under the belief the unit wants to hear your voice and see your actions. So, we had "The Three Bullets".

These are three short, simple bullet comments:

- **Know and do your job!**
- **Be a Warrior!**
- **Remember you are an American Soldier and Act like it at all times!**

I believe these comments could easily and quickly explain my Command Philosophy, intent and vision for professionalism. I did not allow them to be written, put on some cheesy PowerPoint chart or incorporated into a poster to put on the wall. I expected every soldier in the unit to memorize them. I actually carried three inert 5.56 rounds in my pocket. I handed three inert 5.56 rounds to each of my subordinate commanders and expected them to carry them at all times. Any time I spoke to the unit, or subset of the unit, for the next two years, I used these three bullets as the foundation for my remarks and displayed the rounds I carried in my pocket as a visual representation. Changes of Command, NCO Induction Ceremonies, Promotions and Award Ceremonies, Hails and Farewells, Picnics, it did not matter the venue or occasion. I used these "bullets" as the cornerstone. Most people learn from repetition and it didn't take long. The unit quickly inculcated these ideas. Here is a brief explanation of the command vision:

- **Know and do your job!** –

  If you don't know your job, you can't do your job. If you can't do your job, someone else has to do it, so why do I need you?

- **Be a Warrior!** -

  One of the primary missions of the U.S. Army is to "meet the non-negotiable contract with the American people to fight and win the nation's wars." (From the Army Posture Statement 2002). This requires warriors! People with individual personal discipline, intestinal fortitude, a belief in something bigger than themselves and the willingness to sacrifice for the good of the nation.

- **Remember you are an American Soldier and Act like it at all times!**

  Being an American soldier requires CHARACTER and moral courage (see Chapter 4 - Self Leadership "If you can't lead yourself, how can you lead others?"). If someone sees a soldier acting as a fool or without moral courage, compromising their integrity, then they might conclude all soldiers are that way. Whatever you do, people don't just see you, they also see me and every other soldier!

For me, "The 3 Bullets" accomplished two very important things. First, they created Leadership even when I was not physically present, because I used every opportunity to engrain it into the thoughts and actions of the battalion's soldiers, into the very fabric of the unit. Second, they allowed me to meaningfully interface with soldiers one-on-one. I could ask a soldier to tell me one of the bullets and ask what it meant to them. In these situations, I led directly and not through subordinate leaders. It worked for me. In the 20+ years since I was a Battalion Commander I have had the distinct pleasure of interacting with many of the soldiers from that unit. They routinely mention one or all three of these "bullets" and how it has positively impacted their lives.

During our deployment to Iraq one of the achievements I was most proud of was the safety record of our Battalion. A microcosm of the impact of the "Three Bullets" occurred at Base Camp Victory after we

Leaders make the greatest impact at the point of execution. During a 1942 Associated Press Interview, General S. Patton Jr. said, "My theory is that a commander does what is necessary to accomplish his mission and that nearly 80 percent of his mission is to arouse morale in his men." [Edgar F. Puryear, Jr., 19 Stars (New York: Random House, 1971), 260]. These words indicate General Patton believed he did not need to be physically present; but rather, he could ensure his ideas and motivation were always present.

pulled out of Iraq and were preparing to come home. My Executive Officer (XO) shared this short story with me: For safety reasons, we made it an order that no tracked vehicles would move on the Base Camp without ground guides both in the front and rear of the vehicle and, all soldiers involved in moving tracked vehicles would be wearing Kevlar helmets and reflective gear. Late one day the XO saw two soldiers who needed to move a vehicle only a short distance. Rather than to quickly do it with only the two of them–even though chances are no one would know (see "Moral Courage" in Chapter 4 - Self Leadership "If you can't lead yourself, how can you lead others?")--they walked back to the tent area and asked a third soldier to help them move the vehicle. This is a direct reflection of the consistent emphasis of the "Three Bullets" over a two year period.

Not Listening / Paying Attention –

I had a good friend who was a wrestling coach. I once heard him tell his team, "Everyone has seven holes in their head, you learn the most by keeping six open and one closed." Great leaders have conversations with their employees—not one-sided dialogues. In the popular movie "Rush Hour" (Released on September 18, 1998 and Distributed by: New Line Cinema, Warner Brothers, Columbia Pictures, TriStar Pictures, FilmFlex) there is a line, "Do you understand the words that are coming out of my mouth?" Leaders simply can't hear words or say words. Leaders must understand the information, ideas and concepts being provided to them and, conversely, must be able to communicate / project those to the organizations they lead. "When people talk, listen completely. Most people never listen."- Ernest Hemingway.

The importance of applying active listening techniques is critical. When you are in a meeting with your leader or manager or a group of colleagues, it is clear when that person (or people) is so eager to get their next words or points across without internalizing and understanding the information being relayed by others.

Consider how you feel in those situations when the other party is multi-tasking, checking their watch, looking at their cell phone or not being engaged in the conversation.

Not Defining Success or What Right Looks Like - How do we do this? By *fostering an environment in which people motivate themselves to achieve beyond their own perceived capabilities, and face problems for which there appear to be no simple solutions.* It is essential the leader knows where the organization is and where it is going.

When in defense contracting my boss gave me this vague guidance, "Go to Portland!" What do you do with this? You should start asking questions. There are twenty-four towns or cities in the United States named "Portland". There are more in other countries around the world. That said, which "Portland"? What mode of transportation will you use? What are you doing when you get there? What is the duration of the stay? Is anyone going with you? Are you getting the idea? Being able to solve the problem goes directly to our definition of "Leadership". It also goes to communication. You must be ready, willing, able and fearless enough to ask questions and expect the Leader to provide reasonable and cogent answers.

Avoid Shining a Light on Problems –

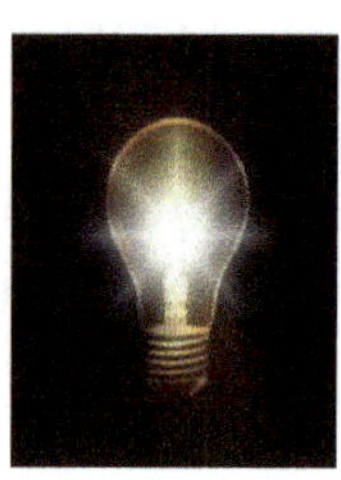

We've heard this before, "Bad news doesn't get better with time." In our experience the earlier a problem is identified, the easier it is to solve. It is a lot easier to pay attention to the fuel gauge in your car and fill-up while it is still running than to drive your car empty and then walk to the gas station with an empty gas can and walk back with a full one. I know, it sounds simplistic but, you'd be surprised. The leader is responsible for everything, including warning signs of an impending problem and 'heading the problem off at the pass.' If you ignore the problem, it will eventually come back as a larger, more complex problem.

A former Brigade Commander once described to me how he routinely communicates with his 3 subordinate Battalion Commanders while in Garrison (e.g., at home station, not deployed). He believed that leading his Battalion Commanders was easier than Battalion Commanders leading their subordinate Company / Battery commanders. This is because the Department of the Army centrally selected Battalion Commanders and, in his words, "There are only two types of Battalion Commanders, good and better." He said one of his battalion commanders would call him on the phone almost every day and discuss information believed to be key, which would allow him to ask questions. He had a second Battalion Commander who sent him a daily email, usually early morning, talking about key information. He could reply to the email or make a call if he needed additional information. Finally, he had a third Battalion Commander who stopped in his office several times a week for face-to-face interactions which enabled open discussion and collaboration. The Leader understood that dictating a formalized form or format to communicate with his subordinate commanders, he likely would not receive the critical information he needed to make informed decisions. Of course, there was still the regularly scheduled "Command and Staff" meeting with the rigid set of information projected on the screen of the conference room, but due to the open and flexible lines-of-communications between professionals, the Leader was rarely surprised by the information presented which allowed the organization to get ahead of most perceived problems before they became actual problems.

Benefits of Good Communications.

There are a wide range of benefits derived from effective communications. Some of the most beneficial are: creating a stronger, more cohesive team; improved organizational morale through positive engagement; generating a shared sense of purpose for the organization; and generating trust.

Creating a stronger, more cohesive team:

Trust (see Chapter 6 - How To Build Trust and to Trust in Others) is one of the most powerful derivatives of good communications. Trust is one of the most effective, far reaching and consistent ways for leaders, managers, administrators, and employees to build strong cohesive teams. When the entire team or organization communicates in a positive way, they build trust with each other, increasing productivity and strength.

Improved organizational morale through positive engagement:

Another dominant derivative of good communication is routine high quality workforce engagement. This, in turn, aids in boosting morale. In any organization, employees will look for–even expect–meaningful communication from leaders. An engaged workforce is characterized by high job satisfaction, feels personally invested in team / organizational success, and self-generates a positive work environment.

Generating a shared sense of purpose for the organization:

A third influential derivative of good communication is a shared sense of organizational purpose. Effective communication generates an environment of positive groupthink with an understanding of the leader' vision and organizational purpose. This positive vision also generates a more productive team. Leaders are now able to *face problems for which there appear to be no simple solutions*, backed with a confident and trusting workforce.

During Operation Desert Shield, I found myself and my team of soldiers on an airfield in Saudi Arabia. The ambient temperature on the tarmac of the airfield was 120+ degrees Fahrenheit! Being on the ground with my soldiers gave me a true appreciation for the conditions and hardships they regularly faced. I consulted the Senior Sergeant on the scene. I called for additional water, directed breaks in shaded areas, removed load-bearing equipment and directed unblousing boots. Conversely, during a training event while stationed in Alaska the ambient temperature was 55+ degrees below zero Fahrenheit. If I were to spend all of my time in the command post tent next to the heater, I would not have been able to properly assess (and mitigate) the environmental risk to the soldiers. This could impact my recommendations to the Battalion Commander. My presence earned trust in my communication and confidence in my risk assessments.

Pitfalls of poor communication:

As you may imagine, many of the results of poor communication are the opposite of those things mentioned above. With poor communication: trust suffers, team cohesion weakens, that sense of belonging and job satisfaction becomes nonexistent, and employee turnover increases which jeopardizes the organizational mission / operations.

Recently, the state of Arkansas passed the "LEARNS Act".[46] One of the results of this Act set the minimum annual salary for an Arkansas Teacher in the 2023 - 2024 school year to $50,000. A noble goal. This is how it was characterized and communicated to the teachers of Arkansas. The practical application of this was not so clean. Today (the year 2024) there are teachers in their first year making $50,000, the highest starting pay for teachers in the United States. There are also teachers with 26 years' experience making, you guessed it, $50,000. There are teachers with "Master Teacher" credentials making, you guessed it, $50,000. Some school districts are laying off classified employees (custodial workers, bus drivers, technology coordinators, among others). These same districts are canceling extracurricular activities, including field trips, low participation sports teams and some events are being scheduled virtual, to save costs. There are others looking at altering schedules to four day school weeks to save on transportation and utility costs. All this, and more, generates the funds to pay teachers because taxes will not cover the deficit created by the LEARNS Act. Not to mention, no reward or pay incentives are tied to teacher experience and advanced education. The communication of this

[46] Eric Saunders. LEARNS Teacher Minimum Salary and Raise Fund. Arkansas Department of Education. May 11th, 2023. https://adecm.ade.arkansas.gov/ViewApprovedMemo.aspx?Id=5469#:~:text=Act%20237%20of%202023%2C%20the,of%20%242%2C000%20in%202023%2D24 - January 29th, 2024

reality is so weak that in one situation an employee being laid-off was notified the day before the Thanksgiving Holiday that they would be released before the Christmas break. This has, in some districts, created a toxic environment where there is no trust, teachers are looking for other meaningful employment and doing the least amount to get by the school year. The secondary, tertiary and quaternary impact of this will be felt in a few years by public school graduates trying to compete with those with a higher education quality. The vision and intent of this Act was positive. The practical application, not so much. Forward thinking leaders will consider the impacts of their decision before executing.

Failure to take advantage of technology:

Today, technology simply is! If you can't use it, you can't communicate. In today's fast-paced world, many skills are considered a baseline merely to remain minimally effective. You must be able to use the skills of word processing, spreadsheets and programs to make presentations and charts. You must also be able to skillfully employ your device for phone / conference calls, text, email, news feeds, research, pictures, video, access to social media, et al. There are many social media and networking options–personal and professional–available, and most people use more than one. Some people today base their value on the number of "followers" they have or the number of "likes" they receive. Communicating with others and taking advantage of the technology is a MUST for any modern leader. As a leader you need to be mindful of advancements, upgrades and new trends for communication related technology. Learning which communication methods and ways your team / organization prefers is important. The more methods you employ the more people you reach. I can't imagine a successful political candidate who doesn't take advantage of all forms of technology. In some instances, the candidate's effective use of technology is the difference between being elected and going home. Not long ago my wife tried to call our granddaughter on the phone several times with no answer and became frustrated. I sent my granddaughter a text: "Call your grandmother NOW!" The phone rang in less than a minute. Remember, one-on-one direct (and in-person when possible) communication is still powerful. That's why politicians still hold rallies, shake hands, kiss babies and sometimes go door to door.

Not giving clear and actionable feedback.

Nearly every employee receives an annual performance evaluation from their leader / manager. Often, feedback is also given throughout the year when the opportunity for development arises. I remember a time when I received feedback from my manager about an email I sent to his manager. During one of our periodic one-on-one managers to employee meetings, I shared that the project timeline may be in jeopardy, due to an issue with one of our stakeholders. He recommended I send an e-mail to his manager, who was on vacation and gave me 3-4 specific talking points to include. Once I completed the draft, sent to him for approvals, I sent the e-mail and assumed we effectively communicated to higher management for further decision. One day later, he asked if we could talk about a problem. He explained that the email I sent was not "executive enough" and should have considered the audience. Naturally, I became defensive but asked what I could have improved about the e-mail. Rather than provide examples of how to improve an important message or provide actionable development advice, he maintained that I was not accepting the guidance and advice given. We then talked past each other trying to articulate our positions without resolution. This was a missed opportunity for the manager to communicate feedback to help the employee grow and develop.

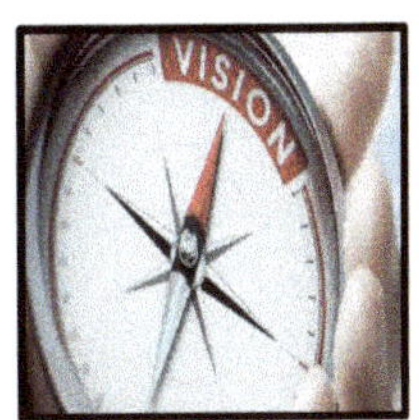

As leaders, we must be able to articulate our vision and intent through all forms of communication. In this chapter, we discussed verbal, nonverbal, visual, and written communication. We must also be able to employ all available mediums to reach a wide and diverse audience to make certain every member of the organization gets the message. Otherwise, we will be left with gossip and inaccurate interpretations of information. As leaders, we must also be willing and able to flex to changing situations and unanticipated results. Leaders should do everything possible to anticipate results, but no one is perfect.

In the case of the LEARNS Act, the vision and intent came from some of the highest levels. Even with these poor results, senior leadership did not implement any changes. Lower levels of leaders, managers and administrators are being forced to deal with the negative results. "Lead the way you want to be led and follow the way you want to be followed." As we noted on Graphic 4 (in the Introduction), most of us will spend the vast majority of our time in a position of simultaneous Leadership and Followership. Communication is a part of everything we do as both Leaders and Followers.

A leader with good communication skills already begins the problem-solving process and can overcome seemingly insurmountable situations. Remember the quote at the beginning of this chapter, it is "impossible to over-communicate." As previously discussed, lifelong learning is one of those areas that require continuous refinement of your communication capabilities.

- Communication is a constant activity. The most effective leaders use all types:
  - Verbal
  - Non-verbal
  - Visual
  - Written
- Sharing information is a powerful tool. Think, "Who else needs to know?"
- Avoid gossip!
- "Bad news doesn't get better with time."
- Articulate your vision for your organization at every opportunity.
- Listen and pay attention.
- Good Communication and associated skills:
  - Creates strong cohesive teams.
  - Improves organizational morale.
  - Generates a shared sense of purpose.
  - Facilitates Trust.
- With poor communication:
  - Erodes trust.

- Weakens team cohesion.
- Employee turnover increases and jeopardizes the organizational mission / operations.

Chapter 6
How Do You Build Trust?

"Trust is like the air we breathe – when it's present, nobody really notices; when it's absent, everybody notices."
Warren Buffett

Trust doesn't happen overnight. It builds gradually, so don't be pushy or try to change your personality to build trust with others. This could have the opposite impact and create distrust. Trust is learned and earned in tough times and maintained in good times. We have talked about the fact leadership is about authenticity and genuine connection to people. Remember: *Leadership is the ability to foster an environment in which people motivate themselves to achieve beyond their own perceived capabilities, and face problems for which there appear to be no simple solutions.* Instead, be authentic, so others know your words and actions are not contrived, letting them know you deserve their trust.[47]

TRUST	
Merriam Webster Dictionary	Reliance on the character, ability, strength, or truth of someone or something.
Cambridge Dictionary	To believe that someone is good and honest and will not harm you, or that something is safe and reliable.
Britannica Dictionary	Belief that someone or something is reliable, good, honest, effective.

[47] Jamie Birt. 14 Tips for Building Trust at Work (And Why It Matters). Indeed. February 3rd, 2023. https://www.indeed.com/career-advice/career-development/building-trust - February 17th, 2024

Synonyms	Confidence, Expectation, Faith, Hope, Assurance, Certainty, Certitude, Conviction, Credence, Credit, Dependence, Positiveness, Reliance, Stock, Store, Sureness
Antonyms	Disbelief, Distrust, Doubt, Uncertainty

- ***Table 6 (Trust): Definitions / Synonyms / Antonyms.***

Trust is a derivative of many things. Look at the common terms in the definitions of "trust" in the Table above: Truth, Honesty, Good, Reliance, and Character. These are qualities proven out over time. They can't be fully demonstrated overnight or in a single event. So how do we earn trust? In a word, **consistency**. Building trust requires consistent truth, consistent honesty, consistent good, consistent reliability, and consistent character. "Whoever can be trusted with very little can also be trusted with much, and whoever is dishonest with very little will also be dishonest with much." Luke 16:10 NIV

How to establish trust:

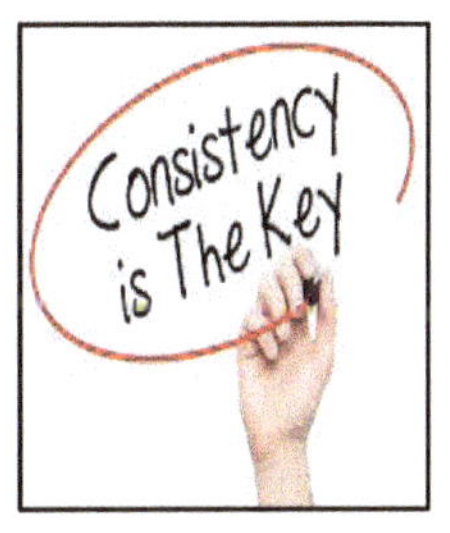

Consistency is key. One effective way to produce consistency is to anticipate and prepare for the inevitable. Have a plan for how you will handle common situations: cell phones will ring and buzz during a meeting; there will be a death in the family; employees will have babies; get married; attend graduations; get sick; experience infidelity; infighting, even lies, stealing and cheating, you name it. During my first week at the Command and General Staff College (CGSC, 1994)--today referred to as Intermediate Level Education or ILE–the school Commandant had all the students (approximately 700 officers) in a large auditorium for a presentation. The Commandant provided some interesting statistics stating that based on the number of students in this 11 month long in-resident school, he could predict: some students will receive a Driving Under the Influence (DUI) ticket, some will pass-away before graduation, some will suffer the death of an immediate family member, others you will fail to graduate because of honor violations, among other sobering predictions. He was very accurate. In fact, four Chaplains, who garner inherent trust, did not graduate because they were found to be copying history papers for submission. Planning or preparing for the inevitable (the future) is not a new concept. When I played high school baseball in the 1970s, the coach would describe a field situation and then ask, "What will you do if the ball is hit to you?" There are many organizations out there whose mission statement is to help you plan for the inevitability of retirement. There are insurance companies of all types; life, health, home, auto, et al. These companies are all about planning ahead for some diagnosis, accident, or natural disaster. My sister-in-law was fond of saying, "I'm insurance poor!" Sometimes planning ahead is expensive. Recently, I heard a series of messages from Pastor Craig Groeschel, founder of Life Church, and he used the term "**pre-decide**." You can 'pre-decide' how you are going to react in a wide variety of situations. This will help generate consistency and, in turn, trust. Let's take a look at those things that simply fell out of our definition of trust, above.

Truth:

If someone is going to trust you, you can't simply be truthful some of the time or even most of the time. Trust requires being truthful ALL of the time. Telling the truth all the time creates predictability. This allows those you lead to consistently know what to expect. The moment you are not truthful, you have introduced doubt in the relationship that never truly abates. We can start using the tactic of "pre-deciding" right here. Long ago, I had a Battalion Commander who had some simple rules for Officer self-conduct, although he did not use the term "pre-decided", he had predetermined outcomes. They included:

NEVER put your integrity in a position of potential compromise;

NEVER sign a report you are not 100% certain is accurate;

ALWAYS have a receipt for every penny of the Army's money you have spent.

He spoke in superlatives, never and always; however, you either tell the truth and have integrity or, you don't; truth is a superlative.

In order to be truthful, you also have to show candor. You can't beat around the bush. We observe this often with politicians. They want to use words and phrases allowing them to be interpreted in different ways. You can pre-decide you will have candor. This doesn't imply you are mean, cruel or insensitive but rather, compassionate and merciful. 20 years ago, I had a young junior officer (Captain) who reported to me. He was a nice fellow. He took pride in being an Officer in the Army. However, he lacked the tools to be effective over the long haul of a military career. As his leader, it was my responsibility to communicate this to him. I told him to consider taking a different path and look at other career options. I gave him an annual efficiency report (known in the Army as an Officer Evaluation Report [OER]) that reflected his average performance but made it clear that his promotion chances were low. This report did not surprise him, but he did take it to heart. Today, he is a successful Senior Manager at a large Banking, Mortgage and Investing Company. By pre-deciding to be candid, he made a well-informed long-term career change which eventually led to long-term success.

Being truthful also requires being accurate. We have all heard the "fish-tale." I caught a fish that weighed 5 pounds but the next time the story is told, the fish weighed 6 pounds and two years later the fish weighed 8 pounds. This is an exaggeration, embellishment, or puffery. This subtle form of altering the truth will also cause trust to fade. It forces those around you to question the veracity of information and, in some instances, spend valuable time verifying data prior to moving forward. In today's culture, many news organizations have teams of "fact checkers" to dig into comments made by politicians…a bit of a "gotcha" squad. One of the local news broadcasts where I live has a segment called, "Let's verify" and digs into viewer-generated questions. You can decide–now–to be consistent in providing the most accurate information / facts available. People can do their own fact-finding if they desire. Being consistent in this area will save time and generate trust.

Honesty:

Again, back to moral courage: consistently doing the right thing and doing things right even when no one is watching. I have often heard the phrase “choosing the hard right over the easy wrong.” The United States Military Academy at West Point has a Cadet Honor Code: "A Cadet will not lie, cheat, steal, nor tolerate those who do." When you accept an appointment to this venerable institution you are pre-deciding to follow this code. This is an individual and personal discipline approach to honesty and integrity. You will not only not “lie, cheat, nor steal” but also hold those around you accountable for their actions. In other words, you can’t simply stand by passively and ignore violations. How often do we hear about or see some bad act taking place and most people pull out their phone to take videos or pictures instead of intervening. We have said this before, leaders are inherently people of *action*. Being willing to stand up for what’s right will earn you both trust and respect.

I remember one instance of West Point’s Honor Code in real-time action. Each military academy places a very high premium on honesty and encourages everyone to be held to a higher standard. The majority of Professors and instructors at West Point are either active duty officers or civilians with a strong affiliation to the military. They are also responsible for spreading West Point’s culture and motto. As part of the school curriculum, cadets are evaluated along three main pillars: academic, military, and physical. In addition to the strenuous academic workload, we also took 2 military-focused courses every semester. In one case, as a Sophomore (Yearling), we were taking a mid-course test for a military development course. I was sitting next to my roommate, who would be a third generation West Point graduate. As the test time ended, the instructor–an Army Major and Academy graduate–yelled, “Cease work!”. You saw 25 cadets, except for my roommate, promptly drop their pencils on the desk. He kept writing for at least 10 seconds past the test time. Once again, the instructor yelled, “Cease work!!!”

and directed his gaze and attention towards the outlier in the group. My roommate eventually dropped his pencil but the damage was done. He sought an unfair advantage and likely violated the school's Honor Code. His actions kicked off an official Honor Board investigation. The Honor Board is composed of fellow cadets and school advisors–many are assigned as liaisons between the school and the cadet company. He was found guilty of violating the Honor Code and was promptly dismissed from the school. In the end, he made a decision to seek an unfair advantage costing him a military career.

Your actions, the ethical standards you hold yourself to, also contribute to your honesty and your ability to gain trust. Deciding ahead of time to do the right thing is a form of Self-Leadership (Phase One). You can simply look back through recent history to find numerous incidents of people who spent years in the spotlight with the air of honesty only to find their ethical standards were flawed: James Orsen "Jim" Bakker of the PTL Club; James Warren "Jim" Jones of The Peoples Temple; Samuel Benjamin Bankman-Fried of the FTX cryptocurrency exchange; Martha Helen Stewart and ImClone stock trading; CIA Director David Howell Petraeus and an extramarital affair. We could make this list VERY long. This is just a small sampling of those who were caught or 'exposed'. There are more whose actions or activities never make the light of day and continue to prey on others' trust for their own personal gain. These events will continue to happen, and everyone should learn a lesson about honesty. But let's simplify the scenario. We all know the person who has coffee at the office and never contributes to the "coffee fund"; The person who never seems to pick-up the check at dinner but orders a meal every time a group goes out; The person who volunteers for the bake-sale and never makes a cookie or helps out at the booth. Yes, these are subtle forms of honesty; however, they can still destroy others' trust in you and bring your integrity into question. Pre-decide to be consistently honest, not just in the big things, but also in the small things … you will gain the reputation of unquestioned integrity and trust.

Good:

Consistently doing good for others will earn you respect. So, pre-decide to be helpful. Trustworthy people tend to go out of their way to help people if they can. Not because of some agenda or perceived reward but because they're genuinely good people. This can also earn you a positive reputation. Maybe you've done all of your work for the day. You could take off early or sit at your desk browsing the internet…or, you could be helpful. If you notice a coworker who is struggling with their own workload, offer to help. Or perhaps, ask your manager if there's anything extra you can take on. Consider helping out the new hire who may not want to ask for help. I spent two years on the Army Staff at the Pentagon (pre 9/11). Traversing the complex and similar looking hallways–especially on my first day–was challenging. That morning, another officer said, "Let me show you where the closest latrine is so you can at least go to the bathroom on your own." Humorous, but true. Just that small modicum of autonomy on the first day was helpful, and as time went on, I learned that the helpful officer was consistently helpful to those he interacted with. He was willing to proofread position papers, review a spreadsheet, and sit in on meetings to provide his perspectives on issues. Not just for me, but for anyone who needed help. His pre-decision to be a nice guy earned him respect and trust from the entire team.

Consistently doing good includes ensuring your actions and behaviors align with your words and internal beliefs. In other words, being Authentic! Pre-decide you will "walk-the-walk" and not just "talk-the-talk!" This comes from discovering your leadership style and using your style to make decisions reflecting your ethics, values, and personality.[48]

Some things to consider:

Think about your leadership image.

How are you viewed or perceived by those you lead? Are you an anomaly, unpredictable and prone to mood swings? If so, people around you become hesitant and lose confidence. Are you seen as unapproachable and aloof? This will cause people to make every effort at avoidance. They will apply more effort finding legitimate excuses to

---

[48] Leading Effectively Staff. Authentic Leadership: What It Is, Why It Matters. Center for Creative Leadership. November 17th, 2020. https://www.ccl.org/articles/leading-effectively-articles/authenticity - February 27, 2024.

stay away from you than to apply their skills and mental capacity on organizational success. Are you perceived as a know-it-all or a "my way or the highway leader?" This will cause your organization to become lemmings. They will be unwilling to present new and innovative ideas for fear of ridicule. This will stifle and crush initiative. On one occasion, I, along with three other Colonels, briefed our commander, a Lieutenant General (3-Star). We did our due diligence: gathered information, developed courses of action, analyzed outcomes, applied screening and evaluative criteria, developed a relative value decision matrix, and presented a pre-brief to a Brigadier General (1-Star) in the unit. The commander scheduled the briefing for 9 PM. We could think of no purpose for this unreasonable time. Looking back, I would call it poor time management. The only people present for the briefing were the Lieutenant General and the four colonels mentioned earlier. The presentation went south from the very start. The General ripped the first chart out of the briefing book and said, "This looks like the work of second lieutenants." To him, our work looked unprofessional and not reflective of senior officers. Then he stated, "This is F…B…S…!" (We will only use the acronym; use your imagination). One of the other Colonels was taking notes as I trudged on with the presentation. In his notes, he wrote the same acronym. In the next 30 minutes, the General used that phrase 47 more times. Soon thereafter,he threw us out of his office with an order, "Tell my Generals I am disappointed in them." I hope it is not necessary to provide a detailed explanation of how this is not only poor leadership but also counterproductive. If you don't respect the people you lead, you are not a leader. From that time forward, we only did the minimum to meet the order of this Commander. There was a preplanned and scheduled change of command coming soon after and we did our best to survive the last few weeks of his command. It is possible to crush your organization. Don't allow arrogance to replace real leadership. From my fellow Colonels, I witnessed true professionalism that night. If they are reading this, THANKS.

<u>Know your strengths and weaknesses.</u>

You do this by pre-deciding to do a consistent and candid evaluation of yourself. Once you begin Phase One (Self Leadership), this becomes perpetual. This gives you the opportunity to capitalize on your strengths and seek to assuage your weaknesses with education, learning, and collected experiences. Bring people into your team with the necessary skills to mitigate your shortcomings. Being truthful with yourself as a leader while understanding your own strengths and weaknesses as a leader is a common theme in our interviews (Chapter 14 - What insights can we gain from Leaders across different specialties?). In our interview with Dr. Beau Sparkman, he discusses a leader understanding their strengths and weaknesses. In doing so, it allows the leader to surround themself with team members complementing them. An example might be a visionary leader who will need people to execute and see a project or vision through to completion. When speaking with Mayor George McGill, he noted that every leader has "shortcomings or flaws" that may not suit everyone. Leaders must recognize their weaknesses and find ways to ensure they don't negatively impact relationships or objective outcomes. "Staying calm" is one of the easiest and best ways to accomplish this. This self awareness and deliberate action based on this knowledge will consistently reflect authenticity and lend itself to trust.

Consensus Building.

You can pre-decide to proactively solicit ideas, opinions and perspectives from those you lead. It doesn't mean you always have to use this input; however, being willing to seek it out will net you trust and respect. Sometimes you act upon solicited input, which will often gain "buy-in" and "full throated" employee support. When we interviewed Ryan Gehrig he said, "When choosing members for your team consider their authenticity coupled with the ability and willingness to respectfully challenge leadership." You want people around you willing to thoughtfully speak "truth to power". Simply being the leader or in the leadership position doesn't mean you know everything. Robert Gould Shaw was only 25 years old when he assumed command of the 54th Massachusetts Infantry during the U.S. Civil War.[49] He is depicted in the highly acclaimed movie "Glory"

[49] American Battlefield Trust Staff. Robert Gould Shaw. American Battlefield Trust. https://www.battlefields.org/learn/biographies/robert-gould-shaw - March 1st, 2024

(Released December 15th, 1989 and Distributed by: TriStar Pictures, Sony Pictures Home Entertainment) as seeking the input of the more mature soldiers under his command. This earned him their trust and their respect.

Work on being a more effective communicator.

Good communication is another way to openly display authenticity and consistency. Communication is discussed in greater detail in Chapter 5 - Communication "Do leaders really communicate or just tell people what to do?" - Learning to communicate with others. You can pre-decide to make communication a priority and develop methods that work for you and your organization.[50]

Clear communication is paramount and helps to clear up misunderstandings or misinterpretations. Avoid overusing technical jargon but spelling out acronyms and use several different mediums to get your message out (written, spoken, video). Having a consistent message and using similar methods to communicate helps to build trust and credibility. Communication experts know that being consistently clear sets the stage for audience engagement.

You also need to be concise. Provide essential information upfront. Many people call this the "Bottom Line Up Front" or "BLUF." This will help keep your audience engaged, grabbing their attention making them more willing to receive your message. This is particularly true when communicating with your leader. We have found many people in the late stages of Phase Three or in Phase Four of Leadership who only pay attention to the topic sentence or the first written / spoken paragraph. If they don't feel it is important to them, their thoughts and time go elsewhere. Being concise saves time by preventing information overload, focuses on the central idea, and facilitates rapid dissemination.

Establishing a consistent schedule also promotes trust, fosters good relationships; again, requiring good communication. Most organizations have a routine update brief with a specific format. As a school teacher,

---

[50] The Sheffield Company Staff. The 3 C's of Communication: Clear, Concise, Consistent. The Brief Lab,. https://thebrieflab.com/blog/the-3-cs-of-communication-clear-concise-consistent/ - February 21st, 2024.

our school principal held a weekly meeting each Wednesday with a published agenda. As a Battalion Commander, I held a "Command and Staff" meeting weekly with a set format. Both of these are examples of tools to help rapidly circulate information to a wide audience.

Reliability:

This is the very essence of consistency. Earning trust through reliability means you are not an anomaly. Are you doing the right things and are you doing them right? This goes to moral courage. Can others count on you and can you count on yourself? Make decisions ahead of time and then you will not have to think about it and you will simultaneously create consistency.

As a Battalion Commander, I made several "pre-decisions." Very early in my tenure as a battalion commander, I determined that our battalion would do everything possible to avoid being assigned, detailed, or tasked to support social events. We did not want to host cookouts and flip burgers and then be the clean-up detail. We did not want to participate in fishing tournaments and bait hooks. We did not want to march in parades and stand in formations. These are all very visible events, the public likes seeing soldiers and many commanders found them fun. My thought was that they had no mission-focused training value for soldiers who were charged with "meeting the non-negotiable contract with the American people to fight and win the nation's wars." The question became, how do you get off the duty roster for these events? We started looking ahead at coming events and would volunteer for any event using live ammunition like live-fire demonstrations, live-fire ranges or events requiring soldiers to put their hands on their actual equipment like displays and demonstrations. This kept the focus on the true mission of the unit. When we were told to go and support a "social event", we pointed out the fact we were already assigned to another task. It worked, and the soldiers of the battalion had more trust and confidence in their combat skills and knew they were not squandering time on nice, but relatively unimportant events.

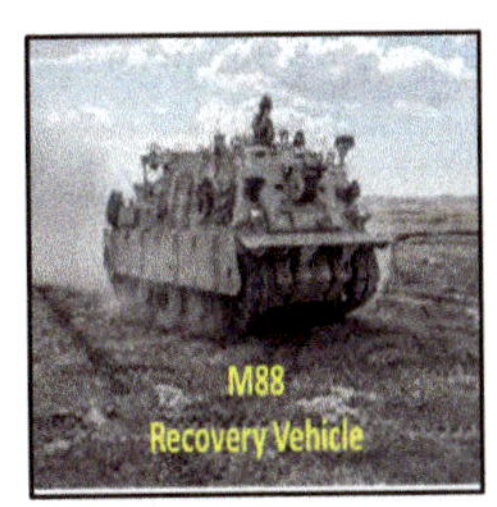

During Operation Iraqi Freedom (OIF) I made the "pre-decision" soldiers were more important than anything - you'd think this is a no brainer. Soon after crossing into Iraq, an M88 recovery vehicle broke down. At 55 tons, nothing else in the battalion (except another M88) could recover the disabled vehicle. We abandoned the non-mission capable (broken-down) M88 and conserved the three remaining for higher priority missions, specifically to recover our M270A1 Launchers if necessary. We left the broken down vehicle unattended to continue our mission. You would think this was natural; however, soldiers are taught strict property accountability, and Battery Commanders spend much of their time in garrison accounting for property. Taking care of and accounting for their equipment is ingrained in them from the very beginning of their service. The action of this pre-decision set the tone for the remainder of the operation. As the battalion moved toward Baghdad and beyond, similar situations occurred many times. Some circumstances involved vehicles being disabled from unexploded ordnance or vehicle accidents. The battalion abandoned non-mission capable (damaged or broken-down) HMMWVs, ammunition vehicles and trailers (still containing valuable Army Tactical Missile rounds), M577A3 command post vehicles and other trucks and trailers. We recorded the location of the vehicles for future recovery, if possible. But no soldier remained behind to guard a vehicle. This communicated that our soldiers were the most valued resource. This earned trust by proving the value of the soldiers and they, in turn, became more confident and more lethal. Soldier-accountability became an overt source of pride for the unit and the battalion's senior Non-Commissioned Officers (NCOs). The 2002 film, "We Were Soldiers" depicts this same value of soldiers. In the movie, there is a scene when the brigade commander asks Lieutenant Colonel Moore, "Hal, how many men do you have battle ready, give or take?" Moore turns to his Command Sergeant Major (CSM) and then replies, "395 exactly."

Another "pre-decision" I made as a Battalion Commander was to always make decisions for the good of the organization over the individual, including myself. In concert with this, I decided we were going to strictly follow the rules governing "emergency leave." These are covered in Army Regulation 600-8-10 "Leaves and Passes." In the spirit of complete transparency, I even had copies of this section of the regulation made and handed out prior to our deployment to Iraq. I knew if an exception was made for one soldier then an exception would be needed for every soldier. While in Iraq, our battalion, like all of them, had soldiers who became new fathers during the deployment. Not once did any of them get sent home for the birth. Having a newborn did not rise to the level of "emergency leave" according to the regulation. I was very consistent on this point. When it came time to redeploy the battalion, I had to send a detail home approximately one week early to prepare things for the battalion's return home. The detail of soldiers I sent home included everyone in the battalion with a new child they had not yet held. This included Officers, NCOs and soldiers. The instructions to the leaders of the detail were simple: Do everything you can, between 8AM and 5PM each day, to prepare for the remainder of us to return home, then, spend as much time as possible with your family. Trust through consistent action.

These are only three examples of "pre-decisioning." Pre-decisions can cover a wide variety of leadership situations and apply to all leadership phases. Pre-decision creates consistency for the building of long term trust.

Character:

Our mental and moral qualities, our character, can also exude or, conversely, suppress trust. What we believe should determine how we act. Again, we can pre-decide to follow a moral code without intentional deviation. You establish this with consistency. When people can look back at a trail of positive past performance and routine success, acquired through hard-work, ethical practices and respect for the people around you, they will get in line to follow you!

As a School Teacher I made the pre-decision that I would not "hug" students. I did daily high-fives, fist bumps, and hearty handshakes, and I even had one or two students who did elbow bumps (think COVID). Even though other teachers routinely "hugged" students, the students quickly realized I would not and came to respect it (consistency). As a male teacher, my belief was I should not be that close to my teenage female students. I wasn't going to allow for any possible perception of impropriety. In concert with this, I did not believe it right for me to be in a classroom, alone, with only female students. I had been a teacher for only a few weeks and an announcement was made that one of the school's athletic teams was to report to the gymnasium. After the exodus, I had only two 7th grade female students remaining. Against school safety policy, I opened my classroom door, told the teacher next door about the situation, and asked her to leave the door open in her classroom, which she did. A few minutes later the School Principal, who was walking down the hall, stepped in and asked why the door was open. I explained the reasoning and he never asked again. I stayed true to my character by staying consistent and respectfully communicating my position to others.

When one searches, "*Who is considered the best leader of all time?*" needless to say, thousands of results and lists appeared. One particular name appearing most often was Mahatma Gandhi. He is considered the Father of the Nation in India. He led the country to independence through nonviolent resistance. His philosophy of non-violence (ahimsa) and truth (satyagraha) inspired movements worldwide. Gandhi's dedication to justice, communal harmony, and civil rights left an enduring legacy, earning him global respect. His emphasis on moral and ethical leadership has influenced political and social figures across generations and around the world, emphasizing the power of peaceful resistance in achieving significant societal change.[51]

When discussing the possibility of a third term as president, George Washington expressed his desire to avoid being, as he wrote,

---

[51] Testbook Staff. Top 10 Great Leaders of the World – Know Most Powerful Leaders in History & Greatest Leaders of 21st Century. Testbook. November 15th, 2023. https://testbook.com/articles/great-leaders-of-the-world - March 1st 2024

"charged . . . with concealed ambition." He was teaching *character* to a nation. On January 1st, 1863, when President Abraham Lincoln signed the "Emancipation Proclamation", he was counting on the *character* of a nation. In his December 8th, 1941 speech to Congress, President Franklin Roosevelt said, "No matter how long it may take us to overcome this premeditated invasion, the American people will, in their righteous might, win through to absolute victory." He was calling on the *character* of a nation. In his inaugural address on January 20th, 2001, President George W. Bush remarked, "An angel still rides in the whirlwind and directs this storm." He was talking about the *character* of the nation.

There are lessons on character for us to learn from and to instill into our own lives. Self-leadership and Lifelong learning will facilitate the inculcation of these lessons. If you want people to follow you and trust you, do a serious and honest evaluation of your own character. Pre-decide to consistently follow high moral standards. You will reap what you sow.

How to maintain trust:
Again, consistency is key. Once you have built trust you must continue to do all the things we discussed in building trust. Do the right things and do them right!

When you are the leader, maintain the trust you have by being consistent in the understanding and respect with which you treat those around you and those whom you lead. Here are some examples:

<u>Answering the phone when your spouse calls and you are at work / in a meeting:</u>

In today's culture everyone carries a smartphone with access to instant information and the ability to be "connected". How many times have you been in a meeting and one of those devices rings, beeps, buzzes, vibrates? The owner sheepishly looks at it and wonders what to do. You can "pre-decide", creating consistency, and remove all doubt. Simultaneously, you can display compassion and respect. Pre-decide, if it is a spouse or child, have them step out and answer the phone with no questions asked and no negative repercussions. That close family member knows the person is on the job and feels like it is important enough to call, let the team member deal with it. Leave it to the person to not answer for others, not family. Remember, the definition of an emergency is different for each of us. Give those around you the opportunity to decide what is an emergency. You will maintain trust, cultivate consistency and even earn respect.

We will speak later in some detail about family leadership however, it is imperative to realize the importance people place upon being present at family events. We have all seen the movies where some bad parenting is depicted: Robin William's character in the movie "Hook" missing his son's baseball game; Arnold Schwarzenegger's character in "Jingle All the Way" missing his son's martial arts exhibition; or Macaulay Culkin being left "Home Alone". We all privately pledge to never be that person or parent. Yet, most of us can look back on some missed event or opportunity. We can "pre-decide" to support those around us and those whom we lead. You can create a culture where it is expected to be at those family events. If someone has a family event, they can ask a coworker to fill-in for them. This will work as long as the person asking realizes they may be asked to fill in for someone else later and must say yes. If you, as the leader, help facilitate this and those whom you lead understand the give and take required for it to work, this can and will be successful. You will maintain trust, perpetuate consistency and facilitate mutual support.

You must "pre-decide" to hold yourself accountable. Afterall, YOU are responsible for YOU! One of the most intense examples I have heard of is Craig Groschel, founder of Life Church, who has stated in an open forum that every keystroke on every electronic device he has is recorded, every text and email he receives is viewable by his wife and his staff, he has even blocked himself from being able to download apps to his devices–someone else must do it. This is accountability at its extreme. I am not suggesting we all go to these extraordinary lengths but try to hold yourself accountable. If you make a mistake, own it before it is called out by someone else. I once said the word "ass" in my classroom. I was talking about the animal, but there is no distinction in a classroom full of 8th graders. I found the School Principal between classes and told him of the incident. I owned the issue. I didn't want him caught off guard with a call from a parent. He was appreciative. Consistently owning your mistakes (we all make them), real or perceived, will garner trust and respect from everyone around you.

Creating reasonable predictability for those you lead is a form of consistently maintaining trust. Can you be counted on? Pre-decide! Do what you say you are going to do. Don't just pay lip service to it. It will be noticed if you fail to do what you say or are forcing yourself into action. Following schedules is one obvious way to do this. Be on time and don't waste your team's time by being late, a clear sign of disrespect to them. Emergency requests better really be an emergency. Here are a few examples:

I spent several years as an Observer Controller (OC) at the Joint Readiness Training Center (JRTC). This assignment required an average of 16 days per month in Field Training or "Rotation" (away from home and loved ones). During one of those years, we had a Change-of-Command. Our new Commanding General issued an order to establish the predictability of time. He said, "During non-rotation times there would be no work on weekends, no work after 5PM on weekdays and no phone calls to someone's home about work." Soon after this order was issued, a Major in the unit failed to follow the order and was issued a General Officer Letter of Reprimand. This is one way to make a point and pre-decide. The General's actions garnered lots of respect.

As a Defense Contractor I received a call on the evening of December 30th asking me to travel to another city on New Year's Day to work on a contract proposal. At the risk of getting heat from my boss, I declined but offered to travel on January 2nd, after my pre-planned family event. However, I failed to ask simple questions: How long will I be there? What will I be doing while there? Who do I report to on this project? et al. Talk about lack of predictability. I was there for over six weeks,

reported to several different people, and my primary responsibilities changed twice. Even if the people around you don't pre-decide, you can. Don't be afraid to ask questions to create a better, more predictable, situation because a better situation may just be information.
Consistency, reasonable pre-decisions, and good communications will foster ongoing trust earned with truth, honesty, earnest good, reliability and visible character.

You can also build trust by being an observant leader. Many years ago, while I was the co-chair for the veterans employee group, our events and professional development teams were meeting to brainstorm new activities for the next quarter. Over time, this core team developed its own approach to solving problems. The group was composed of people with varying levels of professional experience and backgrounds but passionate about veteran issues. Aaron–our vocal and passionate events lead–seemed to have more time on these projects rather than his main job! He would often drive the discussions and influence others to support his ideas or initiatives. His direct and abrasive communication style sometimes impeded others from contributing or offering other ideas. However, we generally did not take offense since his passion also drove many of the impactful events we've held in the past.

As with most volunteer and employee-related resource groups, group leadership and active members change over time. They benefit from a change in leadership to help drive innovative new ideas or initiatives and allow others the opportunity to contribute. Our employee resource group used "term limits" and succession planning to backfill our several leadership and committee lead positions. Every role turned over at least two years or earlier–often when someone left the company for other job opportunities.

In this case, a relatively newer member–Mike–joined the team as our communications lead. During most of the virtual event planning call, he seemed engaged in the conversation but didn't "come off mute" to speak. Near the end of the call, our vocal member pitched an event that potentially created a challenge for our employees. We were contemplating a veteran remembrance walk but had yet to settle on a location. Aaron wanted to hold the event downtown, 20 minutes away from the office. He spent considerable time contacting downtown venues and even developed a pitch deck with routes and other planning details. There was considerable discussion among the group but none of the existing members voiced any real objection. However, Mike finally offered an alternative option, he said, "Let's hold the march at the work location and we'll probably get more participation and impact." After an uncomfortable pause, Aaron explained the amount of work he invested in the event and how we can mitigate any transportation or travel issues later. I immediately saw Mike's body slump into his chair as he physically and emotionally detached from the discussion (and the group). Once the call ended, I immediately messaged Mike and shared my observations of how his opinion was discarded by both Aaron and the broader group (including myself). That discussion gave him the chance to express his frustrations, and he also felt heard. From a leadership lens, Mike appreciated the additional effort to understand his perspective. He also inspired me to challenge Aaron's plan and convinced him to change the march to the office.

Consistency and moral courage go together when maintaining trust. Here is a short story (Author Unknown) to build that point (Pun intended).

The Carpenter's House

An elderly carpenter was ready to retire. He told his employer-contractor of his plans to leave the house building business and live a more leisurely life with his spouse enjoying his extended family.

He would miss the paycheck, but he needed to retire. They could get by. The contractor was sorry to see his good worker go and asked if he could build just one more house as a personal favor. The carpenter said yes, but in time it was easy to see that his heart was not in his work. He resorted to shoddy workmanship and used inferior materials. It was an unfortunate way to end his career.

When the carpenter finished his work and the builder came to inspect the house, the contractor handed the front-door key to the carpenter. "This is your house," he said, "my gift to you."

What a shock! What a shame! If he had only known he was building his own house, he would have done it all so differently. Now he had to live in the home he had built none too well.

How to lose trust: Only you and your actions can give away trust and your integrity. You can't blame anyone else. You are *responsible*. Once it is gone, it is tough to get it back and in some cases you will never get it back. Are you going to let one lapse in judgment, a single

"When wealth is lost, nothing is lost; when health is lost, something is lost; when character is lost, all is lost."

Reverend Billy Graham

event or a single moment cost you a lifetime of building trust and integrity? In our interview with Dr. Patti Conard (Chapter 14 - What insights can we gain from leaders across different specialties?) she said, "The weakest of leaders lack integrity and a lack of integrity can become contagious."

If you read the story of King David, from the Bible, you will find the story of a powerful individual. King David played the harp, wrote poems, killed a giant, led winning armies into battle and was King to a nation. King David also made some really bad decisions negatively impacting thousands of people. He slept with another man's wife and lied about it. The woman he slept with became pregnant. He then tried to disguise it by ordering the husband to war and putting him on the battle's front lines, hoping he would not survive. Later, the child died. Eventually, King David even lost trust in himself. He gave away his integrity and had to go through extreme measures to even get part of it back.

You should understand that doing the opposite of what's mentioned above will prevent you from losing trust. It is possible to lose trust and for it to happen with lightning speed. Here are some examples of reasons leaders–and people in general–lose trust.

Words not matching actions or outcomes:

In other words, saying one thing and doing another. Placating, even in an effort to spare someone's feelings, will erode and destroy trust. Imagine doing a performance review with an employee and your words imply they are doing great but don't provide any examples or evidence. The person will probably leave the review in a good mood. Later, you submit the written report and those 'praise' words don't appear because in reality the employee is marginal at best. Not only have you lost the employees trust but that of those the employee shares the information with. Part of your responsibility as the leader is to provide constructive feedback, preferably in a professional way.

The "Little White Lie":

We tell it to ourselves and then it spreads to others. It is impossible for a single person, even the leader, to have all the answers and or to have expert knowledge of every subject. This can be avoided by accepting input from others who actually have the expertise and knowledge in a specific area. Have you ever seen one of those t-shirts that say, "I don't need the internet, my (partner, wife, husband, significant other) knows everything." Most of us trust people who have skills and knowledge we don't. You can certainly use your skills and knowledge to build trust. However, there are those who will periodically try to hoard their talent and provide others inaccurate or misleading information, leaving out details, or creating unnecessary barriers to important information. Discovery of this type of activity will cause them to lose trust quickly.

Unilateral action:

Most of us truly believe we know best. When people are operating unilaterally, they make their own decisions, avoid distractions from others, and take full credit for any accomplishment or success. However, most organizations operate more smoothly when the members function as a team. People who function as "independent operators" garner less trust. In some situations, this can actually create unnecessary dangers. Consider a military operation or something a little simpler, someone passing on the shoulder of the road.[52]

Don't Trust When Delegating:

In any organization, the unexpected is to be expected. Throughout the year, high-profile projects must be prioritized over the established goals set in the beginning of the year. In one case, I expanded my role by helping the company understand and develop a risk mitigation framework for our third-party suppliers and their compliance to Environmental, Social, and Governance (ESG) standards. The company wanted to get ahead of regulatory reporting by developing a process that would meet regulatory demands and directly impact carbon reduction and other environmentally-related issues. As a relatively new space to consider for a global corporation, we did not have many subject matter experts but relied upon a committee of various stakeholders to help create the overall plan.

Throughout the journey, the regulators driving ESG change in business asked companies to provide "progress assessments" on program developments. We received an information request–with a seven day deadline–to conduct a first-pass and assign "domain owners" for over 1,200 ESG domains and variables! I was already working directly with the ESG workstream but received the task to complete the project directly from my manager. He had some knowledge and awareness of the space and felt I should lead the organization's response.

This project became my top priority for the next week. I had an opportunity to demonstrate I could handle a high-pressure task by

---

52 Joseph Folkman. 6 Top Behaviors That Cause A Loss Of Trust. Forbes. January 24th, 2020. https://www.forbes.com/sites/joefolkman/2020/01/24/42-of-direct-reports-claim-they-are-thinking-of-quitting-due-to-leaders-they-dont-trust/?sh=44fcd8a463e8 - March 28th, 2024

solving a complex problem that required the simultaneous use of several skills. After the first day, I digested the 1,200 line document, created a detailed project plan and set up calls with each impacted stakeholder. By the end of the second day, I completed nearly 35% of the project by assigning an oversight lead to various sections of the response request. I was on track to complete the entire project in five days. On the third day, my manager reached out and asked to discuss the project. He expressed his concern that the project would not be completed satisfactorily or in time. He did not provide any details or further justification for his concerns when pressed for clarity. To reduce his fears, I laid out the problem, guidance received from the primary decision-makers (his manager), project plan, timeline, and any blockers but confidently concluded we were still on track. Several times, he would ask, "How do you know you are done?" or "Who else will be reviewing before we submit?" or "You're hedging." We then had a spirited discussion about my perception that he lacked trust in his employees. As you can imagine, the volume and tenor became louder to the point where it felt like a shouting match. In the short-term, we agreed to table the discussion and re-connect once we've had some "perspective" on the issue but never had an honest and professional discussion about what went wrong and how to avoid this in the future. In the long-term, our relationship became strained to the point where we stopped communicating, collaborating, or sharing common issues and best practices. One-on-one meetings were either canceled or delayed, citing scheduling conflicts. Normal pleasantries were less frequent and the relationship essentially dissolved. I stopped viewing my manager as a resource for professional development or a trusted voice to help resolve an issue or pursue an initiative.

You earn trust with consistency. You can create consistency by pre-deciding for many situations before they ever happen, because they will happen. You continue to build and maintain trust by:

- ➢ Being truthful, no matter the situation.
- ➢ Having the intestinal fortitude to be honest and practice moral courage.
- ➢ Being genuinely helpful to others.

- Establishing reliability by doing what you say.
- Holding yourself accountable and admitting when you are wrong.
- Showing respect to others, even if they are not so respectful to you.
- Knowing your strengths and weaknesses, you have both.
- Accepting reasonable and cogent input and feedback.
- Communicating effectively.

Chapter 7
Leading Others
When is the First Time We Lead Someone Other than Ourselves?

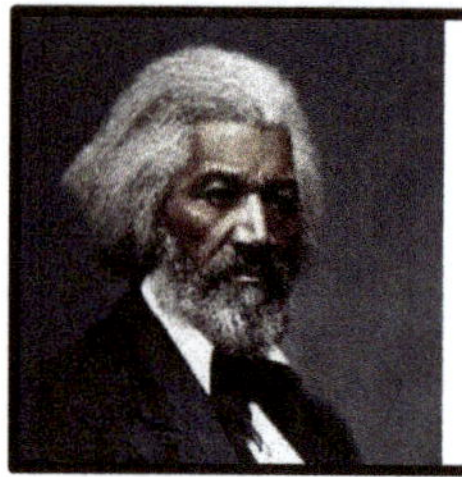

"It is easier to build strong children than to repair broken men." - Frederick Douglass

Leading others takes place in Phases Two and Three. In Chapter 4 (Self Leadership "If you can't lead yourself, how can you lead others?"), we expanded on Self Leadership (Phase One). Here in Chapter 7 we'll expand on Tactical and Operational Leadership (Phases Two and Three). Graphic 3, again, outlines for us the Phases of Leadership.

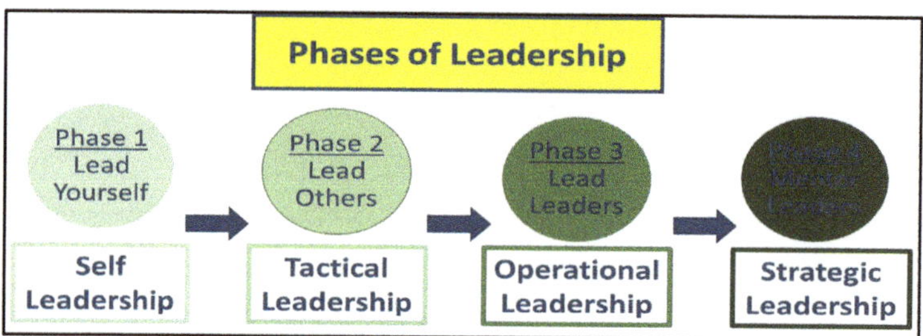

- *Graphic 3 (Diagram): The Phases of Growing Leaders and Leadership.*

Phase Two - Tactical Leadership:

After Self Leadership, chances are the next place you'll practice leadership is in a small group. Likely in a group of friends / a group of fellow students / a sports team / a small group of volunteers / a small group of coworkers / in the family. This is Tactical Leadership. Let's discuss this in a bit more detail.

Leading in small groups means "Being Present". Communication is personal and most often one-to-one. You are receiving and implementing vision and guidance from the next level leader, identifying the strengths of your team members, and using them to the team's advantage. Even at an early age you may lead others. You may find yourself in a group of friends leading them to a social event, starting a new activity like a musical group or kicking off a group of competitive gamers. It is possible you are the leader of a group of fellow students for a graded class project or decorating the school for a dance or homecoming. You could even be the captain of a sports team. If you are leading, there is no requirement for you to be the most outgoing, most gifted musician, reaching the highest level of Fortnite, have straight As, and be the most skilled artist or most talented athlete. You must be able to *foster an environment in which people motivate themselves to achieve beyond their own perceived capabilities, and face problems for which there appear to be no simple solutions.* This includes "being present". Your team, your small group needs to see you. At this level, communication is predominantly verbal. You are present and talking to the other members of the group / team. You are getting guidance and vision from a parent, teacher, or coach. You are articulating the guidance and vision to achieve the best outcomes. You are learning from the experiences of motivating, inspiring, problem solving and communicating. You are discovering what works for you. Implementation of these lessons takes place as you progress through Tactical Leadership. Progression in Phase Two of Leadership can happen in a number of situations. These can include, but are not limited to volunteerism, at work and within the family.

Small group of Co-workers:

You are employing skills and taking advantage of the experience you have gained from other, less formal groups you have worked with. This can be anything from a special project where you are the designated leader or you have the greatest amount of technical experience / education. Leading co-workers on the job most often indicates you have shown potential and expertise garnering the attention of higher level leaders. Often, this can come with some additional incentives like promotion or the potential for a promotion, money, an office, and greater expectations. Like we talked about earlier, in small groups you are "Present". Communication is personal and face-to-face; you are obtaining and actioning vision and guidance from the next level leader to meet team and organizational goals. You are also pinpointing the skills and capabilities of individual team members so they can be utilized to the advantage of the entire team. This is more formal in the workplace than the ad hoc groups we have previously discussed. Along with applying lessons learned from self generated education and personal experience, we are still learning. We are not only gaining more valuable experience and continuing with our own pursuit as Lifelong learners, we are now at a stage of leadership where formal leadership training opportunities are available. We discussed these in Chapter 3 - Responsibility vs Authority. Take advantage of these moments. Although they may be offered, don't be shy about actively seeking out formal training. These can be a great foundation for advancing to Operational Leadership.

In March of 2006, President George W. Bush stated the first pillar of security of the United States was the "promoting of freedom, justice and human dignity." Each one of these finds its early foundation in the family and / or the church. The family is another of those most likely potential starting points for leading others. Remember, in the early founding of this land, known as "The Great Migration", long before we called it the "United States of America" in 1776, but starting more than 150 years earlier, intrepid English and European settlers were led here for three primary reasons: religious freedom, economic opportunities, and political liberty.[53] These people traveled primarily in two types of groups: families (even extended families) and congregations. This required leadership from those who could *foster an environment in which people motivate themselves to achieve beyond their own perceived capabilities, and face problems for which there appear to be no simple solutions.* During the Great Migration these were predominantly Patriarchs and Clergy.

---

[53] United States Citizenship and Immigration Services. FY 2023. https://www.uscis.gov - December 20th, 2023

Leading your family requires you to be, first and foremost, "Present" (sound familiar) and secondly, to "Prioritize" moving the family to the front of the line. Some people, myself included, have attempted to justify my actions by saying we are "providing". What are we providing? "Stuff." And while important, stuff is "Management", not "Leadership". This short written realization appeared in newspapers in the early 2000's in the Lawton / Fort Sill, Oklahoma area. It can still be readily found on the internet. A Senior U.S. Army Officer wrote it; however, it applies to all families and professions, not just the Military.

'Important' vs. 'Urgent' by COL Mark Blum, 212th Field Artillery Brigade, U.S. Army.

My wife and I took our daughter to college a week ago. She's our last child to leave the house as our son has been in college for a couple of years now, and it seems a little empty right now. Phone calls and e-mail will be poor substitute for kitchen conversations, and it is difficult to envision exactly what she's doing, with whom, through a phone line. I suppose we'll have to get used to her being grown up, but I still remember the little girl who loved gymnastics and didn't like to play with dolls.

As I look back, I wonder what I might have done differently if I'd known everything I know now. The Army is a great place to raise a kid, but I think I'd make a few changes given the chance. For instance, I remember a Thanksgiving in Germany as a Major when I worked through the day and all night, only going home for an hour to wolf down some Thanksgiving dinner and then going back to work again. I don't even remember what the subject was, but I now know it wasn't important enough to miss Thanksgiving with my family.

There are a lot of good reasons to spend time with your family, and far fewer good reasons not to. I've been in the field (training) on my share of birthdays and holidays, and there's not too much we can do about that.

Still, here's what I'd change:

I'd leave work every day by 1800 (6 PM) if at all possible and earlier if I could.

We work from before our children go to school until after they go to bed at night sometimes when they're small. How many hours might I have spent with them in the evening if I'd realized the chance doesn't come around again?

I'd save less money and have more fun. I think I'd take more long summer vacations to really memorable places with the kids instead of making the PCS (Permanent Change of Station) move part of the vacation. I'd make it a priority for them to see their grandparents more often, regardless of where we lived. I'd be more selective about the social engagements I accepted, even if it was "expected" that I attend. My kids "expected" that I'd be with them too, and I don't recall any banquets where my presence determined the outcome of the evening. Sometimes I made the wrong choice. I would pay more attention to which teachers my children had and less attention to the grades they made. I'd be more help on school projects and less irritated when they brought one to me for help at the last minute. I get things every day at work at the last minute, for a lot of reasons. I would be more understanding that it happens to kids, too. I'd go to all the PTA meetings, not just some, and every sports. Through the door at night I'd be more absorbed in their worlds. I could have thought about most of those problems after they went to bed. I'd throw a Frisbee more often with the kids and do less yard work. I can rake leaves anytime. We'd clean the house less and spend more time messing it up doing fun stuff. I'd never again lose a day of annual leave (paid vacation). One year I lost 24 days - what a waste.

I once had a boss who talked about the difference between what's "urgent" and what's "important." He hadn't learned that lesson until late in his career, and didn't want others to make the same mistakes. He always worked long hours, even once missing his son's Eagle Scout initiation because of something happening he felt he needed to deal with, but later wished he'd left to someone else.

He had three rules to determine the difference between "important" and "urgent," and if an event were important he'd offer that you should think long and hard before missing it. To him, an event is important if:

1. *It is important to someone who's important to you;*
2. *Your personal presence makes a difference; and*
3. *The opportunity is not going to come around again.*

If those three conditions are satisfied you have a pretty good idea what you should focus on. He would always use this one example: As a Division Commander his unit was having a Warfighter Exercise - a major event for a Division. One of the Brigade Commanders' daughters was starting her freshman year in college, and he indicated he was going to take her and get her settled, and would miss most of the exercise.

As might be expected he was not real excited about one of his senior commanders missing the Warfighter (Exercise), and pressured him to just have his wife take his daughter. The Brigade Commander insisted, even knowing he could be killing his career. After the Warfighter ended he said he gained a great deal of respect for that commander as a result of his decision, and took a hard look at some of the choices he'd made in his own career. His own wife had made him see the wisdom of the man's choice.

Overall, I think military life has been great for my family, and I wouldn't trade it for anything. The choices I've made have been mine, and I haven't always made the right ones for the right reasons. Even so, kids survive parents learning "as we go." My advice is to make your choices wisely. The object for all of us is to make sure we run out of career before we run out of family. For more than 20 years we've had at least

one kid in the house at all times. Now it's just us, which is what we had when we started, at least until Thanksgiving. We're already looking forward to that time this year!

In an interview with Fox News on December 23th, 2023, Mr. Jack Brewer, former NFL player and head of the Jack Brewer Foundation, stated - 70% of all High School dropouts come from families with no father *present*.[54] It doesn't matter why the father is not "Present" (See "Important" vs "Urgent" above).

Being Present as a way to lead the family can be found in many other places. Jason L. Riley, a commentator, author, member of The Wall Street Journal's editorial board and senior fellow at the Manhattan Institute has done research indicating 'Fatherlessness' is one of the 'true root causes' of crime in America. He goes on to state that being present provides role models and teaches children how to behave and how to carry themselves. Mr. Riley also declares, "We know that the correlation between a child coming from a fatherless home and ending up in prison or on drugs, or a single parent himself are much, strongly, more strongly correlated with whether that child came from a fatherless home than it is with race, than it is with ethnicity, than it is from poverty and income level." The solution is for leadership and parents to be present.

If you are going to Lead your family … Be Present! I wish I could say I was always present; however, I am guilty. The wisdom of Mr. Frederick Douglass, with which we opened this chapter can be seen in both COL Blum and Mr. Jack Brewers comments. Take a step back and look at your own family. What do you see?

We've all been at the line of "Important" vs "Urgent" and Being Present … we've made the right decision and the wrong one. Will our new, better understanding of leadership help us make the right decision more often?

---

[54] The Jack Brewer Foundation. April 20th, 2023. https://thejackbrewerfoundation.org/ - January 1st, 2024

It was Halloween, 2007, about 4 PM. I was headed home to take my four year old grandson, who was visiting, to trick-or-treat on the military installation where we lived. On the way out, I saw a fellow Colonel working on his computer in his office. I asked if he was going home to take his five year old daughter (yes daughter, I can't imagine being 50 years old with a 5 year old at home) to trick-or-treat. In a very frustrated tone he said, "No, I have to send out these emails!" I asked if this time next year anyone would remember these emails? He looked up, and then I reminded him that tonight, his daughter would know that Daddy took her trick-or-treating. He did not leave right away; however, about two hours later, we had an impromptu encounter on the sidewalk in the housing area, and we walked the children from house to house together. It was an "important" evening.

The authors of this book bring a wide breadth of family experience to the table. Some of those experiences include: married vs divorced parents; married and divorced themselves; 30+ years of successful marriage; one is adopted and the other is an adoptive parent; children, grandchildren and great-grandchildren; career changes; location changes; even educational growth. All this to say, family leadership is not a "one size fits all situation". Similarities can be drawn and there is vast experience available to you both here and from family, friends and through your faith.

One immutable fact about having a family is the moment you become a parent, you are a parent for the rest of your life. Good or bad, it is not an option and non-negotiable. I remember at the age of 34, while visiting my mother as she was fighting cancer, heading out to a store. She said, "Drive carefully!" I gave her a glance … she followed with, "I'm always going to be your mother." The moment you have children you become a leader, even if you don't want to be a leader.

One of our authors, Bill, is an adoptive parent. This is not an unusual circumstance. What makes this situation a bit unique from most is that he adopted sisters. At the time of adoption, their ages were 10 and 17 years old respectively. Suddenly, these children went from one to two parents on the scene with no history of trust. That earning of trust, going both directions, takes time.

From personal experience, it was one of the most difficult and, simultaneously, most rewarding experiences of my life. You must earnestly decide what is "important" and "urgent" and to be "present." I admit I did not always make the right decision. However, 33 years later it appears I was right enough. We (my wife and I) did homework and are experts at 7th grade math. I coached Little League Softball. We had boyfriends go on family camping trips. We took them shopping for clothes when the TV program "90210" was all the rage. We cooked meals, cleaned up behind them and had "the talks". I taught them to drive. We slipped them a few extra bucks at certain times. I did my best to intimidate boyfriends. I walked them down the aisle.

With divorce, children go from two parents regularly available to only one. Particularly when circumstances create a long distance between the two natural parents. In today's world, second marriages and "blended" families simply are. Mine is no different. In many situations we deal with some of the most difficult leadership challenges imaginable and being present seems near impossible:

- Child support - Most people think of child support as a monthly check. It is way more; it doesn't end with a monthly check. Think about these things as a way to be involved and present:
    - Gifts on Birthdays, Christmas and other Holidays.
    - Transportation.
    - Vacations.
    - Starting an educational fund.
- Communication between the non-custodial parent and the child - This is tougher than you might expect. Prior to the internet and email / text, I wrote weekly letters; called 'long distance'; had to call the house and go through the custodial parent to speak to the children. As technology changed the methods became more available but the children didn't always want the communication.
- Visitation at different times (Summer Vacation / Thanksgiving / Christmas / Key family milestones / et al) - How is travel for

these events going to take place and be paid for? Based on location it can be a lot of plane tickets or driving time.

- Court mandated requirements - health insurance, visitation and if necessary, meeting special needs.
- Trying to make positive memories and making them stick - I created photo books during most visits for them to take home as a visual reminder and, potentially, a future reference of me being present. In addition, we try to remind our kids of those events as time passes.
- Interaction between the children of the now merged family.
- Communications between Divorced / Separated parents.
- Dealing with newly introduced "Step" Grandparents.
- Resentment by the children that may go two ways:
  - To the newly introduced parent … because there is no positive history.
  - To the natural parent for giving attention to someone else.

Certainly, there is more; however, the point is, there is nothing easy here, particularly, at the beginning of these situations. This requires a leader! In the introduction we told you: Everyone, EVERYONE, will find themself leading at some point during their life, regardless of the desire to be there. It doesn't matter if you want to or not. It doesn't matter if you feel qualified or not. If you become a parent, even a step-parent, you will be expected to lead. "Train up a child in the way he should go; even when he is old he will not depart from it." - Proverbs 22:6 ESV.

Thinking of Others First:

Our youngest son is an active football player, starting center for a local high school. Recently, his coach organized a Football Showcase where recruiters and coaches from several Division I and II college teams can directly observe potential talent they may want to consider for their team. In Ohio (like many parts of the country), high school football is a near year-round event for the players and staff. Also, being so close to a nationally-recognized college football school–in Columbus, Ohio–helps to attract more college recruiters and improves a high school athlete's chances of getting a college scholarship–or at least some type of athletic offer. As the Showcase began, the skies opened up with unrelenting rain. For nearly one hour, the players and staff ran drills in the driving rain. Many recruiters slowly left the area, likely to seek dryer conditions. On the way home, we drove separate cars which allowed me to get home before my wife and son. Instead of retreating into the home to wait for their arrival, I anticipated their arrival by finding some towels and hangers (they were both completely wet). One can make a difference by choosing to act, even through small and sustained gestures towards others–especially your family.

Adoption as being adopted view:
One of the authors, was adopted one month after birth to his now-parents. His parents were a typical young couple hoping to start a family while trying to navigate their professional careers. After several attempts of trying to conceive–including many unfortunate miscarriages–they decided to find a child through adoption. There was an adoption office close to my father's office. He went into the adoption agency and began an extensive vetting and interviewing process. In the early 1970's, approximately 175,000 children in the United States found a permanent adoptive home with a family.[55] Sadly, the rate of placements for minority children lagged that of non-minority children. Prospective parents of minority children faced greater hurdles in getting approvals. The agency found them to be a match with a young woman attending Morgan State University. Though they never met, the young woman asked prospective parents to ensure they raise her child as their own–which they did. After my birth, my father resolved to help with the duties of changing diapers, getting up early for feeding, and ensuring I would be exposed to as many opportunities in life. I am eternally grateful to have parents dedicated to my Lifelong development.

Phase Three is **Operational Leadership** - leading leaders. Many of us get to lead other leaders. In some situations, we'll lead leaders with multiple layers of leaders. This creates the need for a long term vision, with definable objectives, communicated across a wide area and nested

[55] Wired Humanities Project. Adoption Statistics. The Adoption History Project. Feb 24th, 2012 https://pages.uoregon.edu/adoption/topics/adoptionstatistics.htm - 24 February 2024

with the leaders above us. This communication must employ multiple forms and mediums to ensure the widest dissemination. The ability to match teams to goals / objectives / strategies is a key skill. You should hire and cultivate the right people to meet those needs. Operational Leaders are responsible for obtaining and maintaining organizational results. At this leadership level, you are looking at the systems used by your organization and making certain they are the most effective and efficient for success.

If, and when, you reach this level of leadership, don't make the mistake of believing you will be followed simply because you attained the position / sit in the chair / hold the purse strings. There will be some of that; however, you will need to prove to those you lead that you deserve to be there.

Leaders are never the best at every task. As a Battalion Commander I had soldiers in the command who were stone cold experts in their areas: Launcher Operations; Fire Direction; Ammunition; Petroleum; Food Service; Tactical Communications; Vehicle Maintenance and repair; Personnel Management; Supply and Logistics and others … you get the idea! The person who is expert in all these areas doesn't exist. During my tenure as a Battalion Commander I had the pleasure of having seven different Battery Commanders. The one I consider the best overall was not a standout in any area; rather, he was solid in every area. This was always the option if you wanted to be certain the job was done. I had a very close acquaintance whose nickname was "Wedge". He would say he was a simple tool, but effective. Think about it: Patrick Mahomes will never run onto the field and position himself as an offensive lineman. There is another player bigger, stronger with more expertise in that position.

A fair portion of your responsibility as a leader in Phase Three is establishing a high-functioning organization. You must identify, acquire, employ and motivate the talent to do so. Some of this talent should be able to perform parts of your job better than you can. You must also have a vision of the future.

During my time as a Defense Contractor, I had team members who were paid more than me, even though I was the designated leader. These people were skilled engineers with unique training and experience requiring years to obtain. They were not leaders. It was my responsibility to employ their skills in the most effective manner possible to achieve success. Success sometimes includes getting past your own ego.

You can't be afraid to delegate authority in order to get the best results. If you have not already figured it out, in Phase Three of Leadership you will quickly discover "you can't do it all yourself." The old saying - if you want it done right do it yourself - throw that out. You must delegate tasks, projects, operations and other activities to people you trust. If you don't trust them enough to delegate to them, you replace them or train them.

> Replace them –
>
> In some organizations, this is easier than it is in others. Every organization has a set of rules (Policies) in place that they expect you to follow headed up by a group of Administrators (remember, Administration influences function and process). Leaders make the final decision. I was once told by one of my leaders … People write policies, people are fallible and there is always an exception to the rule.
>
> Train them –
>
> depending on the situation, this can be time consuming and may not be worth the effort. However, we believe that the leader has an obligation to invest the time to develop your staff or newer employees. This also strengthens trust and allows you to "positively mold" that person's experience. People feel empowered and will retain a level of confidence if Leaders carve out time to be Present and showing "Action. This yields long term success for that relationship and improves the organization.

You must also provide mentorship. This can be done in groups and individually. In the Army, it is common to have Officer / NCO Professional Development classes. As a teacher, we had "Teacher In Service" days where some professional training was provided; the same held true when I worked in Industry. In these situations, they were in groups and were very formal.

I was stationed at the PENTAGON when I was notified of my selection to Battalion Command. My boss at the time was a more senior and seasoned officer who had already commanded at both the Battalion and Brigade levels. From that point forward, we had a weekly meeting in one of the many snack bars throughout "The Building." We discussed everything from Command Philosophy to how best to engage and utilize the Unit Chaplain. During these sessions I took copious notes and eventually found great value from these conversations.

Don't dismiss the impromptu opportunities to mentor those you lead. Remember, a Leader *fosters an environment in which people motivate themselves to achieve beyond their own perceived capabilities, and face problems for which there appear to be no simple solutions.* Sometimes, these impromptu events can have the greatest impact. Particularly, when done in a positive fashion. Most leaders know how to provide harsh criticism, but often forget the "pat on the back" or "at-a-boy" followed with meaningful feedback.

Good leaders are hard to find. They're expensive to hire and harder to keep. But with the right strategies, you can nurture them and turn your organization into an incubator lab for leaders.[56]
If you aspire to Phase Three of Leadership, these are tools you will use.

Most of us will spend the majority–if not all–of our leadership time in Phases Two and Three.

---

[56] Stacey Browning. Three Rules For Successfully Leading Other Leaders. Forbes. July 27th, 2018.
https://www.forbes.com/sites/forbeshumanresourcescouncil/2018/07/27/three-rules-for-successfully-leading-other-leaders/?sh=368c055e55e4 - March 4th, 2024

So:

- ➢ Be Present
- ➢ Communicate often and clearly
- ➢ Know what's Important vs. Urgent
- ➢ Remember, you earn Leadership
- ➢ You don't know it all / everything
- ➢ Delegate
- ➢ Mentor

Leaders are proactive: "For we hear that some among you walk in idleness, not busy at work, but busybodies." 2 Thessalonians 3 ESV.

Chapter 8
Influential Leadership … It doesn't Need a Title
(Phase 4 - Strategic Leadership)

"Vision without execution is hallucination."
– *Thomas Edison*

By all accounts, Thomas Edison never held a public, or appointed office, nor held an official leadership title. He spent most of his life working on inventions and innovations. Yet, many think of him as a leader. Consider some of his inventions: the Automatic Telegraph; the Carbon Telephone Transmitter; the Light Bulb; the Phonograph; the Movie Camera and Viewer; the Alkaline Storage Battery.[57] … His vision allowed him to lead during the Second Industrial Revolution. Through innovation, he influenced the nation and the world. The foundation of his work is still evident today. Yes, there are leaders without titles. However, in today's culture, almost everyone has, or had, a title and many seek a title. The title doesn't make you a leader, it's just a title! Leadership is *the ability to foster an environment in which people motivate themselves to achieve beyond their own perceived capabilities, and face problems for which there appear to be no simple solutions.*

There is a level of leadership and influence where there may or may not be a title. There is likely no official efficiency report for the President of the United States. Who would write a report on the President? There are other forms of evaluation for that position: public opinion; the voting booth; the 25th Amendment; Articles of Impeachment; and veto-proof legislation. Similarly, the President doesn't write reports on the 15 executive department cabinet positions.
If you think about it, you can come up with others who may or may not have a title, yet they have had sway or influence or exercised leadership

[57] Patrick J. Kiger. 6 Key Inventions by Thomas Edison. History. July 18th, 2023. https://www.history.com/news/thomas-edison-inventions - May 18th, 2024

in some arena or way: Elon Musk, Richard Branson, Mother Teresa, George Sorous, Sam Walton, Gandhi, Nelson Mandela, Walt Disney, Howard Hughes, et al. These are most often considered the upper tier of the Strategic Level of Leadership; however, you don't need name recognition to be a Strategic Leader. You do need vision and the ability to mentor leaders.

Phase Four is **Strategic Leadership** - quelling ignorance, articulating vision and mentoring leaders. At this point, your decisions touch every level of the organization and in a few rare situations, entire nations and the world. You are not thinking about tomorrow, next week, next month or even next year. Your attention and focus are 5 to 10 years down the road. You must be able to take a panoptic view of your organization and understand its relationship with other organizations. Your decisions influence every aspect both internal and external to your organization. You mentor others to grow them into strategic leaders. "The difference between a good leader and a great leader is one who learns to anticipate rather than react." - Craig Groeschel, founder of Life Church. At this phase of leadership your vision predicts and drives the need for change.

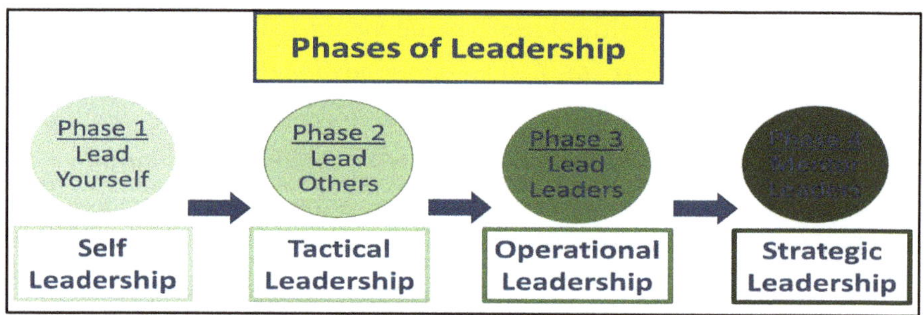

- ***Graphic 3 (Diagram): The Phases of Growing Leaders and Leadership.***

"**Passion fueled by ignorance is dangerous.**"

There are many explosive issues out there today to which this comment can apply. Each one of these issues has many perspectives and many people have their opinions. Some of those opinions are driven by ignorance - they think they are right and will listen to no one else. Just a few examples include Abortion; 2nd Amendment; Campus riots/protests;

Elections; Ukraine; Global Warming; and Social Security. Today's list is voluminous.

There are explosive issues for every generation. Do you remember: the

Ignorance = a lack of knowledge, understanding, or education.

The Brittanica Dictionary

Korean war; Vietnam war; Black Tuesday; Prohibition; the Little Rock Nine; and the Declaration of Independence. Even 250 years ago, there were two major groups - one who wanted independence from England and another believing England and specifically King George III, was our sovereign. There was even one vote, from Congress, against declaring war with Japan on December 8th, 1941.[58] There are issues we have forgotten about, simply because they didn't happen in our lifetime. If you are the leader, do your research. Make decisions based on the best information/facts you have and make every effort to eliminate ignorance from the decision-making process. One of the ways to accomplish this is to have a clear vision for your organization and the ability to effectively communicate it.

Vision –

Comes from within … It's the ability to see success in the future and the path to get there. Again, imagine President John F. Kennedy standing at the podium of Rice University in 1962 and telling the nation we are going to the moon. Notice, President Kennedy not only articulated his vision of putting an astronaut on the moon, he also put a time stamp on it when he said by the 'end of the decade' and he also said 'we' were going to do it. His intent was to provide Americans with a roadmap to inspire toward a challenging vision. Additionally, he said why … "because that goal will serve to organize and measure the best of our energies and skills." To do this, he had to prioritize resources to make

[58]Office of the Historian: history@mail.house.gov. Tally Sheet for Declaration of War against Japan. History, Art & Archives, United States House of Representatives. https://history.house.gov/Records-and-Research/Listing/lfp_036/ - May 3rd, 2024

the vision a reality. We all know the result: Neil Armstong set foot on the moon July 20th, 1969.

Making vision a reality may be one of the toughest things a Strategic Leader will ever do. To be a successful visionary there are several things you must do: Articulate and Communicate your vision; have a Strategy for vision realization; Develop a plan and prioritize resources.

Articulate and Communicate:

Without a vision there is no common understanding of the desired end-state. This often produces a situation with a lot of activity but nothing really getting done. A real vision that is articulated so everyone on the team, in the company or citizen can also see it will bring people together. In his speech on December 8th, 1941, President Franklin D Roosevelt said, "The American people will in their righteous might win through to absolute victory." This galvanized the country for years to come and people were willing to give in every way - paper drives, rubber drives, scrap metal drives, companies retooled their factories to produce weapons, ammunition, tools for soldiers, people lined up at the recruiting stations even lying about their age to join the war effort. We saw "Rosie the Riveter", "Victory Gardens" and the expansion of the "Red Cross." President Roosevelt was also known as the "Great Communicator"[59] and was able to effectively relay his vision at all levels using every means of communication at his disposal. (see Chapter 5 Communication "Do leaders really communicate or just tell people what to do/" - Learning to communicate with others.)

A leader's vision must be clear, focused on success, have long-term implications and be measurable. The vision tells the entire organization where they are going and what it will look like when they get there. As an example, "John the Elder" wrote the book of Revelation in the Bible

---

[59] Franklin D. Roosevelt. Address to Congress- Declaring War on Japan. December 8th, 1941. http://www.fdrlibrary.marist.edu/_resources/images/msf/msfb0002 - May 20th, 2024

to communicate the vision for the future of the world.[60] It's not enough to just articulate and communicate your vision. It must also be exciting enough to spur others to fervently help make the vision a reality.

Today, there is a vision for expanding "Electronic Vehicle" (EV) technology. Those with the vision are touting: lower running costs; environmental benefits; energy efficiency; improved performance standards; and longer material lifespan. There is an entirely different facet of people who don't see the EV vision and are replying with long charging times; unavailability of charging stations (infrastructure immaturity); immature battery technology; range; and price point.

Support for the vision begins with the ability of the visionary to be clear, concise and exciting with the vision. Good communication will enable the visionary to show the importance of the vision and help to get people personally invested in the vision. This means people must understand "why" the vision is important and have a personal reason for aspiring to the vision.

Strategy for Vision Realization:
Strategy should be applied slightly differently in different situations/arenas. Strategy is the path we use to get to the end-state. You can't formulae a strategy unless you have a clear view of the end-state. During my time in the Army, we discussed strategy in terms of how to apply national power: Diplomatic, Information, Military, Economic, Financial, Intelligence, and Law enforcement DIME-FIL).[61] Harvard Business School discusses the strategy in terms of the initiatives a company pursues to create value for the organization and its stakeholders, helping gain a competitive advantage in the market. This

---

[60] L. Michael White. Understand the Book of Revelation. PBS. Copyright 2014. https://www.pbs.org/wgbh/pages/frontline/shows/apocalypse/revelation/white.html#:~:text=The%20Book%20of%20Revelation%20was,1.10). - May 20th, 2024

[61] Air University Library. January 30, 2024. https://fairchild-mil.libguides.com/dimefil - June 25th, 2024

strategy is crucial to a company's success and is needed before any goods or services are produced or delivered.[62]
In academia, strategy is the process by which students learn. It includes, but is not limited to: time management, note taking, study skills, live/virtual/constructive applications and other academic skills facilitating a student's ability to understand concepts and then successfully apply them.

I live less than an hour from Walmart corporate headquarters. You can't swing a dead cat without hitting some version of Walmart (distribution center, corporate offices, superstores or neighborhood markets). Sam Walton believed that "The customer is the king". He always put the customer first and looked for ways to provide value and savings to them. He focused on creating a customer-friendly environment that was welcoming and easy to navigate. He was always open to new ideas and empowered his employees to share innovative ideas. He did everything possible to keep costs low. He was not afraid to introduce new technology. With 2023 worldwide revenues of $611 billion, Walmart is the largest retailer in the world.[63] Who can argue with that vision and strategy?

You don't have to develop a strategy in a vacuum or by yourself. Remember, Sam Walton sought input from his employees, empowered them and was open to new ideas and technology. The President of the United States has 15 Cabinet Secretaries to advise him and, in addition, has a personal, non-titled, "kitchen cabinet" of advisors at his beckon call.

Plan and Prioritize Resources:

---

[62] Michael Boyles. What is Business Strategy & Why is it Important? Harvard Business School Online. October 20th, 2022. https://online.hbs.edu/blog/post/what-is-business-strategy - May 20th, 2024

[63] Dr Ujjwal Patni. Top Business Strategies of Sam Walton. Business Jeeto. Copyright 2024. https://www.businessjeeto.com/blog/top-business-strategies-of-sam-walton#:~:text=Sam%20Walton%20believed%20that%20the,welcoming%20and%20easy%20to%20navigate. - May 20th, 2024.

We've discussed planning in several locations throughout this book with strategic planning in Chapter 2 - Overview of the Leadership, Management, Administration (LMA) Model. Strategic planning is characterized by the identification of long-term or overall aims and interests coupled with the means to achieve them; designed, planned, or conceived to serve a particular purpose or achieve a particular objective.

Your organization will require a plan to execute your leadership vision. People are pouring their energy into reaching the end-state and will need to see some success in order to drive them forward.[64] Think of a football team with a one-win season. That is tough to motivate.

During the Apollo space program each phase had a different goal or end-state that was a building block to the overall strategic vision of putting an astronaut on the moon. This exciting vision was broadly communicated with a synchronized strategy, and had an effective leader able to keep the organization motivated throughout all program phases.

The Army uses the One-Third / Two-Third rule:
This concept is used by commanders in the US Army to manage time when planning for military operations:

One-third - ⅓: Commanders use one-third of the available time to plan, prepare, and issue orders. This time is calculated from when the planning headquarters receives an order from higher headquarters until the subordinate unit begins moving.

Two-third - ⅔: Commanders allocate the remaining two-thirds of the time to subordinates so they can also plan and prepare. This rule helps commanders balance their desire to create a perfect operations order with the time constraints they face.

---

64 Crestcom Staff. The 3 Secrets to Leadership Vision Success. CRESTCOM. April 25th, 2017. https://crestcom.com/blog/2017/04/25/the-3-secrets-to-leadership-vision-success/#:~:text=The%20three%20secrets%20to%20successfully,and%20prioritizing%20long%2Dterm%20goals. - May 17th, 2024

Mentoring Other Leaders –
Strategic leaders can't just sit around and wait for new leaders to arrive, be fully developed and ready to go. As we discussed in Chapter 1 (How to progress through the Phases of Leadership), leaders are grown and cultivated over time. This is accomplished in many different ways both formally and informally: education, training programs, seminars, work experience, Lifelong learning, coaching and yes … Mentoring. Strategic leaders must proactively recognize leadership potential in others and seek ways to develop the potential in order to grow new leaders. If you let leader development become random you should be sitting with Forrest Gump and his box of chocolates because "you never know what you're gonna get."

In every election cycle, there are candidates whose opponents discuss qualifications. There is even one well known situation in which President Ronald Reagan stated,

"I want you to know that also I will not make age an issue of this campaign. I am not going to exploit, for political purposes, my opponent's youth and inexperience."

At the time, his opponent, Walter Mondale, was 56 years old and served as Vice President for 4 years.[65]

Leader mentoring requires a conscientious effort. No matter how busy you think you are or how aloof you feel, if you don't take time to groom and mentor leaders you are proving you don't care about their future.

Identification of Talent:

---

[65] Ronald Reagan Presidential Foundation and Institute. Debate between The President and Former Vice President Walter F. Mondale. Copyright 2024. https://www.reaganfoundation.org/ronald-reagan/reagan-quotes-speeches/debate-between-the-president-and-former-vice-president-walter-f-mondale-in-kansas-city-missouri/ - May 24th, 2024

Start early. An example is Audie L. Murphy, the most decorated soldier in the history of the United States. He lied about his age to join the military during World War II. He was turned down as an enlistee by both the Marines and the Paratroopers. Once in the Army, he was promoted through the ranks from Private to Lieutenant before his 21st birthday. He was given these promotions and leadership positions because his chain of command (Leaders) recognized his propensity to lead. But remember, he did not leave North Texas and join the Army as a leader. He was discovered and given an opportunity.[66]

Leadership potential can be easy to spot if you are actively looking and paying attention. You can see when people are proactive, reliable, thoughtful, looked up to by others … a stand out. You should look beyond the resume … They may not have proper formal education or the optimal progression of work experience. Did you? If you are the Strategic Leader and not grooming talent, are you really the leader you think you are?

Start Mentoring:

Once you've made the discovery, you have to be the one starting the conversation. Chances are they are not coming to you. Not because they don't want to, but because they may be unaware of the possibilities.

Reach out to the person and let them know you have seen their potential. You may find some people ready, willing and able to *motivate themselves to achieve beyond their own perceived capabilities.* You will find others who might need encouragement and this is where you, the leader, are *fostering the environment* and *motivating* them. Get to know the person so you can provide reasonable and cogent advice for them to develop. We've said this before … Doing nothing accomplishes nothing!

---

[66] Arlington National Cemetery. Audie Murphy. May 24th, 2024. https://www.arlingtoncemetery.mil/Explore/Notable-Graves/Medal-of-Honor-Recipients/World-War-II-MoH-recipients/Audie-Murphy#:~:text=He%20was%20Audie%20Murphy%2C%20the,to%20earn%20money%20picking%20cotton. - May 24, 2024

First Hand Mentoring:

Moses led the children of Israel for 40 years. When he died, Joshua became the leader. Joshua had been watching and learning from Moses the entire time. This was a lifelong and first-hand mentoring. You want to give your mentees that personal attention (maybe not for 40 years!). You will want to make sure your protégé gets the right experience, gets challenged, and gains new experience in areas outside their comfort zone which helps to see things from different perspectives. This may mean holding positions in several areas of your organization - Human Resources / Production / Knowledge Management. It may also include stints in different locations - in the United States and / or overseas (depending on your organization).

Remember, this is Strategic level leadership and mentoring. I am sure there may be exceptions to this; however, every General I knew or met, in the Army, spent time at lower ranks being mentored, gaining experience, honing their craft and putting in the time. Not a single person on the Supreme Court of the United States had ever held that position prior to being sworn in. And we have all seen it, the United States Senate puts these dedicated, patriotic men and women through unrelenting questioning in public forums to determine their pedigree and level of experience before making a vote. As you lead and mentor it is necessary to make certain the people under your wing know why you are maneuvering them through many of these roles and positions. I transferred from the position of Secretary of the General Staff (SGS) at a 2-Star command, to the Army Requirements Division at the Pentagon because my 2-Star Commander said, "If you want to keep getting promoted, you have to prove you can do more than move north and kill everything." That was a valuable and insightful lesson.

Mentoring vs. Coaching:

Don't confuse Mentoring with Coaching.

Mentoring normally occurs at higher levels of leadership, over a longer period of time, and is more broadly focused. Earlier, we discussed the value of having a wide array of positions and potentially, even different locations. This takes time to accomplish and requires the mentor to have a projected 'vision' for the mentee.

In our interview with Mr. George Simms, he says, "Mentors challenge you to improve while considering what is best for you. This could mean 'stay and grow', within the organization, or pursue external opportunities." Coaching is normally more narrowly focused, shorter in duration and geared toward specific tasks and requirements. Coaching can happen anywhere: on the sports field; in the classroom; during a training event or exercise; on the assembly line or job site / location. Coaching is normally accomplished by the immediate leader / manager / administrator.

One of the best examples I can think of is the Sergeant coaching a new Private at the weapons range to become a better marksman. This is a simple example; however, it can apply to the budget, property inventory, and even a parent giving a child a driving lesson. Coaching is valuable and it helps people stay on task and focused during learning. It is simply not mentoring.

Observational Coaching –

In this situation, the Coach doesn't make an on-the-spot-observation, but rather holds information until a formal review period / session. This is best used when the Coach wants to show a pattern. Remember, this is not necessarily a negative pattern. An example is a teacher who observes a student's reaction to different methods of instruction and assesses what works best for their students. This also allows the teacher / coach to improve lesson plans.

Success and Failure:

How well your mentee is prepared mentally and emotionally will have a lot to do with how they handle success and failure. How will you prepare them for success? We talk about this in other places in this book, but, as a reminder, we are not gangs of one. When we win the big game, have financial success with a new product or are elected to that coveted position, it is not alone. There are almost always others involved. A teacher, spiritual advisor, other team members and even a previous mentor or coach have provided guidance, encouragement and technical expertise. Mentally preparing your protégé to share the accolades is part of your mentoring responsibility as a leader.

Likewise, they must also be prepared for some failure. Only one National Football League team has ever had a season with no losses - the 1972 Miami Dolphins. I would have to believe there were some missed tackles, interceptions, and wide field goal attempts. So, mistakes will be made and goals will not be attained. Are you going to mentor them to stand tall and take on the mantle of leadership by accepting responsibility?[67]

There are other ways to be an influential leader: be a good example, lead from the front, be present and approachable, words have meaning, be conscious of your choices and be humble.

Be a Good Example:

There are positive and negative situations in every work environment from the production line to the board room. How you cope with these will be seen by others and will influence how others react to the same or similar situations in the future. A good leader will remain poised in pressure situations.

Lead from the Front:

Execute your decisions with confidence; own them. After all, you made the decision. Confidence can be infectious to those around you. There is a line from the old movie "Kelly's Heroes" (Release date: July 23, 1970; Distributed by: Metro-Goldwyn-Mayer). Donald Sutherland, as "Oddball" says, "There you go again with those negative waves." If you are projecting confidence, those around you will notice and respond. Conversely, if you are negative, others will feel that as well.

Be present and approachable:

We have said this before. Make certain you are available and that those you lead know when and where that happens. Set some rules and stick to

[67] Lisa Jasper. 5 tips to coach and mentor future leaders. Insperity. https://www.insperity.com/blog/5-tips-coach-mentor-future-leaders/ - May 17th, 2024

them. I once had a boss with a heavy smoking habit. If you found him in the outdoor smoking area, he was more receptive to discussing various subjects than in his office. This is a good example of being proactive and seeking out support.

Words have Meaning:

Your choice of words can have an influential positive impact or can drive people away. We've been taught to avoid filler words "um" and "like" and have been taught to face the audience or person with whom we are speaking. It is possible to practice and perfect this ability (see Chapter 5 - Communication "Do leaders really communicate or just tell people what to do/" - Learning to communicate with others.). There is one other thought here ... profanity. Do your best to avoid using profanity. I had a supervisor while in defense contracting who said, "Profanity is the sign of an inarticulate mind." Enough said!

Be Humble:

Again, you have heard it before. Being a leader inherently implies you are not alone in your endeavors. By recognizing others, you simultaneously encourage those on the sideline to act in a positive manner.

Being an individual contributor (IC) is where we will initially find ourselves. You don't have any direct reports, and you don't have direct input into the strategic direction of the company or organization. You were hired to perform a specific task and to meet your annual goals and objectives. The organization you join has an established culture, way of doing business, leaders and managers responsible for the direction and success of the business. As with most people starting out in a new job or career, you will likely be the lowest-ranking person in the organization, either due to being a recent college graduate or transitioning from another job or industry.

Over time, you become aware of how your skills can make a greater impact to improve the success of the group or organization. This is when you must become proactive and *seek out a mentor*. This is the beginning of learning how your choices, decisions or recommendations get into the decision-making stream of your Leaders. In Chapter 4 (Self Leadership -"If you can't lead yourself, how can you lead others?"), we discuss self-development and improvement. It is the foundation of how you begin the journey of eventually becoming the leader or manager.

Phase Four (Strategic Leadership) - quelling ignorance, articulating vision and mentoring leaders.

- ➢ Do your research … "Passion fueled by ignorance is dangerous."
- ➢ Have a real vision:
    - Be able to Articulate and Communicate your vision.
    - Have a strategy to achieve your vision.
    - Plan and prioritize your resources.
- ➢ Plan for the future by mentoring future leaders.
    - Identify Talent.
    - Be present and provide first-hand mentoring.
- ➢ Coaching is not mentoring.
- ➢ Even the most strategic of leaders started as an individual contributor.

Chapter 9
Volunteer Leadership

"Leadership is not carried out more through words but through attitudes and actions."
- Harold S. Geneen

Leaders are inherently people of action. This is never more true than in volunteerism. Volunteers are looking for people to emulate. Volunteering and the leadership in volunteer situations creates its own unique set of circumstances and challenges including reward and satisfaction. Many believe the volunteer environment is the most demanding place to lead. There are a few reasons for this:

- There is a perception volunteers are in low-ranking positions within the organizational hierarchy.
- Most people have jobs and family requirements and may have to fight to dedicate the time and energy to lead volunteers.
- There is always a lot of energy at the beginning of a volunteer's involvement; however, this may diminish over time, particularly if people feel undervalued or overworked.
- Without centralized guidance, leading volunteers can become fractured. These multiple points of volunteer entry can hamper the overall effectiveness of the volunteer effort.
- A successful program needs the resources to acquire, train, and retain volunteers. Then, later, recognize their contributions. Volunteer resources like funds, supplies and equipment are often limited.

Here is the Bottom Line, before we look a bit deeper:

- If you are the leader of volunteers: show Respect; give Recognition; be Humble. The quickest way to stifle volunteerism and retention of thoughtful people is to be the "my way or the highway" or the "I know better than you" leader.

- If you are the volunteer, do what you signed up for: show up; be on-time; dress appropriately; be nice (follow the rules / avoid profanity/practice integrity above reproach / don't spend all your time on your phone or device). If you can't do these things, no one will want you around, regardless of your good intentions.

Once people volunteer, they are looking for some structure, guidance and, of course, meaningful leadership that will provide them with what they are seeking. To understand this, it is important to know why people volunteer. So let's take a look at some of those reasons:[68]

Guiding Light - North Star.
Many people volunteer because they have some 'North Star' in their life guiding them. They had a loved one succumb to some particular cancer; they are a veteran or family member inspired to join one of the many supportive organizations; someone may have a special affinity for animals; they may have a close relative or friend already providing support in an organization. Whatever the personal reason, they are all led by that "North Star".

It's Healthy.
Volunteering provides both physical and mental benefits. Some people volunteer to get off the couch or out of the house. One of the authors is retired. Based on my personality and desire to serve, I can't just sit at home. I have routine places I volunteer: one is the local homeless shelter which provides a set of comprehensive services and has an 80% success rate (defined as - people not returning to homelessness for over a year). It gives me a sense of worth and keeps me active both physically and mentally. I teach skills necessary to find and apply for a job (called "Job Readiness"). It is my 'North Star' to get off the sofa by providing me a purpose. It has allowed me to meet some selfless people and to make my local community better.

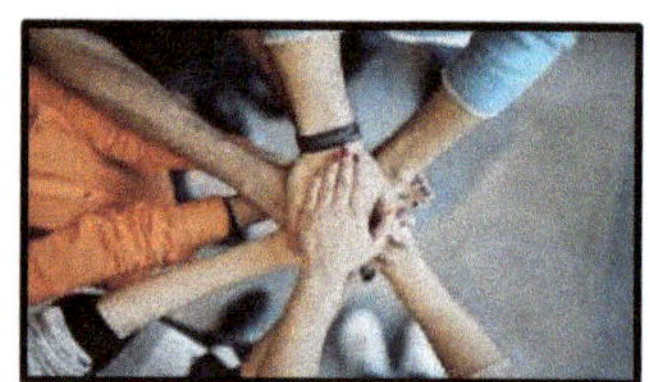

---

[68] Western Connecticut State University. Community Engagement. Copyright @ 2024 https://www.wcsu.edu/community-engagement/tips-for-volunteer/ - March 4th, 2024

Some see it as a way to give back.
They use their acquired skills and finances to make a difference. Communities and organizations see this as very valuable because volunteers generally cost nothing. Imagine going out to help build a house or a wheelchair ramp. Think of the feeling you may get if you install a basketball goal at a park. Volunteering means you are not expecting financial compensation. Many people like to support the efforts and donate their own resources to positively impact their local community.

Some years ago, we moved to the town where we now live and that meant changing places of worship. We visited several local churches and found a home in a welcoming environment that is truly non-judgmental - no one cares how you dress, how many tattoos you have, what your socio-economic status is, what your educational background is, who your parents are or anything else others might think important. The most important factor when considering a new place of worship is their faith – "you confess with your mouth that Jesus is Lord and believe in your heart that God raised him from the dead, you will be saved." (Romans 10:9 ESV). It is that easy! Very soon after our start with this group of Christ Followers, I was invited to dinner with a group of men from the church. We met on a weeknight at a local restaurant. Counting myself, there were 11 men present. After a few minutes I felt a bit out of place. I discovered I was the only person present who had graduated from college, never been addicted to drugs or alcohol and never been to jail or prison (I learned the difference between the two that night). When I arrived home my wife asked me about the event and I shared that the discussion revealed my own hubris, bias and hypocrisy. Today, years later, I count myself fortunate to be part of this congregation. I have the distinct honor of being accepted. I routinely learn from these men who have overcome incredible setbacks to lead their families, this community and our church. If you are truly going to lead, you must know the people you are leading and not allow your preconceived notions to cloud your judgment. It took volunteering for me to learn these valuable lessons.

Volunteering looks good on your resume:
For those without previous jobs or positions, volunteering gives you something valuable to put on a resume. It is also an excellent opportunity to test your skills in a relatively safe environment while observing and acquiring leadership experience. Over the years, you get to know your fellow volunteers and forge stronger, more enduring relationships. You also get an understanding of each person's strengths and weaknesses–a tactic you can apply in other situations. Volunteering will show positive work-ethic, altruism, resilience and provide some quality references. These qualities will never be seen in a bad light! You may also find that volunteering becomes part of your life (think of it as *Lifelong Learning*).

Volunteering becomes part of your life:
Several election cycles ago, I served as the Deputy Voting Location Manager with 20 other poll workers. Most of the poll workers were older and had several years of volunteer experience. Some of our workers were high school juniors and seniors, who expressed an interest in our democracy by gaining first-hand insights into how we run our elections. We assigned them to be Machine Judges, responsible for greeting the voter, escorting them to the ballot marker (to make voting selections), give a brief overview of how to vote, and be available to the voter for any further assistance. The days start at 5:30 am and end after we close the polls and clean up the facility around 9:00 pm. To most teenagers, processing nearly 1,000 voters is not the most appealing thing to do. In the case of our two young poll workers, they continued their volunteerism in college and into their early working careers. One returned to our voting location as an official poll worker, helping refresh the "bench" of those willing to participate in ensuring we have fair and free elections.

Volunteering is an excellent way to build confidence.
There is some debate as to whether confidence is a skill or an attribute. Confidence, like leadership (*the ability to foster an environment in which people motivate themselves to achieve beyond their own perceived capabilities, and face problems for which there appear to be*

no simple solutions), can be cultivated. Confidence is made of our belief in our ability to succeed and our belief we can influence situations in our life. Aim to build relationships with people who appreciate you. Their positivity can help you feel more confident. Those who are negative and try to bring you down often drain your confidence. It is also a way to broaden your network while working to achieve a common goal. It creates camaraderie and a feeling of teamwork. Additionally, it is a productive way to make new friends with likeminded people and build positive relationships.[69]

Volunteering is an avenue for growth.
It also provides an opportunity to understand the needs of your community and the power involvement can have. I recently saw a flier for a volunteer event to clean-up graffiti. The flier touted the success of last year's event, stating:

- 129 volunteers
- Removed 730+ graffiti tags & stickers!

This flier was a great example of previous community involvement and current community pride.

Being involved makes your community more resilient.
Many volunteer activities can provide support to families, improve schools, increase both adult and child literacy, and support youth programs. Cumulatively, this helps bolster the perception of those in the community and creates a new sense of pride. During my tenure as a public school teacher, I had the pleasure to lead students participating in the annual "National History Day" competition. This was voluntary for both the teacher and students. There was no additional pay for being on campus early or late to work with students. There was no additional compensation for forfeiting the daily 'planning period' so students could work on their project in my classroom. There was no special consideration for eating

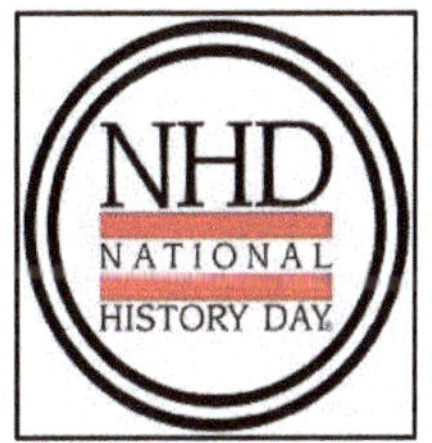

[69] Future Learn. How to build confidence: 5 tips for being more confident. May 18th, 2022. https://www.futurelearn.com/info/blog/general/how-to-build-confidence-5-tips-being-more-confident - March 11, 2024

lunch in my classroom allowing students a space to work. In each of these situations, the students were in need of guidance related to content / method of presentation / research locations and opportunities / work-ethic. Remember, the reward was not going to be the potential crowd cheering buzzer beater or grand slam homerun to win the game. It was more subtle, a possible trip to the local college or university for the regional or state competitions with a story in the school or local news, some pictures with captions on the school social media, maybe a certificate with an associated ribbon or medal. These students also discovered how to learn and have fun doing so. As the leader, be committed to something bigger than yourself. You should be present and be prepared to sacrifice for something you can enjoy and derive personal satisfaction.

Volunteering is a way to promote Lifelong learning. Many situations allow for hidden talents to be exposed changing views on your self-worth. If you are working with not-for-profit groups you can gain a new perspective of government operations, particularly at the local levels.

My mother succumbed to cancer many years ago. After her diagnosis, I volunteered at an event focused on increasing cancer awareness and raising money for cancer research. My purpose was not focused on Lifelong learning, yet I learned from the experience of simply being involved–that was the lesson. I learned about different types of cancer, how different people cope with the stress of the prognosis, how money actually makes it from the event to funding applications and how large, one-time events are organized and operated. It takes a nucleus of dedicated people to make all these things happen.

Being involved promotes civic responsibility, not just in yourself, but also in those who witness the efforts and successes of volunteers. This has the potential to bleed into civic responsibility. Think "see something, say something." It also leads you to even greater responsibilities.[70]

---

[70] Susan N. Dreyfus. Volunteerism and US Civil Society. Sanford Social Innovation Review. August 29th, 2018.
https://ssir.org/articles/entry/volunteerism_and_us_civil_society - March 6th, 2024

Voting Location Deputy and Machine Judge:

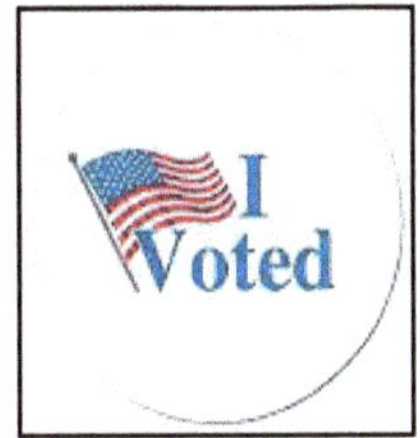

One of the most sacred rights we have as Americans is the individual right to vote. During military service we strive to remain apolitical and not get involved in politics. However, we still encourage everyone to vote and I felt a sense to continue service by ensuring a process to enable voting. After retiring from the military, I missed the sense of duty and service. I also observed the low participation numbers for poll workers and volunteered to become part of our democratic process. I was assigned as a Machine Judge for my first few elections, helping others mark their ballots and ensure their vote was counted. Between the primary elections and a special election, the Board of Elections called and asked if I would consider serving as a Voting Location Manager. They received feedback from other poll workers that I provided the most effective leadership and took the time to train and develop first-time or unsteady colleagues.[71]

You can and will make a difference because every person counts, has value and something to offer. Just remember, if you volunteer, be there, be on time and in the words of the 7 Dwarfs, "Whistle while you work."

With these common reasons for volunteerism in mind, let's talk about some leadership considerations for the leader of volunteers. As the leader of volunteers, you MUST do these things: show Respect, give Recognition and be Humble, and check your ego at the door. It doesn't matter how successful a leader you are in your professional role, this is a different environment. You can never be the "my way or the highway" leader or the "do it or I'll kill you" leader. We have all seen them. This won't work in the volunteerism domain; people will just quit and leave.

Simply saying "Thank You", and doing so with sincerity, is a way to be respectful and simultaneously show recognition. Recently, a member of

[71] From Wikipedia, the free encyclopedia. Volunteering. Wikipedia. 5 April 2024 https://en.wikipedia.org/wiki/Volunteering - May 6th, 2024

our congregation wanted to provide food for our Wednesday Night Youth Group. They decided to buy hamburgers from one of the local fast food restaurants and brought them to the group. If the person wants to give, you let them! It met a need for both the Youth Group and for the person providing the donation (i.e.: Respect - you don't say no). In this situation, prior to serving the food, we publicly thanked and applauded the benefactor. Recognition is a simple way to say, "Thank You". It was that easy.

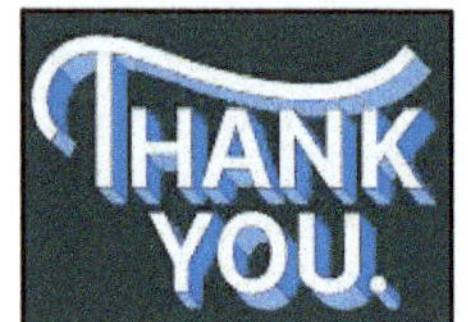

Routinely showing gratitude and recognition to volunteers doesn't need to be complex, time-consuming or grandiose. I know, we've all seen the big ceremonies, dinners and banquets with speeches, awards and honorariums (I just had this vision of the "Oscars", ugh). However, handing out $5 gift cards from Sonic or McDonalds can be very effective. Today's technology makes it easy to produce some fancy-looking certificates with little effort. Even a few positive remarks in front of an impromptu gathering with a warm handshake, done in earnest, is a positive way to show respect, appreciation, and recognition.

Being humble as you lead volunteers is often seen and not heard. We have a gentleman in our congregation who is a leader in our local community, a very successful business owner, well-educated and respected for their routine selflessness. The person volunteers at our Wednesday Youth Group (mentioned earlier). He helps set up tables and chairs for the event, serves food and drinks during the event and helps clean-up (put away tables and chairs, empties trash-cans, washes dishes) after the event. This is leading by example. He could easily just toss money at the group and keep his hands clean; however, his humble demeanor is noticed by the youth and I believe provides a life-lesson to be emulated by others.

Volunteers want to be engaged and one of your roles as the leader is to keep them gainfully employed. To do this, the volunteer leader needs to:

- Listen more and talk less: Make certain volunteers know their ideas are valued. You must earnestly listen to their ideas, ask their opinion, and realize their insights may be better than yours. When you, as the volunteer leader, put their thoughts and ideas into action you have engaged them. This is also a great form of recognition and respect.

- Be considerate of time: Most volunteers have families / jobs /other commitments. Time consumption will impact the volunteer's level of commitment. So, don't be frivolous with their time. You must be on time, don't have long meetings, have a plan and focus on the objective for every event.
- Pay attention to the potential of volunteer burnout. Burnout happens most often when you call on the same person or people over and over. I am retired and folks know it. I am routinely called on for all manner of activities. As the leader, keeping volunteers engaged includes focusing on specific outcomes and being aware of what you are asking. If you are a volunteer, you must be able to say "no" when necessary. You should take responsibility for your own well-being in this regard.
- Understand why an individual is volunteering, that 'North Star' or motivation. We have discussed reasons for volunteering. The motivation is different for each person. Understanding this motivation will assist you in finding a good fit for the volunteer. I spent several years on the Board of Directors for a large, not-for-profit, organization with a large budget. We received the volunteer services of a professional Certified Public Accountant (CPA). This person was willing to donate a few hours per month and our organization received quality (free of charge) support. Motivation, skill, and necessity coming together for the greater good.
- Knowing the skills your volunteers bring to the group will make a positive difference (applying faces to spaces). We have a member of a volunteer group who happens to be Captain of the City Fire Department. He is a certified instructor in Basic Life Support (BLS) and was willing to hold a training class for CPR / AED / choking response along with how to inspect and use fire extinguishers. We now have a "safety team" for our church prepared for many emergencies.

Leading Volunteers: The volunteer leader must be able to handle disagreements on the approach to an activity. Sometimes that also includes being able to lead those on the outskirts of the activity. One year I was asked by a coworker to be his assistant coach on a little league baseball team. I agreed. I did not have a child on the team but thought it may be fun as I did enjoy the game. For a few months I spent several days a week helping at practices and Little League games. As the season came to an end, each of the eight teams in the league picked four players to be on the "All-Star" team and an All-Star game was held with 16 players on each team. Once again, my coworker, who was chosen to be the Leader of one of the teams, asked me to be one of his assistants. The day of the game I was asked to make certain every player had a chance to be on the field in a position they played on their regular season team (unlimited substitution for the All-Star game). Between the third and fourth innings, I moved a player from 3rd base to right field. The father of that player came to me and asked what I was doing. At that point, I was a member of the Management and Administration; however, I had been given some specific *Authority* from the Leader. I explained this to the parents and the effort to make each player feel special. As he walked away he said, "Keep up the good work." I could see him speaking with the other parents. I had led multiple people by speaking to only one.

Just because it is a volunteer group (informal or semi-formal), organization or effort, doesn't mean we throw out structure, guidance and, of course, meaningful leadership to help volunteers with what they are seeking.

You need to have a smooth running / structure for volunteer organizations. Following a set routine, easy-to-use guidelines or having Standard Operating Procedures (SOPs) will make volunteer events easier for the leader and provide a clear roadmap for volunteers.

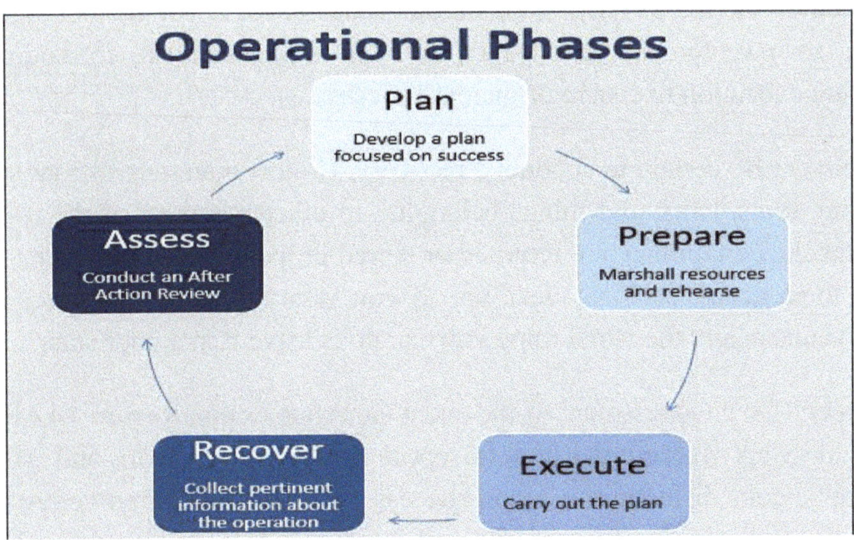

Plan ahead and pre-decide a model to follow for your operations. This consistency will breed a comfortable atmosphere, confidence and facilitate success and trust. The model you employ doesn't have to be exactly like this one; however, every operation, regardless of discipline, has five phases: Plan, Prepare, Execute, Recovery, Assess. There can be more but without these five routine phases success will be "trusted to luck."

Plan: Have a meeting with the key members of the volunteer team. Get cogent input from those team members and develop a plan. Include timelines and required resources in the plan and–if time permits–conduct "what if" scenario planning (i.e.: develop potential back-up plans…"Plan B" or even "Plan C"). Involve as many people as possible in the "what if" session so people know what is supposed to happen. If you do your planning in a vacuum your event will become a dictatorship with a high probability of failure.

Prepare: Marshal your resources and make certain people know their assignments. Produce a timeline that can be easily distributed and then, if possible, have a rehearsal (or at a minimum) a talk-through. Do a talk through of your back-up plans.

Execute: Do the activity. You are the leader! People will be looking at you, so have fun. As the leader, don't be afraid to make corrections during execution to ensure or increase success.

Recover: Be certain to conduct a recovery. Collect materials like tables, chairs, tools, tents, and things belonging to other members of the team and make certain they are returned or stored properly. You may want to use them again. Always clean-up. If you want to use the resources or the venue again, the worst thing you can do is leave it in a poor state.

Assess: Do an assessment of the event–an After Action Review (AAR). Decide what worked and how to repeat it; what didn't work and what must be done differently to attain success; what could be improved; who has the authority to drive the changes in each of these areas you, as the leader, have responsibility for? Once you determine this, you must assign people or teams to implement the changes and hold periodic follow-ups to ensure execution.

I've had the pleasure of volunteering with multiple organizations over the past 40+ years and one of those opportunities was to serve as President of a local Chapter of Ducks Unlimited (DU). This organization conserves, restores, and manages wetlands and associated habitats for North America's waterfowl. These habitats also benefit other wildlife and people.[72] Our local chapter was going to hold a banquet as a "fund-raiser". We had a paid member of the State Chapter of DU come visit with us. They shared a wealth of knowledge and gave examples of how to facilitate such an event. He had pamphlets outlining the "best practices" for conducting a banquet. We found vendors who donated goods and services to sell, raffle and auction at the banquet to generate money to donate to the cause. In order to conduct this banquet and accomplish all of the 2nd, 3rd and 4th order tasks necessary to make it a worthwhile event, it required many volunteers and I am pleased to say we had plenty. Our event was a success, raising over $250,000. This required a structure, with the right skills and quality control.

---

[72] DU Staff. Ducks Unlimited. Copyright 2023 Ducks Unlimited. https://www.ducks.org/ - January 8th, 2024

Fortunately, we also had many members with professional backgrounds in the right skills to promote our success. However, two of our volunteers–who retired from very senior corporate positions–wanted their names to be associated with the group. But, when it came time to do the work, they wanted me to "brief" them (give them a run down) and they would tell me what else we should do.

Most leaders will spend the vast majority of their time in positions where they both lead and have a leader (i.e. are a follower). How we follow sends a message to those we lead. What is your message?

- If you are the leader: show Respect; give Recognition; be Humble.
- If you are the volunteer: Show up; Be on-time; Dress appropriately; Be nice (follow the rules / no profanity / integrity above reproach).
- There are many good reasons to volunteer. Make certain people know what they are.
- Volunteers want to be engaged. When they become idle, they stop volunteering.
- Have a guide for how you will conduct your volunteer event: Plan, Prepare, Execute, Recover, Assess.
- Have fun and make a positive difference!

Chapter 10
Military Leadership

"These scars on my body, were got for you, my brothers. Every wound, as you see, is in the front. Let that man stand forth from your ranks who has bled more than I, or endured more than I for your sake. Show him to me, and I will yield to your weariness and go home." – Alexander The Great

The mission of the United States Military is woven into the very fabric of the nation. Below explains how our nation created a process to establish a military, and the commitment required to serve:

- The Preamble to the Constitution "*provide[s] for the common defense.*"
- Article 1, Section 8 of the Constitution instructs the Legislative Branch to "*provide for the common defense.*"
- Article 4, Section 4 of the Constitution states the "*United States shall guarantee to every State a republican form of government and shall protect each of them against invasion.*"
- Article I, Section 8, Clause 11 of the Constitution gives Congress the power to declare war. It gives Congress the power "*to declare War, grant Letters of Marque and Reprisal, and make Rules concerning Captures on Land and Water.*"[73]
- The Congressional Oath of Office includes the phrase, "*defend the Constitution of the United States against all enemies, foreign and domestic.*"[74] The 118th Congress of the United States, which began its session on January 3rd, 2024, included 98 veterans.

---

[73] Library of Congress. Constitution Annotated. https://constitution.congress.gov/browse/article-1/ - June 17th, 2024

[74] Jennifer E. Manning. Membership of the 118th Congress: A Profile. Congressional Research Service. Updated June 7, 2024. https://crsreports.congress.gov/product/pdf/R/R47470 - June 19th, 2024

- The Military Oath of Office that every service member swears to uphold states, "*I will support and defend the Constitution of the United States against all enemies, foreign and domestic.*"[75]
- Article II, Section 1 of the Constitution includes the Presidential Oath of Office and also includes "defense." "*I do solemnly swear (or affirm) that I will faithfully execute the Office of President of the United States, and will to the best of my ability, preserve, protect and defend the Constitution of the United States.*"
- Article II, Section 2, Clause 1 of the Constitution gives the role of Commander in Chief to the President. It says, "*The President shall be Commander in Chief of the Army and Navy of the United States, and of the Militia of the several States, when called into the actual Service of the United States.*" 31 of the 45 people to have held the office have U.S. Military experience as part of their resume.[76]

It takes **leadership** - *the ability to foster an environment in which people motivate themselves to achieve beyond their own perceived capabilities, and face problems for which there appear to be no simple solutions* - to make this happen.

Just a quick pause. Some of you may want to ask if we are "defending," why does the military travel all over the world? It's simple. We want to project our power forward and defend as far away from home as possible!

Leadership must be applied with:

- An understanding of the environment.
- Realizations that even the smallest things make a difference.

---

[75] U.S. Army. Oath of Enlistment. https://www.army.mil/values/oath.html - June 17th 2024

[76] Caitlin O'Brien. 31 Presidents who served in the Military. Military Times. February 15th, 2021. https://www.militarytimes.com/news/your-military/2021/02/15/31-presidents-who-served-in-the-military/ - June 19th, 2024

- Individual personal discipline is required at every level of responsibility and authority.

Understanding the Environment: There are two distinct tracks of activity in the Military: the "Chain of Command" and "Rank" (see Graphic 7). People can hold positions at various times in their careers in both tracks to become well-rounded leaders. Often, military leadership is viewed as being easier than other industries or situations. However, the dual track a military leader must maintain makes leading even harder. In the end, the military leader is responsible for the lives of ***everyone*** in their command. Should one of their members become a casualty, the commander is responsible for explaining how their decisions led to the death of the family's loved one.

As new leaders come into an organization, they lack an understanding of the current organizational culture and rely upon their team to give them insights into that culture. More importantly, this empowers the team to execute and deliver results–a higher degree of delegating authority. However, at some point, many leaders begin to claw back their delegated authority which can create friction amongst management layers. The Leader has already done your job and should not spend time doing yours. This is why the building of trust is so critical. (see Chapter 6 - How to Build Trust and to Trust in Others)

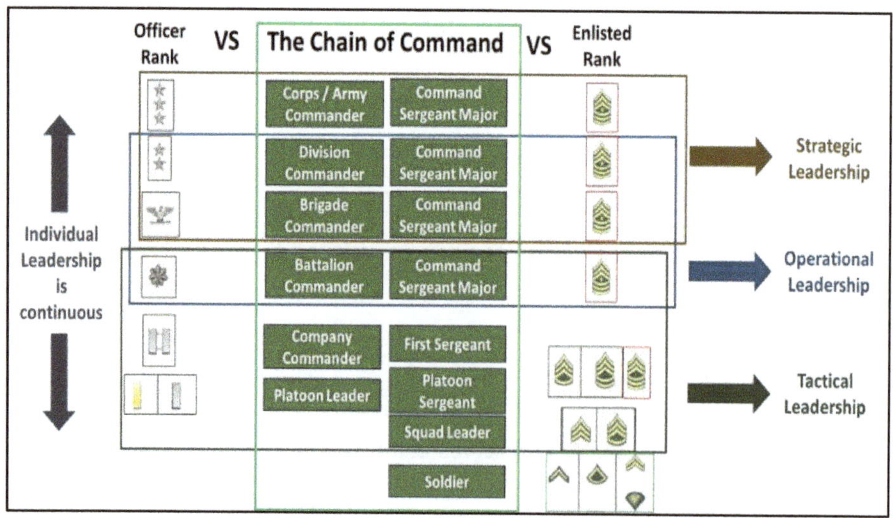

- ***Graphic 7 - "Chain of Command": The path of Responsibility. "Rank": The path of Authority.***

- In the <u>Chain of Command</u> track, people are specifically designated into positions as Leaders and possess the **Responsibility** of the organization. Many are actually designated, via a written order, as the Commander or Leader. The first time I looked at such an appointment order with my name on it, as a new Battery Commander in 1987, it felt weighty. I was now, by name, <u>Responsible</u> for more than 100 soldiers. However, it's not unusual in the military to find an Officer or Noncommissioned Officer (NCO) who is not in a specified leadership position but exercises influential leadership.

- In the <u>Rank</u> track, you will have **Authority** in an organization and respect based on seniority. Most senior leaders have successfully completed commands at lower levels and possess an inherent knowledge and experience base. If you are not in the Chain of Command, true responsibility rests elsewhere. If you are not in the "Chain of Command" your job is to use the Authority provided by the leaders (Chain of Command), along with your experience and your rank, to provide any support you can. Understanding your role in the mission is part of self-leadership. You may also have to exert more influential leadership. Most military people know with Rank comes experience in both tracks.

All of this energy for Responsibility and Authority (The Chain of Command and Rank) is focused on the defense of the United States and its Constitution. Many things go into training and equipping U.S. military forces to "support and defend the Constitution " while meeting "the non-negotiable contract with the American people to fight and win the nation's wars". Anything that can't directly be tied back to it should be a low priority! In many ways, the Military Leader has a clear North Star - Defense - and can create a vision to ensure they meet that non-negotiable contract.

After re-deploying from Iraq, in 2003, I penned an article titled, "Battlefield Decisions of a Battalion Commander".[77] Much reflection has taken place since those days. I realize my responsibility in the Chain of Command, prior to deployment, was to train my unit to get through the first few days. If they made it through the first encounter of a tough situation it would stick, and it wouldn't need teaching again–much like teaching a toddler to stack blocks without having them fall. The next time, the toddler won't need to be taught how to add one block to another.

One of the obstacles we, and many other units, had to overcome in Iraq, was crossing through the Karbala Gap. In the early days of the war, it was believed if Saddam Hussen was going to use chemical weapons, this would be the spot. I remember the very serious discussion with my subordinate commanders in the early afternoon prior to the assault. We conducted training for chemical scenarios at home, but this night it was a real possibility and staring us in the face. We didn't need to encourage soldiers to clean and inspect their gas masks or chemical protective overgarments - most of them did it more than once. Most people look at this as one of those situations that was predictable, not so … we were leading soldiers into the unknown.

Performance Under Pressure Starts with Preparation. The military trains its personnel to perform optimally under extreme pressure so that they're ready when the going gets tough. **Perfect practice makes perfect**. Cultivating resilient service members that thrive under pressure isn't so much about pushing when things get hard, it's more about pre-emptively teaching them the skills to navigate stressful times so they're prepared to dig in when the time comes. We often use the term, *train to standard,* to ensure the tasks are properly trained to the point where the learner can execute independently.

[77] Billy F. Sprayberry. "Battlefield Decisions of a Battalion Commander" Article – July 2004 – The Field Artillery Journal

<u>Effective Communication</u>. Clear, concise, direct communication is crucial in the military; it's also critical to have clear, dedicated channels of communication to ensure the right message reaches the right people.

There is a great leadership movie called "Twelve O'clock High". It was produced by 20th Century Fox in 1949 and featured such stars as Gregory Peck and Dean Jagger (who won an Oscar for Best Supporting Actor). In one scene, two Generals are discussing the problems of one of their subordinate Bomber Groups. During this scene, one of the Generals, portrayed by Gregory Peck, says he knows what the problem is. "It is the Commander's (Leader's) fault, it is always the Commander's (Learder's) fault, it's his job!" This is a powerful comment and goes directly to our definitions of "Leadership" and "Responsibility" in Table 1. The leader can never abdicate the responsibility of the position regardless of who within his command caused the problem!

In all situations, leaders make decisions with the best information available to them. This is also true in the military. How you collect the information may be a bit more unique than in a civilian setting. So how do you know what your soldiers are experiencing? There are several things you can do to find out. In many cases you must set the example and lead with the full realization your every move is being watched.

Infantry "Follow Me" statue at Ft. Moore, GA "Iron Mike"

Trust your Subordinates. Military organizations rely on effective teams to complete tasks, achieve objectives, and accomplish missions. The ability to build teams through mutual trust to maintain effective, cohesive teams in military operations is an essential skill for Military leaders. When moving forward against the unknown, you must trust you have trained your subordinate leaders to do the right things and trust they will do them right.

About three or four days into Operation Iraqi Freedom, we were given the mission to move forward–ahead of the main fighting force–in order to attack a target out of range for ground forces. With the M270A1 Multiple Launch Rocket System (MLRS)--at the time, the most advanced system with the greatest surface to surface range in the world–we moved forward to the designated firing area. This move required us to go beyond the roads and trails crowded with other units. We soon found ourselves with no other friendly forces in sight as we moved through an urban area - the locals were carrying AK-47s / Kalashnikovs. Mixed among the crowds were men in thobes (a traditional longer "dress" worn in the Arabian Peninsula area) with combat boots. Fighting soldiers would often attempt to blend into the civilian population to avoid detection, gather intelligence, or potentially plan an attack against their enemy–us in this case.

I made a radio call to the leader at the front of the unit, one of my subordinate commanders, my co-author David McDowell, and said, "You need to go to weapons red." He responded, "Way ahead of you." There were no other comments. We were moving forward against the unknown and he was ready for responsibility. He was a Leader, doing the right things and doing them right.

I am certain those early days of the war in Iraq are replete with similar situations. However, most of the people in the military find themselves serving in times and areas of relative peace. When there is no immediate threat of war to focus a unit are the times when Leadership truly shows. Where the U.S. military is present around the world sends a message - even one of deterrence … projecting our power and defenses forward -

and the professionalism of those forces is seen by our potential adversaries. Likewise, those training exercises the public never sees and are not advertised in the media, in difficult terrain / at night / in extreme weather / long days away from family, serve to ensure the military is ready for anything and will have the character to excel and win. A quote attributed to both Winston Churchill and George Orwell states:, "We sleep soundly in our beds because rough men stand ready in the night to do violence on those who would harm us."

<u>Work in the same environment.</u> The first 12 days of the war in Iraq (starting on March 20th, 2003), we were at Mission Oriented Protective Posture (MOPP) Level 2.[78] This meant wearing our chemical overgarments and over-boots while carrying our protective mask. Protective gloves and helmet cover were to be readily available. We had trained at home wearing this equipment but not for 12 days! Your rank did not matter. If you were in Iraq, you were wearing this heavy and uncomfortable clothing. Along with this, you had the standard equipment of flak jackets, load bearing vests with ammo / water / weapons and other assorted items. This was in the heat, the sand, the blowing wind (you get the idea) with no break-even sleeping in the equipment. Every leader in Iraq was in the same environment as those being led. Up to that point in my military training (22+ years) I had never worn this equipment longer than a single day. Those leaders and decision makers back in Kuwait and at the Headquarters in Florida, had to trust those on the ground in Iraq for assessments on the impact.

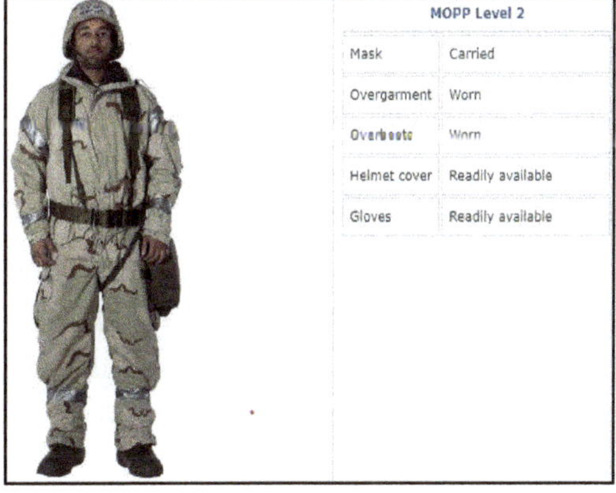

---

[78]U.S. Department of Health and Human Services. June 24th, 2024. https://remm.hhs.gov/militarypercutaneous_ppe.htm - June 25th, 2024

Eat the same food. If you are not eating the same food as your soldiers you are likely not in tune with their energy levels or their ability to perform work. This type of close proximity to your soldiers allows you to make the most informed decision as you get to know your soldiers and understand their challenges or issues first-hand. As a leader in a field situation it is imperative you make fully informed decisions. If your position does not lend itself to this, remember how you felt when it did and trust your subordinate leaders to provide you an honest assessment.

Most soldiers feel it is their right to complain about the food. However, I don't think I was ever in a situation where it was not available. One Meal Ready to Eat (MRE) contains between 1200 and 1400 calories. During most training and operations soldiers are issued three per day or they are made readily available. They may not be your favorite meal; however, soldiers don't go hungry. I once had a peer commander note that sometimes you, the Leader, simply need to ensure they are consuming the meal.[79]

Sleep in the same conditions. During the very first day of Operation Iraqi Freedom (OIF), a really old looking Colonel showed up in my position. He explained he had been recalled to service to accurately capture the history of events as they unfolded. I thought, "I don't have time for this, we're about to begin a combat operation!" He propped his foot on the grill of the closest High Mobility Multipurpose Wheeled Vehicle (HMMWV), pulled out his notebook and started asking questions. I had to point out, even though the sun was up and activity was going on, he was only a few feet from where soldiers were sleeping. Yes, sleep plans are a necessity! Once the Colonel recognized the situation he actually said, "I forgot what it was like." If you are the

---

[79] Stephen Biesty. USS Constitution Museum. Daily Calorie Intake of an 1812 Sailor and a Modern Combat Ration. Copyright 2011. https://ussconstitutionmuseum.org/wp-content/uploads/2018/09/Daily-Calorie-Intake-of-an-1812-Sailor-Dinnertime-Sailors-Eating.pdf - April 9, 2024

Leader on the scene, don't hesitate to respectfully point out or provide pertinent information. Even though he out ranked me, I was responsible.

Workout and train in the same conditions: We've mentioned this before, the leader is constantly being watched and evaluated. Are you, as the Leader, physically fit enough to set the example and hold yourself to the same training standards as those you lead? Do you attend training; are you seen doing tough physical training (PT); do you wear your seatbelt, kevlar helmet, and body armor; do you look like a Soldier and hold your subordinate leaders to the same standard; and more? In order to be a credible leader, you can't be an anomaly to the Soldiers you lead. They must know you are fair, consistent, and present. Your personal involvement will have a positive impact. This means being seen *doing the right things* and *doing them right*. This requires character, integrity, honesty and the willingness to always demonstrate those traits.

Remember what it was like. It is not always necessary to endure every hardship. Sometimes you must remember what it was like when you were a follower or subordinate leader at the tip of the spear. Imagine yourself in those all too familiar situations. You can also proactively seek input and insights from your intermediate subordinate leaders who may be out front. If you are willing to do these things, you will create a deeper connection with your subordinates. Actively seeking this input will provide you with the situational awareness to make the best decisions possible and earn more trust as a leader.

Continuous Training. Training is ongoing in the military— it's part of the job. It's how service members get better at their jobs every day. When you are not holding one of the positions in the "Chain of Command" you will be in a position, based on your "Rank" within management and / or administration supporting the Leaders. Every NCO and Officer in the military understands this. These are serious requirements; yet some do not take them as such. In order to meet the mission of defending the United States and its Constitution, units must be resourced, trained to high levels and be led by Leaders who embrace continuous improvement. In the build up to our Iraq deployment

(February 2003), there was significant attention paid to individual and collective/unit training and certification. Even the best leaders can't do it all and there were many great people in management and administrative positions with authority to help make things happen. We fielded the most advanced weapon system at the time, the M270A1 MLRS. Every personnel position in the Battalion was filled with the appropriate rank and skill level; we also had a Maintenance Support Team of 25 skilled personnel attached to us; we were provided every nut, bolt and tool on the assigned Table of Equipment. We were also provided the land, fuel, ammunition and other needed resources to conduct a 10 day training exercise (December 2002) to make certain we were at the top of our game because "**perfect practice makes perfect**."

We named this exercise "Razor's Edge." The exercise started with individual tasks and transitioned to collective and unit-level tasks. Once the mission was briefed to leadership, this gave the NCOs–responsible for directly training and managing soldiers–time to work with individual soldiers as they progressed to the collective tasks at the Battalion Level including a fire mission utilizing every M270A1 MLRS in the unit (19 - when you included the float launcher). This was 10 days of the most valuable training we could have had and improved how individuals worked together and allowed us to focus on safety procedures in every task. I once heard a football player say, "the separation is in the preparation." The reason his team was winning was because they prepared the best they could for each game. What set them apart from other teams wasn't their facilities or their skill, but their *dedication to preparation.* The same held true for us. The separation was indeed in the preparation. We deployed, executed every mission given us and returned home with a safety record I will continue to boast about. We did not lose any time for a single soldier for a safety-related injury for over six months. More importantly, we re-deployed all soldiers back to their families without the loss of life, limb, or eyesight! This is a testament to the leaders at every level of the Unit. Organizations anticipating great things prepare for great things.

The Smallest Things Make a Difference:
We were notified of our deployment at 9:21 AM on a Saturday morning and began loading our equipment for movement. 80 hours later we were on the way. There were people of all ranks and positions in the chain of command involved. During the pre-operations brief, the first General in my chain of command, a Brigadier General, (1-Star) Commanding the Corps Artillery, came to the rail loading point to get a first-hand look and to talk to me. One of the things he asked was, "Do you have everything?" I responded, "No". We were missing 3 items on our Prescribed Load List (PLL - repair parts available for immediate use when necessary). I explained to the General these items were readily available on the Post in the Logistics Warehouse. I further explained the people managing the Warehouse told me it was their "go to war stock". Using some pointed and colorful four-letter vernaculars, I asked, "Where do you think I'm going?" After a chuckle, the General left and returned an hour later with the parts and the Warehouse manager.

Leadership / Responsibility vs Rank / Authority.
On the tail end of our deployment, when we pulled out of Iraq, we were re-positioned on one of the several "Base Camps" in Kuwait. The base camp had tent areas for sleeping, areas to park our vehicles, portable latrines and even some portable shower facilities. There were even two large tents (imagine circus tents - big) being used as dining facilities. We pulled into this base camp in the early hours of the morning and, as the sun rose, subordinate leaders started getting things organized. After a quick discussion with the Battalion Command Sergeant Major (CSM), subordinate commanders and the staff, we decided the uniform on the base camp would include weapons, gas mask, one canteen and required kevlar helmets be worn in moving vehicles and, in the vehicle parking area. All other individual combat equipment - body armor and load bearing vests could be stored. At this point, the CSM and I went to the Camp Commander's HQ Area (think of this as City Hall to visit the Mayor) to introduce ourselves. He immediately notified us that the uniform on the camp included all individual combat equipment because other units on the camp were preparing to go North and they needed to be focused. I explained this particular Battalion's focus was my

responsibility and this would be our uniform while inside the confines of the camp. Being responsible means other commanders have the authority to determine the focus of their units as they deem necessary. Later that afternoon, I was informed soldiers from our Battalion were not being served meals in the dining tent because they were not in the correct uniform as defined by the Camp Commander. The CSM and I walked to the dining area and took the place of the food service personnel and made certain our soldiers received dinner. Needless to say, the Camp Commander was upset and made calls to several more senior officers. I'm not certain what transpired in those calls; however, from that point forward there was no question about our uniform. It would stay the way I and the CSM agreed upon. This proved two things: 1) when you are responsible, be responsible 2) this small act of serving food showed the soldiers we cared about even the smallest things related to their comfort and wellbeing - loyalty to your people is a good thing.

Individual Personal Discipline: If you have ever been in or around a military unit on a regular basis you will note there are many traditions, mottos, oaths, codes, values, and other pledges to instill honor and motivation in U.S. military forces. Personal discipline is necessary to "defend the Constitution against all enemies–foreign and domestic." One of my favorites is the Non-Commissioned Officers (NCO) Creed. Even though I was not an "NCO", I took the time to memorize this creed. As a leader of leaders, I found it a valuable tool. There are two lines I use most often. The first, "No one is more professional than I. I am a noncommissioned officer, a leader of Soldiers." If I ever found my subordinate leaders not performing up to standard, I would simply ask them to quote the first two sentences of this creed. There was no need to make up new rules or establish a new standard. In most circumstances simply reminding them of the creed they follow was enough to create motivation and inspiration.

The other line from the NCO creed I found most useful in training or teaching subordinate leaders was, "Officers of my unit will have maximum time to accomplish their duties; they will not have to accomplish mine." Sometimes just asking, "Why do I need to be here?"

was enough. Most professions and organizations have their set of "creeds" and or "values". If you want to lead more effectively in your chosen field of endeavor, take the time to learn them.

NCO CREED

No one is more professional than I. I am a noncommissioned officer, a leader of Soldiers. As a noncommissioned officer, I realize that I am a member of a time honored corps, which is known as "The Backbone of the Army". I am proud of the Corps of noncommissioned officers and will at all times conduct myself so as to bring credit upon the Corps, the military service and my country regardless of the situation in which I find myself. I will not use my grade or position to attain pleasure, profit, or personal safety.

Competence is my watchword. My two basic responsibilities will always be uppermost in my mind–accomplishment of my mission and the welfare of my Soldiers. I will strive to remain technically and tactically proficient. I am aware of my role as a noncommissioned officer. I will fulfill my responsibilities inherent in that role. All Soldiers are entitled to outstanding leadership; I will provide that leadership. I know my Soldiers and I will always place their needs above my own. I will communicate consistently with my Soldiers and never leave them uninformed. I will be fair and impartial when recommending both rewards and punishment.

Officers of my unit will have maximum time to accomplish their duties; they will not have to accomplish mine. I will earn their respect and confidence as well as that of my Soldiers. I will be loyal to those with whom I serve; seniors, peers, and subordinates alike. I will exercise initiative by taking appropriate action in the absence of orders. I will not compromise my integrity, nor my moral courage. I will not forget, nor will I allow my comrades to forget that we are professionals, noncommissioned officers, leaders!

After Defending: So, what happens when defending the United States and the Constitution while in uniform is over? We've all heard the phrase, "Thank you for your service." I've had people say this phrase to me many times. It happens most often when wearing a shirt or cap in public indicating military service. There is a comment often attributed to George Washington indicating a nation should be especially judged by how it treats veterans. My father said, "The words *homeless* and *veteran* should never be in the same sentence." Veterans leave the military and try to fit into a society that does not always understand them nor know how to properly leverage the skills and values veterans acquire during military service. Despite the challenges in "re-integrating" into society, veterans continue to *serve*.

Veterans make significant contributions to their country, including continuing to serve their communities through volunteer work, advocacy, and other public service. Veterans Day is designed to thank living veterans for their service, recognize their contributions to national security, and defense of the nation and the constitution, and acknowledge all those who sacrificed.

Veteran Superpowers: Today, there are more than 18 million living veterans in the United States, representing about 6% of the country's adult population.[80] Based on a vast assortment of factors, the experience for each of these 18,000,000 is unique. Some of these factors include: What branch they served in; what was their speciality; what was the political climate at the time; how long did they serve; what was their rank; did they deploy and if so, where; how old were they when they joined; what was their socio-economic background or conditions; what was their education level; et al. Regardless of the individual experience most veterans leave the military with real skills as mechanics, cooks, logistics specialists, law enforcement, communications, heavy equipment operators, truck drivers, or any of the 160 designated career

---

[80] Katherine Schaeffer. The changing face of America's veteran population. The Pew Research Center. March 19th, 2023. https://www.pewresearch.org/short-reads/2023/11/08/the-changing-face-of-americas-veteran-population/ - November 27th, 2023

fields. A veteran's experiences can have a lasting and profound influence. The majority of veterans join the military as young adults–an important time in life for shaping values, beliefs and attitudes. Because they were socialized into the military culture at a time when they were malleable, many will have adopted military values and ideals as their own.[81] This encourages many organizations to provide preferential hiring for veterans because of the skills and attributes they obtained in service to the nation.

They bring with them what we will call 'Veteran Superpowers'. They:

- ➢ Are Present
- ➢ Are On Time
- ➢ Are Respectful
- ➢ Are Professional
- ➢ Are Problem solvers
- ➢ Are Loyal
- ➢ Have Integrity
- ➢ Place Service Before Self
- ➢ Accept Responsibility

"Thank you for your service" - And I heard the voice of the Lord saying, "Whom shall I send, and who will go for us?" Then I said, "Here I am! Send me (Isaiah 6:8 ESV)." Think about what that means: "duty" is drudgery; however, "service" is done with joy! These valued members of our society have a heightened awareness of the cost of the freedoms we enjoy as Americans. They feel the need for Civic Duty. Civic duties include obeying the law and cooperating with first responders, serving on juries, paying taxes and educating others in upholding the Constitution of the United States. These same people also set an example for others in Civic Responsibility. Civic responsibilities are steps voluntarily taken to support the community–our Civil Society. Civic engagement takes those responsibilities further by working on problems affecting everyone in the community.

---

[81] Open Arms Staff. Understanding the veteran experience. Open Arms. https://www.openarms.gov.au/health-professionals/about-veterans-and-their-families/understanding-veteran-experience - July 1st, 2024

Chapter 11
Does your Title Make You a Leader?

President Truman had a no-nonsense approach to decision making. The sign, *"The Buck Stops Here"* on his desk reflected his belief he was ultimately responsible for the actions of his administration.

Most organizations advance individuals into leadership positions because they have demonstrated potential for additional responsibility and are promoted based on that potential. Remember, being promoted only means you are promoted; it doesn't make you a leader. In our interview with Dr. Patti Conard (see Chapter 14 - What insights can we gain from leaders across different specialties?), she mentions "merit-based" promotion. They have shown the capacity for Leadership: *"the ability to foster an environment in which people motivate themselves to achieve beyond their own perceived capabilities, and face problems for which there appear to be no simple solutions."* This is not always the case. There are still situations where people end up in leadership positions, but they are not leaders or have lost sight of how to lead effectively.

In some instances, these same people have lost sight of the responsibility they hold. Some have been leaders, or in leadership positions, for so long and have amassed so much responsibility they believe they have become infallible. Most of us have heard the cliches: 'Believing your own press' or 'Power corrupts, absolute power corrupts absolutely'. President John Adams said, "Because power corrupts, society's demands for moral authority and character increase as the importance of the position increases." I saw this further elaborated one afternoon when every Brigade and Battalion level Commander and Command Sergeant Major in the Corps Artillery were at lunch together–a group of nearly 40 leaders in varying leadership positions. The Corps Artillery Command Sergeant Major stood and said one simple thing, "We are all perfect!"

He paused and said it again, "We are all perfect and that's how we got here!" He was being facetious, but he was reminding us of our humanity and that we are prone to mistakes. All leaders are guilty of being fallible. The following series of vignettes demonstrate this. The key is to learn from the mistake and to have some humility.

Being present - Several years ago I was invited to represent an organization of which I am a proud member. This organization has over 40 locations in the United States and around the world. This conference lasted three days and over 1,000 people participated. Due to the scale and size of the event, we expected to see and interact with the organization's senior leadership. Not once did the Senior Representative (face of this global organization) show up. On several occasions, the direct subordinates of the Senior Representative apologized for his absence, citing his busy schedule. As a Leader, what you spend your time on is a display of what is important to you. There is no nuanced excuse for those you're supposed to be leading, you're just not there. Be Present. A quick reminder … We have all seen the news stories of a President of the United States showing up at a Dining Facility / Mess Hall in a combat zone to have Thanksgiving with the troops. Regardless of political party, this is a powerful image and message.

Being Available When Needed - In one position I served in the Army, my immediate boss was a civilian. He was a member of the Senior Executive Service–equivalent to General Officers in the military. In one of my first meetings with him after arriving in my new position he told me, "No matter what I'm doing, I'll always have 5 minutes for you." Several weeks later I was preparing to make a decision. I was certain I would require some 'top cover' and decided it would be best to get a few minutes with the boss. I went to his office to discover he had several people seated there in a meeting. His administrative assistant informed me he was busy and that it would be later in the day before he would have time. I told her about the "5 minutes" and that I needed to speak with him. The administrative assistant sheepishly went into his office and whispered to him. Moments later everyone left his office, and he waved me in with no questions asked. He was indeed good to his word and was always available when needed. He made himself available for the people who reported to him–even if the timing interfered with his day. This also earned him great respect among those in his organization.

Being on time - One of the most professional things a Leader can do in any situation is to be on time. In the days leading up to our deployment to Kuwait and later into Iraq (early 2003), a more senior officer (Brigadier General / 1-Star) wanted to go on a morning run with the Battalion (over 400 soldiers) I had the privilege to command. The General planned on meeting us at 6 am at a predetermined location, run with the Battalion, and then give a motivational speech to the unit. On the day of the run, the Battalion formed up at 5:30 am, completed warm-up exercises, and was present at the predetermined location on time. We waited 30 minutes for the General to arrive and there was no sign of him. Pressed for time, I decided to start the run. About one mile into the morning run the senior officer ran up alongside me, demanded I stop the formation of 400 soldiers running, and began to berate and yell at me. This was in plain view and earshot of most of the soldiers. Clearly, this is NOT Leadership–on multiple levels. There was no motivation or inspiration for me or the soldiers of the Battalion. The intent of the group exercise was to display and inspire camaraderie. We finished the routine morning run and the senior officer spoke to the unit. However, his previous outburst and display of unprofessionalism ensured his words fell meaninglessly on the assembled group of soldiers. Being present and on time shows what is truly important to you as the Leader. This also includes *what* and *where* you spend your time. Your organization will see and value actions, not words. Being "Present" and "On-time" is about leading yourself (see Chapter 4 - Self Leadership "If you can't lead yourself, how can you lead others?").

Don't forget what it was like - I spent time as the Secretary of the General Staff at a unit commanded by a Major General (2-Star). Early one morning the General called me into his office and gave me instructions for a short project. At the end of the verbal instructions he stated, "You should be able to have it for me by the end of the day." With respect, I let him know it would take several days. He looked at me puzzled. Then I explained the sequence of events and tasks required to successfully deliver the project. This included doing the work, getting the work reviewed by the multi-functional Staff and Chief of Staff, resolving and reconciling any comments they made, then the Command Sergeant Major and Deputy Commander had to approve the plan before it came back to him. Still, the General seemed a bit put-off, so I reminded him over the past 14 years (the amount of time I had been in the Army at the time) he had been a Colonel, Brigadier and Major General. He had forgotten what it was like to be me. Remember, leading Leaders doesn't happen overnight. They are grown with experience and education. Don't forget where you came from and how you arrived in the leader's position.

Leadership (positive influence on people) **vs Dictatorship** (my way or the highway):[82]
There are still other people who have ascended to or maintained leadership positions by acting like a dictator, micromanaging or are unwilling to change or adapt. No title, resource, management skill nor expert ability to administer will make you a Leader. As we have stated many times in this book, Leadership is about the *positive influence of people*.

The fallacy is thinking that getting a job done or reaching the objective is leadership. No! How you achieve the outcome or reach the objective is just as, if not more, important. A "Dictator" can reach the objective but, at what cost?

- Was the "juice worth the squeeze?"
- Did the operation have an unusually high casualty (resources) rate?
- Did achieving the goal bankrupt the organization?

[82] Marissa Foster. "Leadership VS Dictatorship." November 20th, 2022. https://guyanachronicle.com/2022/11/20/leadership-vs-dictatorship/ - March 16th, 2024

➢ Did you or your team have to compromise your integrity or ethics in order to meet the end-state?

Many people often don't see the difference between a Dictator and a Leader. The graphic below shows specific characteristics of each style. Even some good leaders fall into the "dictator" category but listen to the feedback from trusted sources (including subordinate leaders and employees) to re-align their leadership style towards inspiring others again.

Dictator	Leader
Know it all	Inspires and Motivates
Seeks Power & Ignores Feedback	Seeks Input
Places Blame	Accepts Responsibility
Stands Back	At the Point of Execution
Unilateral	Encourages
1-way Communication	Transparent Communication
Demands Respect	Earns Respect
Self Centered	Mission Driven

- ***Graphic 8 - Differences between a "Dictator" and a "Leader."***

Look at some names of well-known dictators in history: Adolf Hitler, Suddam Hussein, Napoleon Bonaparte, Idi Amin. Is it possible to apply our definition of leadership to these individuals? You decide. Did they *foster an environment in which people motivate themselves*? As an example, in Napoleon's case, at Waterloo, his arrogance and overconfidence led to nearly 25,000 casualties on the French side![83]

In my last position in the Army, prior to retirement, my immediate supervisor was a Major General (2-Star). All of the senior staff in the command were issued a "BlackBerry" (yeah, we're dating this story). This created a situation where communication was expected to be rapid, responsive and continuous. One night the Major General sent me an email at 2 am and I saw the message around 6 am. At 2 am, I was asleep

[83]Brown University Library. Waterloo 1815: The Aftermath. https://library.brown.edu/cds/askb/waterloo/aftermath.html#:~:text=The%20battle%20of%20waterloo%20was,23%2C000%20for%20the%20Allied%20army - July 17th, 2024

and did not see the message until later. When I arrived at the office in the morning there was a written note waiting for me to call the Major General. I did. Once I had said, "Good morning, sir," I never spoke another word for the remainder of the call since the Major General "chewed me out" for not answering the email during the night and then hung-up. I've yet to understand this reaction. I would suspect if we were to go back to this person today and ask about the situation they would have little to no recollection. But his actions and behavior is something I have never forgotten. *Fostering an environment in which people motivate themselves to achieve beyond their own perceived capabilities* was not achieved in that call.

Micromanagement is a pattern of managerial behavior marked by excessive supervision and control of employees' work and processes, as well as a limited delegation of tasks or decisions to staff.[84] It creates a lack of trust within your team and for your subordinates. In the realm of leadership, micro-management carries a negative connotation because it is viewed as an impediment to a successful organization and a poor influence on employee morale. What drives people into this morass?[85]
Understanding the reasons behind micro-management is key for a leader.

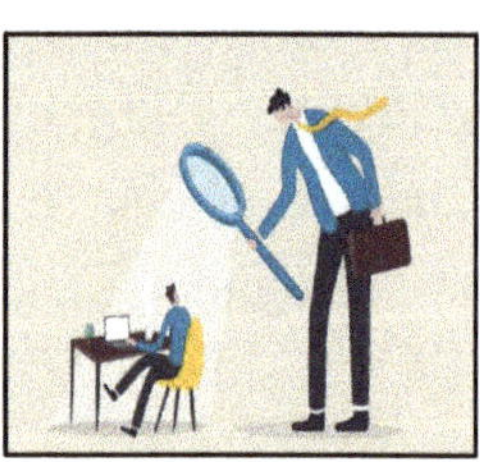

It allows leaders of micro-managers to develop plans for subordinate leaders to overcome this to be more successful. Many organizations can increase productivity by mitigating micro-management tendencies.[86]
Some signs of micromanagement include:

---

[84] Bilyana Petrova. "What is Micromanagement and How to Deal with it?" October 24th, 2023. https://www.slingshotapp.io/blog/what-is-micromanagement - March 20th, 2024.
[85] Julia Neves. "Micromanagement: Why is it killing your business and what to do about it." Day.IO. 25 August 2022. https://day.io/blog/micromanagement-why-it-is-killing-your-business-and-what-to-do-about-it/ - April 10th, 2024.
[86] Jo Banks. "5 Reasons Why Managers Micromanage." July 28, 2023. LinkedIn Corporation © 2024. https://www.linkedin.com/pulse/5-reasons-why-managers-micro-manage-jo-banks/ - April 4th, 2024.

Never learned how to delegate: Some current leaders and managers grew up in environments where the leader retained complete responsibility and authority. They never witnessed an example of how a good leader behaves. They have not experienced healthy work relationships. In the past, the micro-manager has been outperformed, believes they have been betrayed by their team or feels their team can't meet expectations. Inevitably, micro-managers feel driven to be overly involved in every task to ensure some modicum of success.

Their team can't handle it: Some micro-managers believe his or her employees are not able to handle the workload or satisfactorily provide deliverables. In some cases, this may be true, but a strategic leader invests in understanding their baseline skills and works with the employee to improve their performance and effectiveness. By controlling every aspect of the work, micro-managers hope to minimize the risk and maintain a false sense of security.

Look at me: The leader / manager needs to be the center of attention or has a conscious (or unconscious) need to feed their ego. Some leaders see the success of the team, or its individual members, as a threat to their personal success and advancement. They feel if they are not in total control they lose power.

Asking to be carbon copied (CC'd) on every email: Directing that you, as the leader, be included on all email traffic is a great way to erode trust in your organization. Along with stifling initiative, it will also stunt the growth of leadership in the people around you. It also will hurt you personally! Do you really have the time to read every email and siphon through every detail? Do you have the mental capacity to apply the vast flow of information created in this situation, particularly in an organization larger than just a few people? While the Secretary of the General Staff at a 2-Star Headquarters (Command and Control of thousands of soldiers and civilians) we had a new Deputy Commander assigned. Just a few weeks after arriving, he called me and directed he be included in all email traffic including the Commander, Chief of Staff and the Command Sergeant Major. This was in addition to the information he already receives from those falling directly under his own purview of responsibility and authority. About a week later he called again and exclaimed, "Uncle!" He asked NOT to be included in every message as this overwhelmed his inbox and added more work to his daily responsibilities.

'Be careful what you wish for, lest it come true!' The origin of this saying is Aesop's Fables, the world's best-known collection of morality tales (circa 260 BC).

It's Easier to do it myself: How often have we heard this old cliche? The leader taking this approach is creating several problems. First, this person will eventually become overwhelmed with the simple volume of the requirement, not to mention the need for expertise in multiple disciplines. If the requirements are physical in nature, it may simply require more than one set of hands. Next, by failing to teach others the task, this leader is breeding incompetence. The leader is not *fostering an environment* of growth and learning. If you are attempting to do it all yourself, the organization will move at the speed of one… you. This approach loses sight of the big picture and overall objective when they are immersed in the details of all the 2nd, 3rd and 4th order tasks required. Nolan Ryan has the most career strikeouts in Major League Baseball history. During his 27-year career, he struck out 5,714 batters. However, if he ran out to the mound by himself with no position players he would lose every game.

Looking over the team's shoulder: The micro-manager wants to know what everyone is doing all the time. Let's face it, it's annoying. If the leader is standing there watching every move it has the side effect of causing stress and even mistakes, because the team is not focused on the task but rather what the boss is seeing, thinking or saying. There are times when "micromanaging" seems appropriate. For example, if you are teaching someone a new and dangerous task, you want to give detailed guidance and training. Once you are satisfied, they can perform independently, you "loosen the reins" and allow them to do it themselves. Think about learning to fly a plane, eventually there will be the first "solo" flight and after that, you'll be flying with passengers.

Constantly wanting updates: Weekly check-ins and status reports are standard. Most organizations have these formal meetings. In the Army we had "Command and Staff Call". In Defense Contracting we held "Weekly Situation Reports" and "Budget Reviews". In Academia "Professional Learning Communities". Regardless of what you call them, they can be very healthy for the organizations. Peter Drucker (an Austrian-born American management consultant, educator, and author, whose writings contributed to the philosophical and practical foundations of the modern business corporation) said, "What gets measured, gets done". However, when updates are being expected daily (or more frequently), you can be sure you're being micromanaged or you're being a micromanaging boss yourself. These constant updates create wasted time because people are filling out reports or focusing on creating slides rather than focusing on objectives.

No room for initiative: Delegating is a must. The leader can't do everything. However, when the leader dictates both the "what" and the "how" they are micromanaging and suppressing the initiative of others. Because they don't trust others to do their job, micromanagers tell employees what to do without leaving room for creativity and initiative. Especially if the job is in a creative area. Being constantly told how to perform a task can be very frustrating and discouraging. The Leader also misses the opportunity to leverage the insights and day-to-day experiences of their employees. Perhaps the employee comes up with an innovative solution to a problem–but the micromanager's approach stifles creativity. This also reduces the chances employees will be engaged enough to feel empowered to think, speak and act independently.

Most successful organizations and leaders use some form of quality control or quality assurance (QA/QC). We have said previously that it is impossible to proofread your own work. It is important to make certain standards and metrics are met (remember Peter Drucker - "What gets measured, gets done"). However, as the leader you should encourage initiative. After all, you hired the most qualified person for the job to achieve success.

Steve Jobs said, "It doesn't make sense to hire smart people and tell them what to do; we hire smart people so they can tell us what to do.''

Never satisfied: Micromanagers are never satisfied and are constantly complaining. If you regularly look for faults, errors, mistakes and liability that is exactly what you will find. There are times and occasions for this; however, if you are truly a practitioner of leadership you are looking for opportunities to *inspire*, *motivate*, promote growth and drive success. Micromanagers think they encourage perfection, but they are actually draining the motivation out of their employees.

Focusing on unimportant details: Micromanagers are fixated on control. Many of them latch on to the smallest detail having no real impact on the goal or objective. It's easier to deal with the small unimportant stuff. The big stuff is tough and "fixators" tend to avoid addressing them until it can no longer be put off. One of the first taskings I had as a newly minted Battalion Commander was to have my unit stand in formation and march in a review for a retiring Brigadier General (1-Star). My orders were simple, to have every available soldier in the formation. I failed! During one of the last rehearsals for the event, my Brigade Commander discovered my unit Chaplin was not in the formation and participating. For this I was chewed out in front of the entire complement of the battalion's soldiers. A better leader would have pulled me aside for a private discussion. If the answer was not satisfactory, then give me a one-way conversation. I, as the follower, should have been more proactive. Even though I did not feel he handled the situation correctly, I still failed. I did not follow the orders and they were simple.

Micromanagement stifles individual initiative, creates unnecessary work thereby wasting resources and stunts the growth of an organization.[87]

Why Change? Organizations change for different reasons but every organization will have to change at some point. Changes can be 'Reactionary' or 'Proactive'.

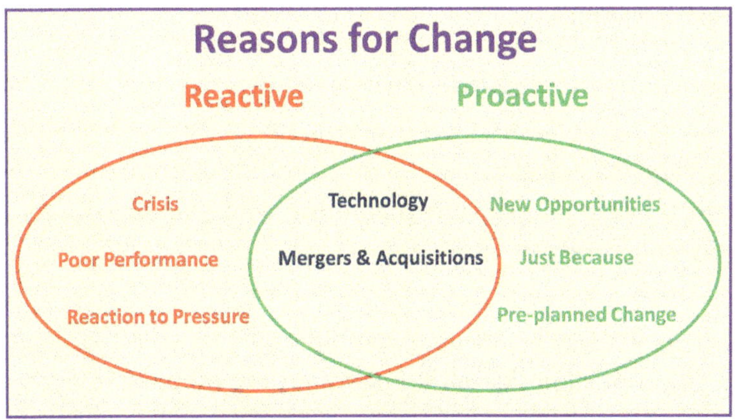

- *Graphic 9 - Reasons for Change.*

Reactive Change:

Crisis - September 11, 2001 is one of the most dramatic examples of a crisis in the United States in the past 50 years. It caused untold numbers of organizations like the airline and travel industries to evaluate their current processes and make significant changes to their safety-related protocols. It drove the creation of the Transportation Security Administration (TSA) and the Department of Homeland Security (DHS). It also forced an entire generation to re-evaluate how terrorist activities impact their daily lives.

The 2008 Housing Bubble collapse forced significant changes to the financial services and housing industries. This mortgage crisis was triggered by risky lending practices. When interest rates froze, borrowers could no longer afford their payments, and the housing market crashed. As massive foreclosures ensued, the fallout spread

[87] Julia Kagan. "What Is a Micromanager? Impact, Signs, and Ways to Reform." December 30, 2022. https://www.investopedia.com/terms/m/micro-manager.asp - March 16th, 2024.

throughout the global financial system. The Treasury Department had little legal authority to act and even less funding authority. As a result, Congress passed the Troubled Asset Relief Program (TARP) in October 2008, which provided the Treasury with $700 billion to fight the crisis.[88]

Poor Performance - We normally see this when an organization's financial goals and objectives are not being met or other organizational needs are not being satisfied. Changes are required to close these gaps. Today (2024) you don't have to look far to find news stories about Electric Vehicles and the success or failure of manufacturers. Some are even considering cutting manufacturing and waiting to re-enter the market in later years.

Reaction to pressure - A great example of this was the recent (2023) Writers Guild of America strike in which the organization was seeking more pay and residuals from streaming services and programs. External pressure from viewers–who demanded new programming–also impacted negotiations.

Reactive and Proactive Change: See Graphic 9. Some changes can fall into both Reactive and Proactive categories.
Technology - New technology can produce change; however, it most often comes with a need for training of the workforce. Think of the example we provided in Chapter 1 (How to progress through the Phases of Leadership) with the fall of "Blockbuster" and the new streaming technology allowing for the rise of "Netflix". Blockbuster failed to adapt to the technology, and Netflix embraced it.

Mergers and acquisitions - Combining companies into a more efficient organization often produce cost savings. These cost savings are generated by cutting redundancies which, in many situations, means

---

[88] Yale School of Management. US Government Crisis Response. Copyright 2019. https://ypfs.som.yale.edu/us-government-crisis-response#:~:text=The%20Treasury%20itself%20had%20little,use%20to%20fight%20the%20crisis - August 4th, 2024

workforce reductions (layoffs) that are never popular and must involve proactive leadership to navigate change.

Proactive Change:

Potential new opportunities - This also means having a vision. When a leader identifies a need or an opportunity in their market area, they drive the change to facilitate their organization's ability to take advantage.

Just Because - One great example is a sports team. The team may have the best coach of all time but makes a change simply to make a change. The legendary football coach Bear Bryant successfully coached four other teams before becoming the head coach of the University of Alabama with a tenure of 25 years.

It sounds like a good idea - In some situations, an organization may not have made a change or done anything new lately and something just sounds good. Think about how many times you have seen the container for your favorite cola change (shape, color, design, logo, etc).
Pre-Planned Change - Products don't last forever (new technology). I have the vision of 8-track tapes, Vinyl Records, Cassette Tapes, and Compact Disks, and today we have streaming services.[89]

Change with Purpose: I joined the Army in September 1980 and retired in December 2009. During my tenure, I saw several purposeful organizational changes. Some were technology-driven: the Bradley Fighting Vehicle, Abrams Main Battle Tank, Meals Ready to Eat (MREs), Laptop Computers, Satellite and Digital Communications, Kevlar Helmets. Some were financially driven: Base

[89] Robert Swaim. "Nine reasons organizations need to change." PEX Network. August 1st, 2024. https://www.processexcellencenetwork.com/organizational-change/columns/why-organizations-change-and-what-they-can-change - March 16, 2024

Realignment and Closure (BRAC) and Military Downsizing (Force Reduction). Some were driven by world events: the fall of the Berlin Wall, the terrorist attack on the World Trade Center (9/11), and the introduction of Google. In every one of these situations, a leader had to make hard, forward-thinking decisions and simultaneously make certain their organization came out the other side of the change healthy. Otherwise, there was a detrimental impact on the organization, potentially even the death of the organization. However, in each of these change situations, it is possible to recognize the need for the change.

During this same period, I also witnessed more esoteric changes in nature. I saw our uniform change from utility uniforms (OD Green Fatigues to Battle Dress Uniforms (BDUs) to BDUs with the Big Collars (I know some Army veterans may be chuckling) to Army Combat Uniforms with velcro and everyone wears a Black Beret. There were new awards introduced like the Army Achievement Medal and the Combat Action Badge; it's almost as though we applied the idea of "everyone gets a trophy". I spent an additional ten years working in the Defense Contracting Industry. We had so many structural reorganizations, that the term "reorg" became the punchline of humor and an excuse for lack of action by some leaders. What's the point? Change, simply for the sake of change, costs! It costs mental energy, time, money and human capital to implement. All necessary meaningful changes require proactive communication and understanding. Make certain the change you are driving is consequential and worth the cost.

<u>Change and Vision with Guidance:</u> While still the Secretary of the General Staff, we had a "Change of Command". Soon after the change of command, the new Commanding General directed me to create a revised "Certificate of Achievement" for use to recognize exceptional performance but not rising to the level of other medals. It would have his signature on it and could be given to military personnel,

civilian employees, volunteers, and family members associated with the command. So, I discussed this with others, came up with several options, had a skilled graphic artist generate digital sample certificates, had them reviewed by the staff and Chief of Staff, determined a recommended new certificate, acquired the approval of the Command Sergeant Major and Deputy Commander then sent them into the new Commanding General, confident in the work done. The next morning, I found the entire packet torn in half lying on my desk with no explanation. At the first opportunity, I asked the Commander about the packet. He responded, "I don't know what I want, but I'll know it when I see it." If you have no idea what success looks like, or vision, and can't communicate it to others, how do you expect to *foster an environment in which people motivate themselves to achieve beyond their own perceived capabilities*?

Change and Vision with Attention to Detail:

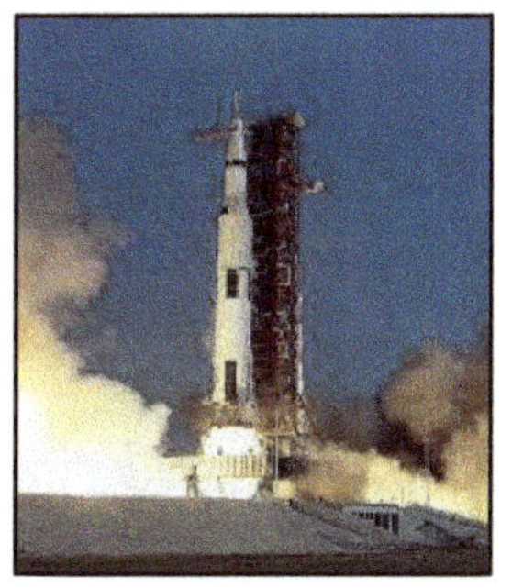

In the introduction to this book we mentioned President Kennedy's grand vision: America will go to the moon! It's critical leaders reduce their big visions into small, digestible components for those who follow them. There were 14 Apollo missions between 1961 and 1972. Each of those missions had different goals and objectives; however, they were linked building upon the success (and failures) of the previous mission which allowed the overall vision of putting people on the moon to be realized.[90]

In our interview with Dr. Beau Sparkman (Chapter 14 - What insights can we gain from leaders across different specialties), he talked about the importance of surrounding yourself with team members who complement your skills. There is no excuse for a leader who can't reduce their vision to actionable details for their followers.

---

[90] National Air and Space Museum Staff. Apollo Program. June 5th, 2023 (https://airandspace.si.edu/explore/topics/spaceflight/apollo-program#:~:text=Afghanistan%20War-,Many%20 - March 20th, 2024

This same process can be seen in the Bible. Nehemiah had a vision for the entire 2.5-mile wall around the city of Jerusalem to be rebuilt–leading to a more robust city–but his recruits couldn't act or begin to conceptualize how to achieve that lofty goal. Instead, Nehemiah gave them specific jobs, often assigning individuals to work on specific areas of the wall near where they lived. Simplifying the tasks helps employees understand how they can support the overall goal without feeling overwhelmed.

Unwilling to grow and learn in an evolving environment: Most of us have heard some version of this well-known saying, "Insanity is doing the same thing over and over again and expecting different results." (I have seen it attributed three different ways: Rita Mae Brown, Albert Einstein, Al-Anon or Alcoholics Anonymous). If the leader is not open to the reality of change, they will eventually fail. Earlier, we discussed the downfall of "Blockbuster" and the rise of "Netflix". Blockbuster failed to understand and react to the changing landscape of home entertainment. Others learned from this example and look several steps ahead in almost every arena. "The Only Constant in Life Is Change."-Heraclitus.

There are only 13 companies on the Fortune 500 list that are over 150 years old. It's not surprising, that these are big, iconic corporations you know well—like Colgate, Palmolive and DuPont—and, also not

"Leadership is a combination of innate traits that you're born with and experiences you gain along the way. That is what shapes you as a leader."
Michele Buck (CEO of The Hershey Company)

surprising, many of them are banking giants. Give credit to the Leaders who created the vision which helped to create such long-standing organizations. Conversely, the average age of a Standard and Poor's 500 company is only 21 years. Research indicates organizational inertia and lack of long-term vision are the primary reasons for companies' short-lived S&P 500 lifespan and success.[91]

The Leader should be thinking about evolving threats or opportunities to maximize the chances of long-term success for their company or organization. When will we use teleportation as transportation? When will microchips be implanted in our brains, possibly phasing out schools? When will we transfer our human consciousness into some robot?

Management and Administration are not interchangeable with Leadership: Some people reach a leadership position because they showed great skill as managers or administrators (remember, Leadership = *people*, Management = *stuff or resources* and Administration = *procedures*). They may have exceptional academic credentials (remember, "being educated only makes you educated").

Being seen and heard - I spent several years teaching in a school district with two people in Leadership positions who, on paper, looked like the ultimate leaders for academia. Both held Doctorates in education-related specialties. One had more than 20 years in education and the other more than 40 years. Both were experienced educators having spent many years in the classroom as teachers and serving as school Principals. One was a school Superintendent. Both were excellent Managers (influencers of stuff) and Administrators (influencers of procedures). In other words, buses ran on time, budgets were made and followed, and websites with state-required information were maintained. Everyone knew them. They sent emails and signed and published policy letters but were rarely seen. In four years, each only came to my classroom twice. Each time, I had to invite them to ask for feedback only to be told, "I love your enthusiasm" or "Your students love you." I never received constructive feedback to make me a better teacher or motivation to do more. On paper, their credentials made it nearly

---

[91] Scott D. Anthony, S. Patrick Viguerie, and Andrew Waldeck. Corporate Longevity: Turbulence
Ahead for Large Organizations. Spring 2016. INNOSIGHT. https://www.innosight.com/wp-content/uploads/2016/08/Corporate-Longevity-2016-Final.pdf - October 3rd, 2024.

impossible to question them and most of the district staff were averse to speaking up or asking questions. However, neither was able to motivate the teachers or support staff (who used their own Self Leadership to develop). They didn't have our book to guide them! I tried a couple of times only to be told by the Principal not to upset the apple cart. Holding the position doesn't make you the leader even though you have the title.

Over-identification with those you are trying to lead - Several years into my time as a classroom teacher, our school had some workforce turnover. One of the teacher replacements was fresh out of college without an education degree and thus had a "Provisional" license. This young teacher didn't have the benefit of the "practicums" and "student teaching" required with an education degree. Very early in the school year this teacher made a judgment error by allowing the teenage students to call him by first name. From that moment, you could watch the student's respect for this teacher slowly dwindle until he had no control over his classroom. There must be some separation between the Leader and the led. Our school principal routinely said, "We must differentiate ourselves from our students." I have to believe in the early 1960s, Vice President Johnson didn't call President Kennedy "John". There are Leaders in positions needing to give instructions/orders carrying a level of danger with them. If the leader is too familiar with the people being led this becomes difficult. This is particularly true for the military and first responders. What we find is leaders don't necessarily need to be liked. However, if they are not respected, they will never truly lead. If you *foster an environment in which people motivate themselves,* you will inherently be respected.

> Earlier we referenced a scene from the movie "Twelve O'clock High". It was produced by 20th Century Fox in 1949. There is a closely related scene where the two Generals are discussing the problem with a subordinate unit. They conclude the commander, COL Keith Davenport, is the problem (i.e., the lack of leadership). The Major General says, "On paper, Keith is the best commander we have." His deputy, played by Gregory Peck, says his leadership problem is "over-identification with his men." Implying the

commander can't make tough decisions because he is too friendly or familiar with those whom he is expected to lead. The leader must differentiate themself.

Followership: If you are going to lead, you must also know how to follow.[92] We have all heard this phrase, "Follow the way you want to be followed." This is an important concept. Most of us will spend most of our time as leaders in positions where we are both a leader and a follower. The people you lead will be watching how you react to your leader. You must make certain you are setting the example because it will be reflected right back at you. Followership is straightforward: take guidance without public criticism, support the boss/program/project, be a good team member, *know and do your job* so someone else is not saddled with your requirements. One of the best displays of followership takes place in the books of Deuteronomy and Joshua in the Bible. Joshua followed Moses for 40 years and then led the people of Israel into the "promised land."

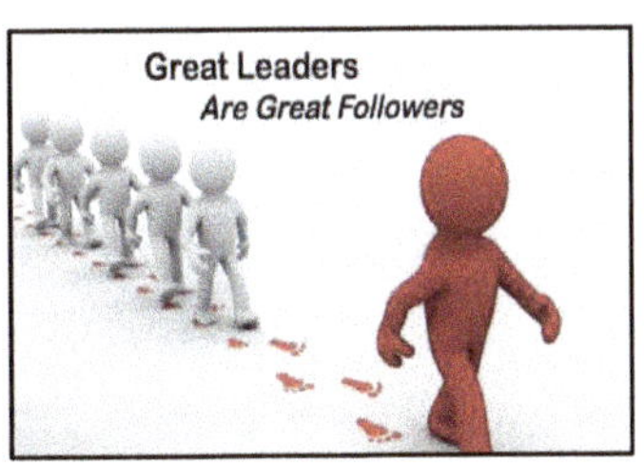

Good followers must be able to take the guidance issued by the leader and put it into action. It is important–both as the leader and the follower to make certain the guidance is legal, moral and ethical. If you have misgivings, speak up sooner rather than later. The key is being able to discern the difference between guidance your leader provides that you may not agree with versus something truly wrong/unethical.

Good followers have a good work ethic. Good followers are hard-working, motivated, dedicated, pay attention to detail and work through challenges. Leaders have a responsibility to *foster an environment in which people motivate themselves to achieve beyond their own perceived capabilities, and face problems for which there appear to be no simple solutions.*

---

92 Željko Zidarić. "To be a good leader you first need to be a good follower ???". LinkedIn Corporation © 2024. https://www.linkedin.com/pulse/good-leader-you-first-need-follower-zeljko-zed-zidaric/ - April 10th, 2024.

Good followers are competent. You can't follow unless you know and do your job. True leaders will employ hiring practices to fit the right person to the job or task and make training available, ensuring followers have the tools for competence. This is the leader setting the conditions for followers to achieve success. Remember, it is the leader's responsibility if the follower fails!

Good followers can speak the truth to the leader. The follower has the responsibility to provide the leader with respectful, knowledgeable and accurate feedback from their perspective. This permits the leader to adjust when necessary. A follower can't knowingly let the project fail. If the leader is one of those who are unreceptive to feedback, consider going up a level; however, do so humbly and with respect.

Good followers have discretion. When I was Secretary of the General Staff, one of the first things the 2-star General I supported told me was, "Sometimes your credibility is based on what you don't do and what you don't say." In other words, know when to use discretion.

Good followers are loyal to the organization and, at appropriate times, to a good leader. Lack of loyalty can cause problems and can most easily be identified by poor effort, disparaging speech and willful incompetence.

Good followers work for the good of the organization not for personal gain. Good followers know their personal success can't be realized unless the organization succeeds first. It doesn't matter how many touchdown passes the Quarterback throws unless the team wins the game.

Good leaders will give the public credit to good followers. There is a common saying, "An organization is only as good as its weakest link." Good leadership will help set conditions for good followership and success.[93] "The mark of a good leader is loyal followers; leadership is

---

[93]John S. McCallum. "FOLLOWERSHIP: The Other Side of Leadership." Ivey Business Journal. Sept/Oct 2013.
https://iveybusinessjournal.com/publication/followership-the-other-side-of-

nothing without a following." Proverbs 14:28 ESG

Make your leaders' decisions yours: As we have noted on several occasions in the book, the majority of leaders will simultaneously lead and follow. It is imperative to make your leaders' decisions yours. Even when you don't agree with the decisions/direction of your leader, you must still be able to carry out the guidance with enthusiasm and vigor. It's not optimal but, there are some mitigation strategies; influence or lead your leader; ask questions and look for the positive; openly challenge your leader; and understand your boundaries. None of these are easy; however, the word "easy" doesn't appear in any definition of leadership we have reviewed.

Influence or lead your leader: There are several times to do this. If your leader seeks out your input, give it! Do so respectfully but provide cogent input you believe will positively influence your leader. In some situations, your leader may be making decisions without complete information. If this is the case, provide the information they may have been missing and include the 2nd, 3rd and 4th order impacts and the associated risks. Framing the new information in a fashion focused on success versus risk of failure is likely to gain the most positive result. Simultaneously doing consensus building with your contemporaries so you are speaking to your leader with one voice will also lend sway to the discussion. Sometimes even a slight change or compromise, even though it is not ideal, is progress and will allow you to get behind a plan.

Ask questions and look for the positive: Early on we discussed asking questions. It is never wrong to make certain we understand the intent. It can be easy for initial reactions and emotions to turn into anger and clouded judgment. Consequently, the ability to ask reasonable questions to clarify information is key. A question asked in the right way is also a method of influencing your leader. Additionally, even if you disagree,

leadership/#:~:text=Followership%20is%20a%20straightforward%20concept,what%20is%20expected%20of%20you. - March 28th, 2024 asking questions–looking for benefits and merit in the guidance–provides you with positive points to share with your team. It will also aid in reducing friction during the execution of the direction. Even when decisions are driven from the top down, finding the positive "nugget" will open the door of passion for the work.

Openly challenge your leader:

I think we have all heard the phrase "Nuclear Option", this is it. In this situation, you are assuming great risk. You're willing to lose your job, (in the Army) being relieved of your command or position by clearly stating you will not follow the guidance. This option of last resort should only be used when:

- You believe there is an unnecessary physical risk.
- You feel the health of the organization will never overcome the guidance.
- You are convinced your integrity is on the line (think: unethical, illegal or immoral).

This action does indeed show your leader/leadership you are serious. They must either remove you or reevaluate their decision.

Understand your boundaries: Is your credibility within your organization strong enough to withstand a disagreement? When you and your leader are not routinely on the "same page" you need to take a hard look at your options. There are several things to consider: maybe the disagreements are over small things, and you should focus on "the big picture"; maybe the problem is yours! You must decide if your expectations are out of touch with reality. You are the only one who can decide if it is time to seek a different path.[94]

"Praise in public, criticize in private": A quote that's been around for a long time. The modern attribution is to the great football coach, Vince Lombardi, who wrote, as part of an explanation about building a team,

---

[94] Ben Brearley. "Following Orders When You Don't Believe In the Direction." The Thoughtful Leader. Copyright © 2024 Thoughtful Leader. https://www.thoughtfulleader.com/following-orders-without-believing/ - April 10th, 2024.

"Praise in public; criticize in private." Praising in public breeds loyalty, generates status, shows appreciation, strengthens teams, relationships, demonstrates value and makes private criticism more impactful and palatable.

Remember, there are exceptions to every rule. There are times when it is better to 'praise in private' and an experienced leader recognizes this:

- ➢ In the moment: If a leader witnesses a small positive action then a sincere immediate acknowledgement is in order. These "on the spot" recognitions show you are paying attention.
- ➢ Acknowledging the same person over and over: When a person routinely does outstanding work while others rarely do. Over recognizing can cause perceived jealousy issues within the team. Consider something more long term like a bonus, given privately, or potentially even a promotion.
- ➢ Perception: When there is group success, even though it is clear there is a stand-out, often generates animosity.
- ➢ Praise for one reflects negatively for another: If praising one person openly criticizes another, there is the potential to drive a wedge in the team.
- ➢ Is it truly praiseworthy? Sometimes people produce a personal best. It may not reach the level of a great performance.

The key for your effectiveness is to do the right thing for the situation, rather than relying on generalized advice–no matter who said it.[95]

- ➢ Some essential actions of leadership:
  - ★ Be present
  - ★ Be on time
  - ★ Don't forget what is was like to be a follower or subordinate leader
- ➢ Be a Leader, not a Dictator.

[95] Tina Lewis Rowe. "Insights, Information & Inspiration." April 29th, 2008. https://tinalewisrowe.com/2008/04/29/praise-in-public-lombardi/#:~:text=%E2%80%9CPraise%20in%20public%2C%20correct%20in,%2C%20but%20praise%20them%20openly.%E2%80%9D - April 4th, 2024.

- There are “Reactive” and “Proactive" reasons for change. Make certain you are driving meaningful change, otherwise you are wasting resources.

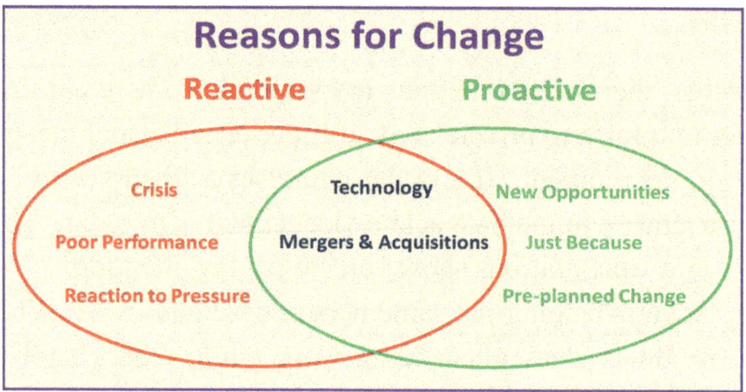

- ***Graphic 9 - Reasons for Change.***

- Signs of a Micromanager:
    - ★ Fails or refuses to delegate
    - ★ No confidence in the team
    - ★ Craves the center of attention
    - ★ Seeks unrealistic levels of information and details
    - ★ Wants constant updates and reports
    - ★ Stifles initiatives
    - ★ Is never satisfied
    - ★ Focuses on minutiae
- Management and Administration is not interchangeable or synonymous with Leadership.
    - ★ Being seen and not heard
    - ★ Differentiate yourself from those you lead
- If you are going to lead, you must also know how to follow.
- Make your leaders' decisions yours. Carry them out with the same vitality as if you made them.
- Praise in public and criticize in private.

Chapter 12
Corporate / Work Leadership

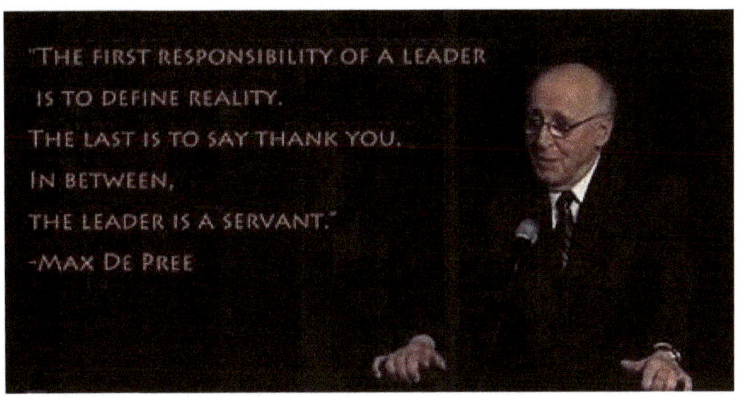

Max De Pree, in *Leadership Is an Art*, wrote, "The first responsibility of a leader is to define reality. The last is to say thank you. In between, the leader is a servant."[96] This recognizes the importance of people in helping leaders realize success in "maximizing shareholder value." Departments are created and maintained to improve a product or service–often aligned to a company's quarterly or annual results. Business performance is typically measured using operational metrics and key performance indicators (KPIs). For the manager, their individual success is often driven by these business and operational metrics. These are then translated to the individual, generally aligned to three general areas: how well the employee delivers business results, how well they support clients and customers, and teamwork and leadership. Each is designed to provide the employee a roadmap towards a "strong" performance year while giving the manager a framework to evaluate how effectively the individual contributed to organizational goals.

Military Transition Experience: In 2022, approximately 174,000 people separated from military service–82% under honorable

[96] Warren Bennis. On Becoming a Leader. Basic Book. Philadelphia, PA. 2009.

conditions.[97] Of the population that actively seeks employment in the corporate or non-governmental sectors, most veterans experience some level of adjustment when transitioning out of uniform. They no longer have to stay physically fit or show up to every accountability formation

amongst a host of other rules and regulations–all designed to maintain the military's "good order and discipline". They have joined the labor market in hopes of finding a job or role replicating the experiences of Leadership they had while in uniform.

Both authors have experienced this transition. This was one of the things inspiring us to write this book and shed light on how the strategic leadership insights we learned and observed can be applied in a variety of worlds or situations–including the corporate sector. Leading in an organization with the mission of defending the US Constitution when compared to being a productive member of a for-profit group are different worlds. *Inspiring people to achieve to their maximum capabilities*, however, is universal.

In one environment, we see leaders who are responsible for the training and development of their employees (soldiers). With a predictive promotion framework, there is time and space dedicated to ensuring your employees are given multiple opportunities for self, group, and organizational development. There is an implied responsibility of leaders to ensure each person under his or her "charge" is technically and tactically proficient. Each person has a clearly defined role and is expected to perform that role–especially in combat.

In the corporate world, however, that guiding principle or North Star is more nuanced.

---

[97] Military One Source Staff. 2022 Demographics Interactive Profile of the Military Community. Personnel Separations. https://demographics.militaryonesource.mil/chapter-2-personnel-separations - August 3rd, 2024.

How do you define corporate success? From the perspective of the leader, driving and/or motivating the team to achieve those strategic goals is the key. How well you learn the culture and apply your skills to help organizations achieve those goals is the key for individuals. Development is occurring at both the leadership and followership levels. This, in turn, improves the organization with better versions of leaders, managers and administrators.

Characteristics of Successful Leaders: In most situations, we've observed a common set of traits for those who are considered good leaders. Leadership requires flexibility, adaptability and the ability to delegate. Today's work environment has a much faster tempo and its complexity places greater demands upon leaders and an individual's time. You can't do it all! You will also need a suite of skills and capabilities to become an effective corporate leader.

- Leader brings the weather – You set the tone and direction of the organization and its people. They will observe and adjust to how the leader acts and behaves. As humans, we experience a host of emotions, problems, and setbacks. It can be hard not to bring those problems (or negative energy) into other settings, but the Leader has to work on "compartmentalizing" their problems and ensure they don't transfer negative behaviors to the team.

- The Ability to Change – The best leaders embrace change as not only an inevitability but also as a stepping stone to progress. They also help their employees manage through change and communicate the impact of changes to all levels of the organization.

- Innovation – Having the confidence to challenge existing norms is essential to modern-day success. The way things were done rarely will be effective in future situations. Often, the conditions or set of assumptions change and evolve into more complex problems. Being creative in how to frame problems and crafting solutions to those problems is the key.

- Cooperation – The best leaders are willing to work with others regardless of differences in pay grade. We've noted before, the Leader cannot do it all–they must delegate but also have an appreciation they can (and should) leverage those around them. Effective leaders know their strengths and generally use those skills to improve their own development while strengthening the team through collaboration.

- A Willingness to Learn – Elite leaders attend seminars and training sessions to expand their horizons. They also build teams around them with a diversity of thought. Those voices provide different perspectives which helps the Leader grow.

- Patience – A willingness to wait is essential in a society increasingly moving toward on-demand results. Moving too fast before having a clear understanding of the problem can lead to applying the wrong solution. Conditions change and evolve throughout a problem or crisis. Those changes need to be factored into any proposed solution before execution. This concept also applies to career development. After a while, you've become an "expert" at your role and feel you should be considered for growth opportunities (e.g. promotion). Investing the time by staying in a certain role longer than you want can help you work on self-development areas.

- Resilience – Some view being resilient as only being tough. "Just rub some dirt on it!", "Push through the pain". While physical endurance or determination is an element of resilience, we posit that toughness also includes mental and emotional strength. The leader possesses the ability to remain calm and effective through periods of severe stress. For example, when the project is not on track but there is no clear solution, the leader must be able to shoulder those additional stressors and do their best NOT to transfer negative stress to the team. You need the team to focus on solving the problem, not worrying about the worst-case scenarios. Stay the course no matter what hurdles arise!

- Emotional Intelligence (EQ) – Emotional maturity highlighted by self-awareness is central to growing as a leader, professionally and as a person. You are able to regulate your emotions and that of others (as best you can). In the corporate sector, this capability has become an important factor in many personnel decisions. In fact, a 2023 study found 75% of hiring managers apply some level of EQ rating for hiring, promotions, and salary increases.[98]

- Empathy – Empathy brings employees together, creating a family-like atmosphere and is also a sub-component of EQ. Empathy towards others (particularly employees) is understanding the importance of work-life balance, having an appreciation for the perspectives of others, and demonstrating you actually care about other people.

- A Willingness to Listen – Communication is a dialogue as opposed to a monologue. In the Communications chapter (Chapter 5 - Communication "Do leaders really communicate or just tell people what to do?" - Learning to communicate with others.), we noted active listening is an important component towards being an effective communicator. When listening to others, you receive the information being presented instead of forming a response in real-time. Additionally, being open to the views of others builds team trust, allows employees to be more authentic and candid about their issues, challenges or opportunities.

- Coaching for Impact – The Leader has an obligation to provide effective development support to their direct reports and employees. Coaching should be designed to drive employee behavior towards making an impact (improved performance). It should occur often (weekly) and when there are "on the spot"

---

[98]Rachel Wells. Emotional Intelligence No.1 Leadership Skill For 2024, Says Research. Forbes. January 5th, 2024. https://www.forbes.com/sites/rachelwells/2024/01/05/emotional-intelligence-no1-leadership-skill-for-2024-says-research/ - August 22nd, 2024

opportunities to give an employee insights into how to do things better the next time. The focus is forward-looking and aspirational, not backward-looking. "Be shepherds of God's flock that is under your care, watching over them—not because you must, but because you are willing, as God wants you to be; not pursuing dishonest gain, but eager to serve; not lording it over those entrusted to you, but being examples to the flock." 1 Peter 5:2-3 ESV.

Individual skills development: Becoming a Strategic Leader begins with self-leadership, identifying and actioning your areas of development. Lifelong learning includes identifying your weaker areas, taking steps to improve them, and establishing and maintaining your *image*. This is how you see yourself and how you want others to see you. Your *brand* is how others see you and what they say when you're not around. This also means you are taking an honest and clear-eyed assessment of yourself. You can't chart a path towards success without knowing your starting point. This self-assessment can take on many forms but generally follows the same path. You are "tested", designed to understand the skills or capabilities you do well, things you don't like, and those areas where you can grow and improve.

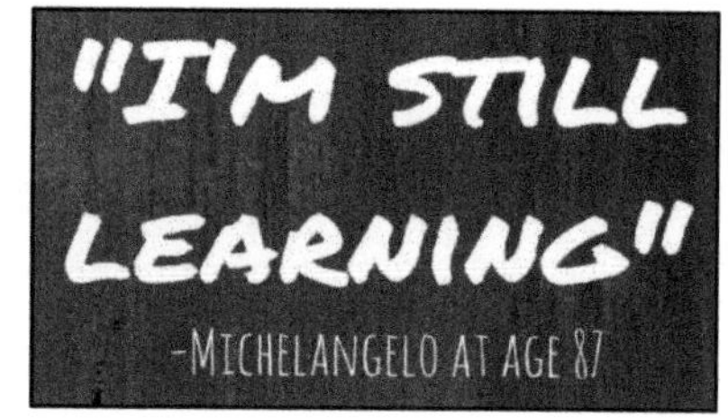

Self-paced and instructor-led courses will deepen your understanding of the business organization, how the business operates, and detail the current processes in use. You are improving your own understanding while using your own skills—to be a more productive and effective individual contributor. Hold yourself accountable and set a career plan including your development goals (e.g. learn a new skill, uplift existing skills, network). *Graphic 10* shows a multitude of places to access continuous learning. As you can see, there are dozens of ways you can begin, sustain or improve a desired skill set.

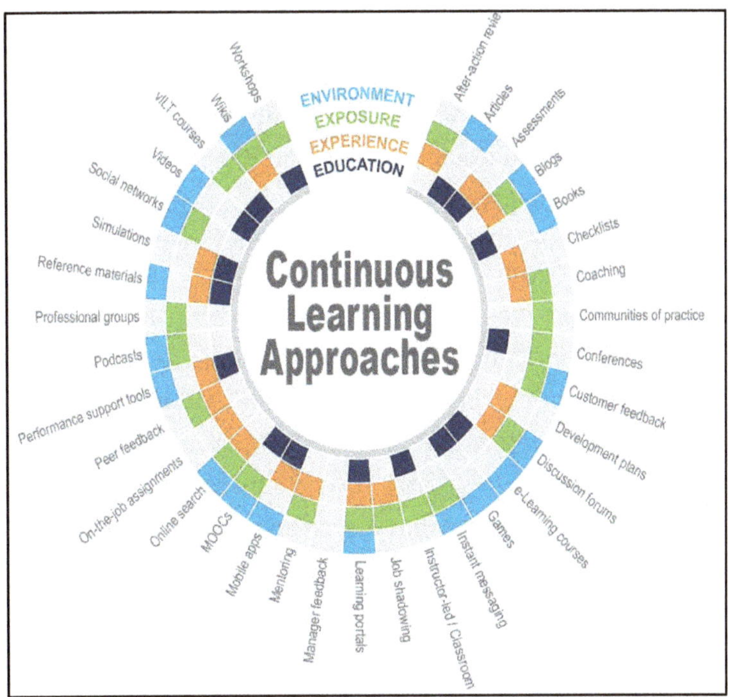

- ***Graphic 10 - Meeting the Need of the Modern Learner.***

Managers are typically given access to enhanced training to become better managers and to uplift their administrative responsibilities. They also get development and insights to improve how they can support the team and organization to drive business results. Often, these development goals are aligned to capabilities–tangible categories or sub-categories. In many cases, these capabilities are also how people are evaluated for promotions or positions of greater responsibility.

These include, but are not limited to:

- <u>Build the team.</u> How well a manager recruits, on-boards, and integrates resources (people) into the specified team. The manager also has to consider how team members will interact and work together. Team "harmony" is an important consideration for building effective and well-performing teams.

- <u>Coach for impact.</u> Not only do the leaders understand the capabilities of their workforce and how to employ them, but they take this concept to the next level by knowing how to motivate those resources (people) to achieve the greatest impact. This impact is seen in how well the team or group is meeting their business goals and objectives. It also means coaching employees to improve themselves!

- Empower the team. Once the team is built, the leader delegates authority. As we noted in Chapter 3 (Responsibility vs. Authority), the leader always retains ultimate responsibility for the organization they lead. They delegate authority to subordinate leaders and employees which drives the employee or individual to take greater ownership to perform their job. Empowered employees have a stronger connection to the work they are performing and often take pride in their efforts. They have their own "space" in which to independently operate.

- Drive performance. Getting the most out of employees requires an understanding of their capabilities and how to employ them. We've noted techniques and tools an emerging leader can take to help them get to know their people while assessing their strengths and development areas. In addition, the Leader must have a clear understanding of the organizational goal and how their team fits into the overall objectives.

- Set clear directions and provide clear guidance. Part of guiding the team towards optimum performance is giving out clear and actionable guidance. Remember the telephone game where a group of people are in a line? One person starts and whispers a phrase into the ear of the next person. Eventually, the message reaches the end of the line where we find the final message is nowhere close to the original message. Admittedly, this speaks towards communications but also provides an opportunity to be deliberate about how to create and message a task or set of projects a leader wants employees to focus on.

- Foster feedback. It is rare for people to want to hear they could have done something better–especially after you think you did your best. It is a humbling experience and many often choose to ignore or downplay what they are told. However, one of the most effective ways to improve is to embrace insights from others. After you've finished working on a project with others it is the best time to solicit feedback (and advice). You can ask them what things you did well, things to improve upon, and anything you may have not observed. Being self-aware does not mean you see all your blind spots.

- Guide careers. There are some managers and organizations who don't support employees moving to another role–either within the company or externally. Some reasons include:
  - The employee is so valuable, their loss would hurt the team. These are often the high-performing workers who should probably be guided towards a larger platform.
  - The employee is doing most of the work. Without the employees' contributions, the manager would likely be exposed as not carrying their own weight.
  - The employee does not know anything else. Similar to keeping someone in the dark, the manager withholds development information from the employee.

Rather than hold back or restrict an employee, the leader invests in personnel development. Their focus is on the best interests of the person, not how the loss of the employee will impact their goals. A good leader should be honored by employees wanting more for themselves. It shows how well you build, trained, and developed your team.

Corporate Leadership Miscues:

One of the most striking differences between the military and corporate is how leadership is defined and put into practice. A survey of recently separated veterans with established positions in for-profit companies overwhelmingly cited the *lack of leadership* as their primary reason for seeking another job–both internally and externally.[99] One of the many misconceptions we've corrected throughout this book is managing is not leading. Often, the manager's focus is on their individual performance without embracing the idea of lifting up the team or employees. Company goals for managers are not focused on employee development but on individual merit and achievement. There is a lack of an *inherent need* for a manager to truly connect with their employees. Soldiers and employees can see through the veil of a manager who is not invested in them, their problems or their goals. But when they see and experience a genuine and authentic leader, employees will "Follow you through the gates of Hell and then a little bit on the ice!" This was a routine comment from a former commander of ours, MG(R) James Boozer.

From a military standpoint, it is easier to rally and focus on the profession of people because you have a North Star and a unified mission. You can point those at all echelons (administrators and managers) towards the goal. To apply a military-style type of leadership (focus on people), the leader must create a new North Star to re-create and mimic the type of environment where military leadership thrives.

Soft skills are more important in this space. These are often unspoken behaviors, mindset, emotional intelligence and social patterns.[100] We've all observed those managers who lack self-awareness or an inability to "read the room". Why is there a disconnect between how corporate leaders and managers see themselves when compared to how their employees see them?

Below is a listing, with some vignettes, of those areas in which aspiring corporate leaders tend to fall short:

Not giving clear directions or instructions:

---

[99]Dr. Stephen Barden. Military Leadership in the Corporate World: The Balance of Power Series. Copyright 2020. https://www.stephenbarden.org/2021/03/23/military-leadership-in-the-corporate-world-the-balance-of-power-series/ - 27 March 2024

[100] Boris Groysberg, Jeremiah Lee, Jesse Price, and J. Yo-Jud Cheng. The Leader's Guide to Corporate Culture. Harvard Business Review. Jan - Feb 2018. https://hbr.org/2018/01/the-leaders-guide-to-corporate-culture, 27 March 2024.

There is a scene in the hit movie "Apollo 13" (Released by Universal Pictures on June 30, 1995) where the people at NASA tossed a pile of seemingly unrelated items on the table and were tasked with making an air filtration device using only these items. After considerable deliberation and brainstorming, they managed to build a working device. Then, instructions for the three astronauts–who would need and use the filtration device–were prepared and relayed to them. Without clear instructions they would not have been able to perform the task and lives would have been lost. This is an extreme example; however, as *the leader you are responsible*. If you start with a void of guidance, you are going to get nothing or be disappointed with the outcome.

Failure to share available information with the team:

In a previous role, I was part of a team where each member managed their own projects and initiatives. While some of our projects were similar, they were unique enough to where we presented the status of our projects to the broader team every two weeks. To the manager's credit, he established a culture of sharing information and best practices. He also encouraged team members to back each other up for times when the primary is out of the office for an extended time. One of our members–who focused on piloting services with third parties–went on paternal leave. A few weeks into his leave, my manager asked me to take the lead in onboarding a supplier to pilot a new capability they presented to our team in the past. During the initial sync call, my manager gave me bits and pieces of the background and overall problem set. I confirmed the next steps with my manager, and he agreed with the course of action. A few days later, he came by my desk and exclaimed that I was not meeting his expectation of resolving the problem in one week. He mentioned that when the other employee is given a similar task, he approaches and solves the problem much more efficiently than me. The manager showed a different level of trust and communication. His decision not to share all information, confirm assumptions, and find a way to share his vision (or problem) extended the project for nearly 30 days.

Lack of self-awareness:

Most people would recognize this as having a blind spot. That thing you can't see but others can. Strange facial expressions during a meeting or virtual call, negative body language, or even audible responses when you hear something you don't like. Your team will interpret those signals in ways the leader did not intend. Consider asking your trusted advisors about your mannerisms or those things which tend to "offend" others. Be selectively "vulnerable" and share that this is a development area.

Blame game or Transfers Accountability to Employees:

Responsibility always resides with the Leader. They are placed in positions based on their implied ability to produce results. When things go wrong, finding the root cause is important to help prevent the issue from occurring again. Once the team learns of a problem, they spend too much time on figuring out, "Who shot John?". Instead, the Leader needs to stay focused on navigating the team out of the crisis. Pointing fingers erodes trust among employees and diminishes how the leader is seen by others. We can look at the success of Sam Walton and the rise of WALMART. Mr. Walton actively sought input from members of the team at every level and today they are the most prosperous retail organization in the world.

Finds faults without explaining the standard:

Feedback is looking at what *has been* done and how it could have been done more effectively and efficiently. Advice is a look forward on how things *can be* accomplished for peak effectiveness. Either way, you must clearly communicate expectations before setting someone out on a task and be clear about how things went after the tasks have been performed.

We're sure many can resonate with a situation where you did not get clear or actionable feedback. This is different from not being willing to accept feedback from others–this requires humility and self-awareness. The manager also has a responsibility to provide feedback without breaking into dysfunction. Once, I was working closely with my manager after learning about a mini-crisis in one of our programs. His manager was more involved in the program but was on extended vacation. We debated whether we should inform his manager of a brewing problem during their time off. Instead of presenting a problem, we agreed to send an informational email explaining the problem and steps we took to temporarily resolve the issue. He dictated a few specific bullets, and we settled on a final version. After I sent the e-mail to his manager, he came to my desk and offered on-the-spot feedback. He said, "I think the message you sent missed the mark." It was rare that I sent messages to my boss's boss and felt that an "unprofessional" note may hurt my standing in the organization. I pulled up the e-mail and asked him to provide me specific feedback on how "WE" could improve this message. His non-verbal cues told me that I did not understand how to receive his feedback. He focused on how the email would be received by senior leadership. After this interaction, I lost trust in collaborating with my manager out of fear of experiencing another miscommunication. Ironically, I asked the senior manager for feedback from the e-mail. That manager remarked, "I appreciate receiving your note and knew the team would resolve anything in my absence".

Not investing the time to develop your people:

Each new year in an organization brings the hope and opportunity for advancement by setting your goals and objectives with your manager and overall team. Companies spend time 'hindsighting' and determining next year's opportunities and risks. Managers get their higher level guidance and incorporate those goals into–hopefully–measurable metrics to track and evaluate an employee's performance. During that initial performance and goal setting review, the employee is made aware of what success looks like for the upcoming year. After the initial performance review, the employee focuses on achieving those goals, progressing projects according to importance level and impact to the business. Effective organizations encourage weekly or bi-weekly touch bases–to ensure the employee is tracking and appropriately working towards their goals. This also is a chance for the manager to evaluate employee performance and offer support, coaching, and guidance. As the year comes to an end, the manager and employee meet to discuss employee accomplishments and assess against objectives. Often, a manager doesn't want to cause tension in the relationship and does not offer course-correcting guidance.

Unwilling to help:

As a Defense contractor I was involved in the writing of several contract proposals. My role in the proposals varied but typically included technical writing, past performance and technical review. On more than one occasion I was the lead for the project known as "Proposal Manager". One of these was a particularly large contract and my boss, two levels higher, showed up at the facility where the proposal was being written. He said he had come to "help." I thought it was great, we are going to have an excellent opportunity to win the work. What actually happened is he spent two weeks sitting in the office next door to the proposal room and regularly called me in for a status update and to tell me what I should be doing. He never wrote a word, proofread any portion of the proposal, reviewed the pricing, spoke to the assembled proposal team or mobilized any additional resources. I am not even certain he read the requirement. On a few occasions, early on, when I asked questions his response was, "Google it!" I stopped asking. His presence became a hindrance and was simply time-consuming. We did not win the contract. If you are the leader and offering help: **bring it**; marshal more or better resources; roll up your sleeves and do some work; motivate and inspire; teach me. If you are simply going to sit on the throne and give orders, you are wasting everyone's time, including yours.

Wasted Resources:

During my time as a defense contractor, I noted one of the most glaring weaknesses in our organization was the competitive Price to Win (PTW) process for assessing how competitors will offer solutions to meet customer requirements. Our group was routinely out-bid by our competitors and after the bid, there would be the inevitable review, scrutinizing the PTW to determine where we went wrong. Over time I was allowed to attend PTW training. First, I was sent to a one-week course on PTW for beginners. The expenses included airline tickets, hotel for five days, meals, and of course the training. There were multiple people from our organization in attendance. A few months later there was a second, more advanced, session with all the same expenditures. We spent considerable resources associated with this training effort. Even with all this training, I was never on a PTW team. In fact, we continued to use the same people as in the past. The results

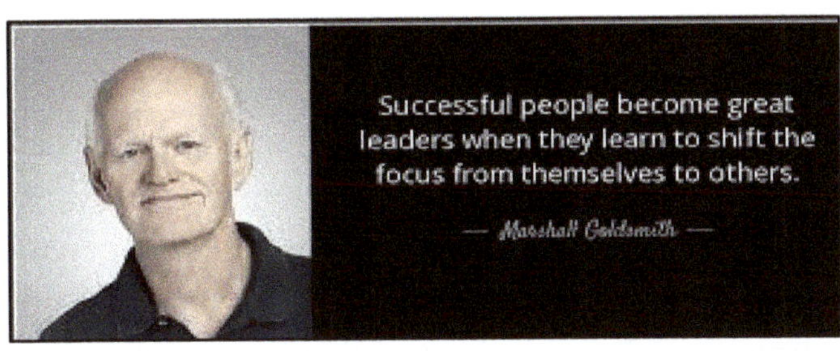

did not change. We wasted resources and accomplished nothing.

Would your employees say you are a good manager or even a leader? The goal is to become a ***Genuine*** and ***Authentic*** Leader, who happens to be in the corporate space. Someone others look towards for guidance, advice, vision, and purpose. They have authentically connected with their employees and have empowered their subordinate leaders with the same. These are the leaders we say, "I would work for that person anytime and everytime." They have left an enduring mark on others by inspiring people to become better versions of themselves–regardless of the reason.

Chris Kane explains that the prime directive of a good leader delivers results (Chapter 14 - What insights can we gain from leaders across different specialities?). **Influential leadership** is the method Chris uses to deliver those results. The leader must show others they are able to be influenced. The goal is not to convince or persuade but to develop another type of psychological safety conveying, "I'm here to enable and support your needs". You show an ability and capability to be a follower. In a sense, the leader is giving up a portion of their "power" to others but, in reality, they are establishing a foundation of trust and mutual support.

Corporate leadership is often described as Organizational Leadership–a general idea that leaders and managers are responsible for motivating teams to achieve a goal or mission.

According to the 2023 Global Leadership Forecast, the top 3 concerns of CEOs are: 1) attracting and retaining top talent 2) developing the next generation of leaders and 3) maintaining an engaged workforce.[101] These people and resource issues outweigh more traditional problems including business concerns and market conditions.

A common blunder among unsuccessful corporate leaders is taking charge before understanding the organization, how their people operate, and what opportunities exist to improve. This "Lone Wolf" mentality does not message one is willing to follow or be open to being influenced. They disproportionally rely upon their past experiences without understanding the uniqueness of their current environment. Adding to the "isolated leader" concept, some leaders also lack self-awareness of the difference between confidence and arrogance (see Chapter 4 - Self Leadership "If you can't lead yourself, how can you lead others?").

- Selflessness – Put the collective interest ahead of self-interest for the greater good of the company.

- Clarity – A clear vision for the enterprise sets a realistic objective to strive towards.

- Humility – Real leaders understand the bigger picture is not about them and does not focus on their own personal interests.

- Authenticity – Authentic individuals are trustworthy, credible, and respected.

- Versatility – Elite leaders have skills extending beyond narrow expertise.

[101] Stephanie Neal, Rosey Rhyne, Jazmine Boatman, Bruce Watt, Mindy Yeh. Global Leadership Forecast 2023. Development Dimensions International. Copyright 2023. https://assets-us-01.kc-usercontent.com/469992e5-7cbd-0032-ead4-f2db9237053a/19c8dfff-4c5a-4c39-b046-f9bb074513d7/Global%20Leadership%20Forecast%202023.pdf - August 4th, 2024

- Cultural Intelligence – Leaders must be willing to expand their cultural horizons and prove willing to understand the cultural nuances of a truly diverse workforce.[102]

Change Management:

Managers embrace process, seek stability and control, and instinctively try to resolve problems quickly—sometimes before they fully understand a problem's significance. Leaders, in contrast, tolerate chaos and lack of structure and are willing to delay closure in order to understand the issues more fully. They are self-confident enough to operate in chaos or uncertain change. In this way, business leaders have much more in common with artists, scientists, and other creative thinkers than they do with managers.[103]

- Technology accelerates workplace expectations and the expected level of performance.

- Concentration – Zero in on well-defined goals and relentlessly pursue them.

- Preparation – Put in the time and effort necessary to reach the targeted goals.

- Flexibility – Be willing to adjust plans as necessary considering the dynamics of the situation.

- Motivation – An energetic leader with intrinsic motivation will inspire others to give their all.

- Prioritization – Designate what is most important and pursue it with passion.

Understand your "Space" within a Space:

---

[102]Dawn Heiberg. The top 20 leadership skills you need in corporate America. May 10th, 2024. https://firstup.io/blog/the-top-20-leadership-skills-you-need-in-corporate-america/ - August 3rd, 2024

[103] Abraham Zaleznik.Managers and Leaders: Are They Different? Harvard Business Review. January 2004. https://hbr.org/2004/01/managers-and-leaders-are-they-different - August 13, 2024

In the military, understanding your space means being both tactically and technically proficient. This also means having an understanding of how your unit aligns and coordinates among other units, vertically and horizontally. The same is true in nearly every other space or industry. For example, you move to a new job or a new role. You will be acclimating to a new set of people, and organization with established rules and norms while learning your role.

Performance, Image and Exposure (PIE):

During my third year of working for my first company after retiring from the Army, I was reporting to a manager who liked to move fast and challenge existing processes and procedures. When presented with a set of options or solutions, he would often ask "why not" or "what if" questions and would push forward with an idea or thought while bringing others along with him. I never experienced a "dreamer" for a manager. His approach to problem-solving was much faster and less deliberative than the bureaucratic processes and rules of the Government.

He also introduced a framework he has used throughout his career to help him prioritize career development. The PIE model, Performance, Image, Exposure[104] is an often referenced framework to help an individual think about how to allocate their time spent on performance or promotions. Rather than pose the issue as a conflict between the individual and those a leader supports, we posit that exposure and image are also part of how others see the leader or manager.

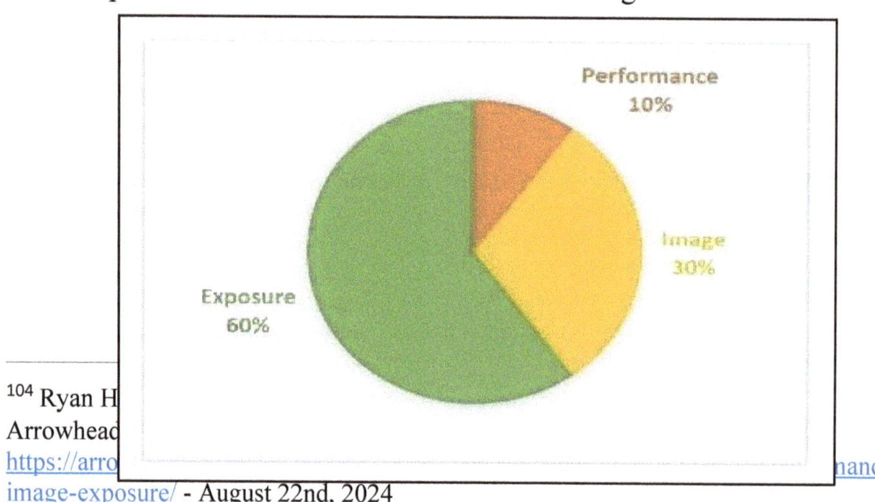

[104] Ryan H
Arrowhead
https://arro nance-image-exposure/ - August 22nd, 2024

This model focuses on how an individual can successfully position themselves for positions of greater responsibility. Most major companies and corporations offer an entire universe of training designed to help employees navigate their career mobility aspirations. There is less material available on how to become a better Leader or how to effectively manage people. How does individual achievement fit into the concept of Situational leadership? Dedicating 90% of your time cultivating your personal brand and image surely takes time away from developing a team or people. How does a Leader (or prospective leader) balance the need to focus on people, organizational goals, and their own individual career advancement?

While your performance may be strong and worthy of appreciation, the challenge is showing others of your efforts and capabilities. This means being an advocate for yourself. You care most about your career–it's personal! After investing time in self-discovery, learning how to improve your development areas, and performing at high levels consistently, you work on telling others, often through networking and exposure.

Many corporate leaders will attest to the importance of a network, cultivating professional relationships, and having mentors and coaches to help successfully navigate your career. Those relationships are often started through some sort of **networking**. This word conjures up all sorts of images and pre-conceptions. You are in some after-hours event with co-workers and others vying to gain business contacts or further their own careers. However, networking has become an essential tool for successfully navigating the corporate world. You can learn about potential areas of interest to you, job opportunities, or get referrals. You might even make a new friend.

Chapter 13
Leadership Fears: Crippling!!!

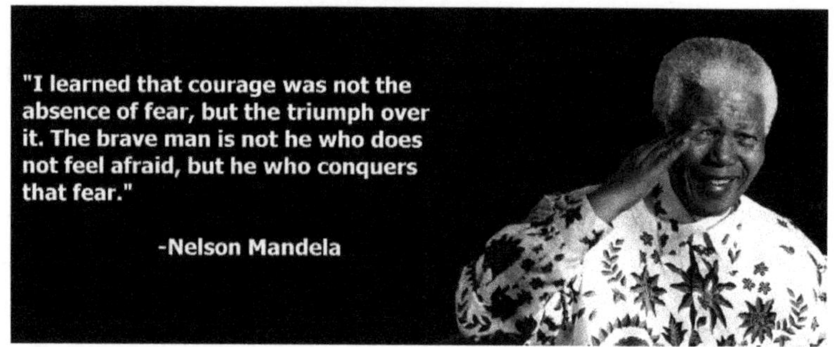

Most people are perfectly content to let someone else lead. There are a myriad of reasons for this, all of which start with some type of fear, self-doubt or a lack of confidence. Here, we are going to discuss some common fears associated with leadership and why many people shy away from "stepping up" and some of the ways to overcome the feeling and lead - *foster an environment in which people motivate themselves to achieve beyond their own perceived capabilities, and face problems for which there appear to be no simple solutions.* The most often repeated command in the Bible is, "Fear Not," this is because you are never alone.

Fear of Responsibility:
This is simple; some people are unwilling to shoulder Leadership simply because they have figured out it comes with Responsibility. In Chapter 3 (Responsibility vs Authority), we specifically discuss responsibility and what that really is. This too can be overcome. Identify your weakness, which in this case is a lack of self-confidence. Proactively use your Lifelong learning time to: put yourself into leadership situations with less stress (think volunteerism - Chapter 9 - "Volunteer Leadership"); get a mentor; increase your technical skills; break the overall situation into small parts and deal with them individually; take the time to actually learn from prior situations. We've talked about this, leaders are grown and cultivated - use your lower-level leadership opportunities for your growth.

Fear of failure:

Fear is not a bad thing. It is a natural human instinct and can protect us from bad things. Think about a fire or jumping from a high level. There are ways to mitigate fear (wearing a seatbelt or a lifejacket). These are the most basic of ideas. However, everyone will fail at some point … We miss the three-pointer that would've won the game, we fail the test, we don't get the promotion at work or miss-out on a new opportunity. For some people this fear can become crippling to the point where they don't even make the effort to reach success.

Remember the leader is "responsible" for everything. For that reason, some will try to remove the word "failure" from their lexicon. They will replace it with some synonyms - breakdown, letdown, misfire, foul-up or just tough luck. It is still a failure. The line from Shakespeare's Romeo and Juliet comes to mind, "A rose by any other name is still a rose." A failure by any other name is still a failure. As leaders, we must employ strategies to mitigate this fear.

Have realistic expectations:

As a teacher, I had a young student whose stated life goal was to be a Top 10 NBA Draft pick. A lofty goal by any standard; Kobe Bryant was drafted 13th and Peja Stojakovic a 14th pick overall … Tom Brady was the 199th overall pick in the NFL Draft. Leaders must also have realistic expectations. This can be accomplished by setting intermediate goals, having team members with the right skills for the job, realizing you don't control. You guide while understanding there are factors beyond your control like the weather, the enemy, or even the loss of a skilled team member.

Controlling your Emotions:

I can tell you from personal experience the most difficult thing for a soldier is to move forward into the unknown. In the days leading up to March 20th, 2003, the initial assault into Iraq by the United States, we had intelligence reports, maps, satellite imagery and other forms of information. However, we didn't know if Iraq would use SCUD missiles, if chemical weapons would be used, how committed our foes were to their cause, if those dressed as civilians were really radicals willing to carry a suicide bomb or if we would encounter minefields /

roadside bombs / hidden traps. The people around you, will look to you as the leader in order to determine how you are dealing with the high intensity situation of moving forward and your mere calm presence will quell anxiety for many. An unseasoned leader should plan for the first of these situations they encounter. Seek out the counsel of more practiced leaders, don't dwell on "what-if-isms", use your Lifelong learning time to research other leaders who have successfully weathered intense situations or simply take a few deep breaths. Once you, the leader, can control your emotions it will be easier for you to help assuage the concerns of your subordinate leaders and team. Matthew 6:27 ESV tells us: "And which of you by being anxious can add a single hour to his span of life?"

Solution before Execution:

Most people can solve a problem, once it is CORRECTLY IDENTIFIED! Albert Einstein famously said, "If I had an hour to solve a problem I'd spend 55 minutes thinking about the problem and 5 minutes thinking about solutions." Make certain you actually know what the problem is before you plan a solution and begin execution. In

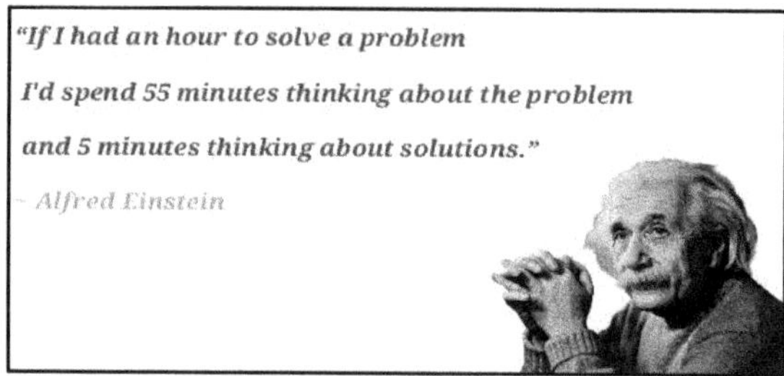

the end this will save you time, energy and resources.

There's no such thing as a Perfect Plan:

There are leaders who attempt to make a perfect plan. They try to think of every contingency. While they are making this perfect plan, their team sits idle. An imperfect plan executed well, by competent and energized people will generate success. If you trust you have hired, trained and properly resourced the people around you, you don't need a perfect plan.

Keep It Simple Stupid (K.I.S.S):

A good leader will be able to break down what appears to be a daunting requirement into smaller parts. This allows the team to focus on smaller, more recognizable goals. We have referenced the Apollo Space Program several times in the book. President Kennedy didn't say, 'Let's go to the moon' and then put Neil Armstrong in a rocket. There were years of tests, calculations and prior flights that didn't go to the moon. All this work went into mitigating failure.

Remember, fear can be a good thing. It can keep your mind focused on the objective / goal. This can include the 2nd, 3rd and 4th order requirements allowing you to stay on the critical path for success–fear can have a negative impact. It can stop you from trying unique solutions and stifle your creativity. If you control your emotions and set realistic goals you can conquer the fear of failure.[105]

Fear of success:

Success breeds expectation from others. How many artists have we seen have one hit song or one good movie? How many athletes only have one good season? How many leaders land that one big contract? The expectation for future success is high. How do you celebrate success? How do you reproduce it? Being fearful of success is tough to see. All leaders want to be successful. Some leaders may try to replace "success" with "just doing the best you can" and yet still fail. For instance, saying, "We did our best, what else can you ask?" This might be acceptable in a sporting event or on a school project; however, when people's lives or livelihood are on the line … it is simply not a good answer.

Yet, "doing your best" implies success (i.e.: this is the mentality that 'everyone gets a trophy'). It's critical to define success in concert with organizational goals and objectives aligned with the vision of the next levels of leadership. Remember our earlier comment from Zig Zegler, "If you aim at nothing, you'll hit it every time."

---

[105] Síle Walsh. Leadership and the Fear of Failure. Linkedin. January 29th, 2021. https://www.linkedin.com/pulse/leadership-fear-failure-sile-walsh/ - May 29th, 2024

Learn to celebrate your successes. Recognize team members with a public "thank you" or a personal "handwritten" note. If it is a big achievement, consider a special certificate or even some financial reward. Many leaders don't take the time. Some may not even realize they have achieved success because they don't stop to reflect or ruminate. Celebrating success, even in some small way, will help drive future success.

Do an after action review (AAR). Take time to bring the team, or at least the key members, together and discuss what succeeded; what worked, what didn't, can we do it again? This will help you build confidence that success can and will be replicated.

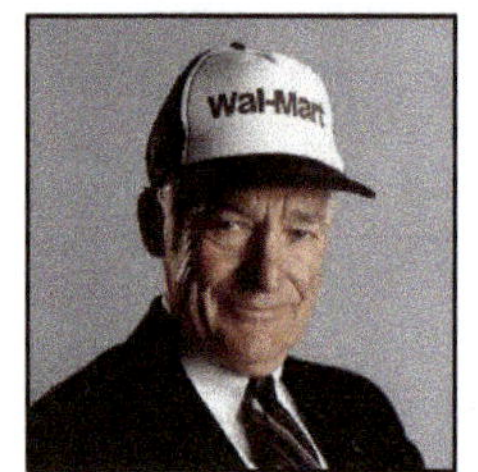

Walmart started with one man. In 1962, Sam Walton began with just one store and one mission: to help people save money so they could live better. Mr. Walton's vision is still there today. Walmart stores are all set up in the same general fashion. They choose store locations on similar terrain and arrange store items to provide familiarity to shoppers. They buy in bulk in order to provide lower prices. They figured out what works and put it into practice over and over again.[106]

Fear of Risk:

President Theodore Roosevelt said, "Far better it is to dare mighty things, to win glorious triumphs, even though checkered by failure, than to take rank with those poor spirits who neither enjoy much nor suffer much, because they live in the gray twilight that knows neither victory nor defeat." (i.e.: No guts, no glory). On his inauguration day in 1933, President Franklin D. Roosevelt said, "... the only thing we have to fear is fear itself—nameless, unreasoning, unjustified terror which paralyzes needed efforts to convert retreat into advance." (Again: No guts, no glory).

---

[106] Wal-Mart Staff. Walmart Careers. Walmart. Copyright 2024. https://careers.walmart.com/ - February 6th, 2024

History is replete with risk takers. Some risks led to failure, some led to success and others led to failures they learned from leading to eventual success.

The Great Depression of the 1930s was one of the most significant and widespread economic crises in modern history. The stock market crash of 1929 triggered a chain reaction leading to bank failures, widespread unemployment, and a sharp decline in economic activity. At the heart of the crisis was a lack of financial regulation and oversight, which allowed banking and financial leaders to take excessive risks and engage in speculative activities. When the bubble burst, banks were unable to meet their obligations, leading to a wave of bank failures and widespread panic.[107]

Try to imagine how the world would be different today had the Allied forces of World War II not stormed the beaches of Normandy, France on June 6th 1944. General Eisenhour could have said … it looks too hard, and many people would have agreed: heavy German defenses; reports of poor to marginal weather conditions; daunting terrain; coordination between the major contributing nations, United Kingdom, Canada and the United States along with at least 10 other nations providing what they could; attacking from both air and sea. Our leaders assumed the responsibility of the risk. In fact, before the D-Day landing on June 6th, 1944, General Eisenhower, commander of the invasion force, wrote two letters for public consumption. One was released, praising the efforts of the soldiers and sailors who successfully gained a foothold into Nazi-occupied France. The other was not. It was written in case of disaster, then filed away. General Eisenhower wrote a curt message pointing to

---

107 FasterCapital Staff, Historical Examples of Systemic Risk, Copyright 2024. https://fastercapital.com/startup-topic/Historical-Examples-of-Systemic-Risk.html - February 7th, 2024.

himself as the blame for any defeat. He was the leader; he was ready to take responsibility.[108]

The Wright Brothers are widely credited with the invention of the first successful heavier than air vehicle flight. Did you know during their success, they also suffered failure? The brothers survived eight major crashes and in one of those, they had a passenger who died. They assumed risk and overcame failure to lead the way in heavier than air flight.[109]

Fear of being an imposter:
Imposter syndrome is the psychological experience of feeling like a fake or a phony despite any genuine success you have achieved. It can show up in the context of work, relationships, friendships, or just overall. It's a very common and frustrating phenomenon because it holds us back from the self-confidence we've earned and deserve to feel.[110]

As the leader, you don't know everything! Many leaders fail to own this fact. Notice I didn't say "advertise" it. However, you must embrace your vulnerabilities and find a way to mitigate and / or assuage them. There are many ways to do this: surround yourself with smart, capable people; educate yourself in the vulnerable area; create an experience, over time, by taking small steps outside your comfort zone. In our interview with Dr. Beau Sparkman (Chapter 14 - What insights can we gain from leaders across different specialties?), he talks of the fact he is a "visionary" and actively seeks team members who are excited in the execution phase of his business.

---

[108] Peter Feuerherd. What Eisenhower's Unsent Letter Reveals About True Leadership. JSTOR Daily. June 6th, 2017. https://daily.jstor.org/what-eisenhowers-unsent-letter-reveals-about-true-leadership/ - February 7th, 2024

[109] Smithsonian Staff. The Wright Brothers. National Air and Space Museum. https://airandspace.si.edu/explore/stories/wright-brothers - February 7th, 2024

[110] Arlin Cuncic, MA. Imposter Syndrome: Why You May Feel Like a Fraud. Verywell Mind. Jan 19th, 2024. https://www.verywellmind.com/imposter-syndrome-and-social-anxiety-disorder-4156469 - February 12th, 2024

A great example of this was seen in basketball. In the 1997 National Basketball Association (NBA) Finals, Michael Jordan drew in the opposing defense and then passed the ball to Steve Kerr so he could take the winning shot. It took a tremendous amount of vulnerability for Michael Jordan, arguably one of the greatest NBA players ever, to put his reputation and the game's outcome in somebody else's hands, but he did it, and they won.

This fear can be paralyzing for the leader who worries their perceived strength in a particular area will be exposed as inadequate. Overcoming this fear requires embracing vulnerability and being authentic. Growth arises from genuine connection and shared experiences. Overcoming this fear often starts with realizing no one is perfect–we are all flawed and imperfect. Remember, leadership is not about perfection but about authenticity and genuine connection.

Fear of not meeting expectations:
Don't overcommit. You and your organization should do what you do well and not try to do everything! If you lead an Auto maintenance organization… Don't sell steak and lobster! Most leaders are prone to over-commitment. You must learn to say "no"! A lesson I am now learning.

I recently retired from my third (what I call) "real job." I now receive monthly retirement checks from several professions and I receive social security. People think being retired means I am either fishing or watching reruns of 'Andy Griffin' and 'Gunsmoke'. Not even close. Being retired, and an experienced leader leaves me time to give back and do quality volunteer work. This includes: routinely volunteering at a local homeless center where I teach job readiness skills; provide safety oversight and help with set-up and clean-up for a church youth group; lead safety oversight for the congregation of the church where I attend worship; judge at local and regional National History Day competitions; and individual stand-alone events and speaking roles. It gives me a great sense of purpose and value. It also creates feelings of potentially not doing enough or of being perceived as lazy if I do say "no." What started off as just showing up and trying to provide a quality volunteer effort quickly crept into over-committing. I am routinely asked for help or volunteer in a wide variety of efforts. I was recently approached by an organization whose primary stated mission is building homes, creating independence and a better life for others. A noble cause. I declined. I possess absolutely no skills in the construction arena and, as noted earlier, I am already applying the skills I have accumulated over the past 60+ years to what I believe are worthwhile endeavors.

Make certain you know where your proficiency and real skills lie. Remember: If you lead an Auto maintenance organization… Don't sell steak and lobster! Prioritize your time and your organization's time for quality in your area of expertise. I recently read an online review for a local burger restaurant stating … "don't order the fish sandwich" … No kidding! Set realistic expectations and focus your organizational growth in areas related to your primary purpose and in line with your competencies. Embrace an attitude of continuous improvement, focusing on progress and learning from mistakes. I have heard it said, most people learn more from a mistake than getting it 100% correct the first time. Learn when to say "no."

Fear of comparison: There is always someone bigger, stronger, faster or smarter with superior skills. So what? If I were to ask, "Who is the better quarterback, Tom Bradey or Patrick Mahomes?" There would be a big debate and the battlelines drawn. Stephen Hawking, considered by many to be one of the greatest minds of the late 20th and early 21st

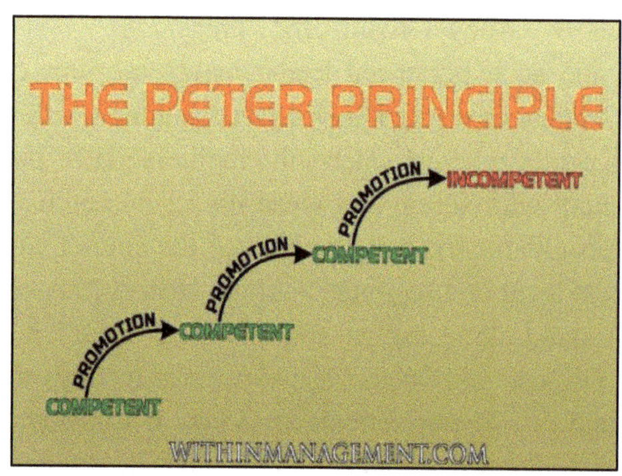

century, never won the Nobel Prize.

To quote The Peter Principle, "In a hierarchy, every employee tends to rise to their level of incompetence," suggests people are promoted to their own individual level of ineptitude.

If you experience this fear, then you need to realize no one has the exact combination of skills, education and experiences as you. While a defense contractor, my boss called me and gave me a mission I thought was daunting. I considered the task for a few hours and called him back asking, “How do you want me to approach this?” His response was, “Use your organizational skills, I think they are the best I’ve seen.” This is the idea of using your best skills and attributes to overcome your own weaknesses. It worked out well and the task became less intimidating.

The more you compare yourself to others the more you breed doubt and insecurity. By cultivating a real appreciation for your own accomplishments and an unbiased knowledge and honest assessment of your unique set of capabilities and shortcomings, you can stride forward with confidence.

Don’t be threatened by others, learn to celebrate the successes of your team or organization thereby promoting a positive mental attitude perpetuating future accomplishments. Remember, you can’t measure yourself or your organization's success based on someone else's perceived standards. You also can’t determine success based on history. Only one person, Neil Armstrong, will be forever known as the first person to step foot on the moon; however, what a great accomplishment for the next person to stand there.

Fear of loss:
The fear of loss in an organization can be stifling. Some people actually spend a lot of time pondering backup plans for this type of event. It may be easiest to think about this from the standpoint of an athletic team. No matter how good the quarterback of the team may be, if they run out to face the opposing team alone they will be crushed. There must be 10 other players on the field, all performing their team roles correctly, to

achieve success. The poet John Donne said, "No man is an island, entire of itself, every man is a piece of the continent, a part of the main." We must also remember, eventually the great quarterback will move to a different team, age, retire or have an injury keeping them from the field or hindering their effectiveness. Regardless of the situation, the team will continue to take the field. I spent 28 years on active duty in the United States Army. I am proud to have had the opportunity, yet, it proves I was not, and am not, indispensable. The Army was there for over 200 years prior to my joining and is still there even though I am no longer active in the organization.

It's key to remember during times of loss, it is also a time of new beginnings. When one person steps away, for whatever reason, there is always someone there ready to show their capabilities. A new quarterback, soldier, engineer, teacher or leader (etc).

To overcome the fear of loss, acknowledge loss as an inevitable part of things. You have to lead yourself and refuse to let fear or the fear of loss be the driving force for you and your team/organization. Instead, adapt to the situation by finding people and resources who provide fresh perspectives, renewed energy and the ability to grow. Remember, with loss comes new opportunities. Charles De Gaulle said, "The graveyards are full of indispensable men". It reminds us that anyone can be replaced, and the world will continue functioning without them.

"It's lonely at the top.":

Most of us have heard this idiom. Merriam-Webster dictionary indicates it is used to say powerful and successful people often have few friends. This is another form of fear. In our interview with Dr. Patti Conard, she talked about seeking out mentors. Even the most powerful people have trusted advisors. Think about the President of the United States. There are 15 executive departments: the Secretaries of Agriculture, Commerce, Defense, Education, Energy, Health and Human Services, Homeland Security, Housing and Urban Development, Interior, Labor, State, Transportation, Treasury, Veterans Affairs, and the Attorney General.[111]

---

[111] The White House. The Cabinet.
https://www.whitehouse.gov/administration/cabinet/ - February 16th, 2024

These people provide advice and make decisions under the authority of the President. Then there are the unofficial advisors. This is a group of trusted friends, associates and even mentors to the President commonly referred to in colloquial terms as the "kitchen cabinet".

Can you imagine the pressure on President Abraham Lincoln leading a country at war with itself? Even with a full Cabinet of Secretaries he had two close trusted advisors who were routine visitors to the White House, Anna Ella Carroll and Frederic Douglass. Two people, who, at the time, were not legally allowed to vote but were willing to speak the truth to the President. Regardless of your level of leadership or size of your sphere of influence, you need to have people you can trust; to give you a straight answer; to speak truth-to-power; to be an expert in your area(s) of weakness; to bounce an idea off of; to provide mentorship. Having this cohort does not alleviate your responsibility as a leader; however, it will make it easier to carry the burden of leadership.

"When in command, command." This statement is attributed to Admiral Chester Nimitz during the battle of Midway in World War II. When you are at the top, you must step-up. That's why you are there, regardless if you have fear or not.

Fear of being "Outshined":

I don't care who you are, there is always someone bigger, stronger, faster, smarter, better looking, smoother, with a better Grade Point Average (GPA) or higher intelligence quotient (IQ). The person at the perceived top is called the G.O.A.T - Greatest of All Time. Even then, there are debates: Michael Jordan or LeBron James, Tom Bradey or Patrick Mahomes, Babe Ruth or Hank Aaron, Ford or Chevrolet. You get the idea. There are those rare employees with superior attributes who may work for you. Don't lose sight of your leadership responsibility to the "mission". But be mindful you also have an obligation to develop those high performers without allowing "professional jealousies" to creep into your leadership style. Be humble enough to learn how to improve your leadership skills and style–even if offered by your employees/subordinates.

This may drive you to be concerned about getting enough credit for yourself, your team or your group's accomplishments I was invited to join an employee development, mentorship, and project-based program for one department within the firm as the North America program lead. The program was designed to provide development opportunities for junior-level employees seeking upward advancement and exposure. The program lead–powered by her passion for helping others–convinced the Department Head to support growing the program in the upcoming year and encourage their direct reports to also get more engaged. A colleague–aspiring to get promoted–ideated, planned, organized and executed a mentorship program for 50 employees. She embraced the idea of bringing in others who can help propel an initiative and readily shared credit for successes. She worked with Department managers to identify 10 real-world problem areas supporting 5 to 6 operational areas which became projects. We assigned 6-7 participants to various projects including process improvements, reducing backlogged tickets, customer experience enhancements and assigned one team the task of figuring out how to globalize the program. In the first year of the program, we focused on our North America footprint and in the second year, targeted India and the Philippines as another cohort. Early in 2023, Jane's direct manager (and mentor) took another role. Her new manager, Lois, had an existing relationship with the Department Head and asked to be assigned as the Executive Sponsor for this program which seemed poised to scale past regions and become a global program with significant visibility. The globalization team–spread out over four geographic regions–met bi-weekly for six months and finally was ready to present their program growth recommendations. While it was clear Jane was the propellant for the program–from inception to a durable and effective program–Jane's manager–who only attended one preparation call–publicly took credit for providing thought leadership and program direction. What is the reason NOT to elevate and uplift your employees? The impact of that public non-acknowledgement of her employee's hard work and dedication–for three years–is likely the primary source of resentment and loss of trust in management.

We have discussed this previously, "bow's we take together." A good leader realizes there are contributors all around them. In fact, if you are truly a leader it means you have followers.

Confidence vs. Arrogance:
A dangerous line to toe is the ability to have trust and confidence in yourself without being arrogant. Confidence is the ability to have trust in your own abilities or a feeling that you can reliably handle situations–with humility.[112] In addition, a confident person is focused on the problem and how to develop a solution, not themselves or the emotions they feel as a result of the problem. On the other hand, arrogance is the need to prove you are right when compared to others. We've all seen examples of this: the person who dominates a group discussion and does not allow others to contribute or speak; the person who plays "Devil's Advocate" without offering any ideas to move the issue forward towards resolution; or the person who either name drops or tries to prove they are the smartest person in the room (or on video chat). While we all have some level of arrogance, it must be tempered with humility and a realization others might have better ideas than you.

Confidence is also gained through past experiences. Over the course of our careers we amass individual experiences, both positive and negative, that we "add" to our ruck sack of life. When presented with a new problem, we draw upon those experiences to identify and execute effective solutions. The self-leadership phase is a great place to develop and hone your personal confidence (see Chapter 4 - Self Leadership "If you can't lead yourself, how can you lead others?"). Here are some tips for how to understand the differences and nuances among these terms.

---

112 Tracy Brower, PhD. Confidence Without Arrogance: Why You Should Stop Trying To Be The Smartest Person In The Room—6 Tips To Avoid The Arrogance Trap. Forbes. January 13, 2020. https://www.forbes.com/sites/tracybrower/2020/01/12/confidence-without-arrogance-why-you-should-stop-trying-to-be-the-smartest-person-in-the-room-6-tips-to-avoid-the-arrogance-trap/ - July 9, 2024

Why Confidence is Important:

- Focus on ideas, not yourself. When you're challenging the group or playing devil's advocate, be sure you're doing so because *the idea* is important, not because you believe *you* are important.

- Respect others' points of view. At the same time, you may have confidence in your own ideas, you need to acknowledge the value of others' ideas as well. Your advocacy for your thoughts shouldn't overshadow people who may think differently.

- Listen and seek understanding. Perhaps the best evidence of respecting others' points of view is listening and asking questions to understand unique perspectives.

- Invite different opinions. When you're sharing something new or different, rather than seeking agreement, ask whether others see things differently.

- Share early. People are more convinced to try something new when they have the opportunity to shape the solution. They also feel included and empowered to help create a solution.

- Cooperate. Find common ground and collaborate with others.

Ask for Advice not feedback.

- Feedback is backward-looking — it leads people to criticize you or cheer for you.

- Advice is forward-looking — it leads people to coach you.

- Figure out which sources to trust.

- Decide what information is worth absorbing — and which should be filtered out.

- Listen to the coaches who have relevant expertise (credibility), know you well (familiarity), and want what's best for you (care).

Avoid Burn-Out: Have you ever run a marathon? I have, most runners will tell you the hardest mile of a marathon is not mile 26; runners rarely quit with the finish line in sight. Most runners find the toughest going is somewhere between miles 18-22, that's where things get really hard. The Leader's journey is much like a marathon. Many leaders drop out on those lonely mundane miles between the middle and tail end of their careers. Burn-out is something everyone faces. Over the course of your leadership career some form of burn-out will likely creep up on you more than once. You must learn what works for you; however, here are some methods that have worked for many people to avoid or relieve burn-out.

<u>**Have some quiet time**</u> –
Take time just to think or "ruminate". We heard this in our interview with Ryan Gehrig (see Chapter 14 - What insights can we gain from leaders across different specialties?). Find the time that's just yours (morning, noon, or night) and make it a routine. Use it for reflection, time in your faith, or to simply clear your mind. Think about something other than the leadership role you find yourself in.

<u>**Delegate**</u>
(part of Phase Two and Three - Tactical and Operational Leadership, Chapter 7 - Leading Others - When is the First Time We Lead Someone Other than Ourselves?) – It's easy to get in the trap of, "I'll just do it myself." There is a point of diminishing returns when anyone performs more and more tasks by themselves. When a leader delegates, they do at least two things: 1) they create time for themselves to apply mental and physical energy to other requirements 2) they create opportunities for growing leaders by providing experience followed by an after action review. As you advance to higher levels of leadership, you are eventually going to reach a point where you literally "can't do it all yourself."

<u>**Make sure family is a priority**</u> –

As previously mentioned in Chapter 7 (Leading Others - When is the First Time We Lead Someone Other than Ourselves?), knowing the difference between what is "important" versus what is "urgent". I, and many others around me, have made this mistake. One day you will look back and realize your family is too important to routinely be put on the back-burner. Of the 21 years I spent in active duty military service, I spent nearly nine years deployed or in the field, preparing to deploy. I missed several special once-in-a-lifetime events from my children and extended family. I will never get that time back but realize–going forward–work-life balance is crucial to maintaining my long term success. Burn-out begins with poor time management. James 4:13-14 (ESV) says, "Come now, you who say, "Today or tomorrow we will go into such and such a town and spend a year there and trade and make a profit"— yet you do not know what tomorrow will bring. What is your life? For you are a mist that appears for a little time and then vanishes."

Take care of yourself – Sleep Well:

you really need rest. I'm not talking about eight hours in the bed; however, make certain the rest you do get is a quality rest - wash your face, brush your teeth, dress comfortably for sleep, turn out the lights and put your devices (cell phones etc.) somewhere else. Don't sleep on the couch; don't use sleep aids like drugs or alcohol. Some leaders mistake burn-out for just being tired.

Eat healthy:

If you are living on a steady diet of coffee and pastries both your body, and your brain, will turn to mush. Try some fruits and vegetables or try to have a more balanced diet.

Exercise regularly:

workout, go for a walk, play tennis, ride your bike, find something that works for you.

Mental health –

Just like we exercise and train our bodies to strengthen and avoid future physical problems, taking care of yourself should also include an assessment of your emotional and mental state. When we feel stressed or tired, we tend to look for a quick fix, such as adding caffeine so we can work a little later and sleep a little less. Some even look to more addictive options. These are short-term solutions with the potential for long-term problems. Take a moment and consider your long and short-term solutions. The stress of Leading–in any situation–has a cumulative and additive effect. I'm most alert and ready for a challenge when I've gotten rest, spent time with friends, exercised, and eaten a decent meal. Having someone to reach out to: a family member; a friend; a religious or spiritual leader; a mental health professional; a support group, can make all the difference. Set aside regular time for your faith and make it a priority (regardless of what religion you practice). Psalm 23 ESV ends with the statement, "He restores my soul." Make sure you're allowing enough time to restore your soul.

Show Gratitude –

Say "please" and "thank you": kind words go a long way toward a productive environment. A simple handwritten thank you note can have a profound long lasting positive impact; not only on you, but also on the person receiving the note. As a school teacher I would often ask my students, "What does it cost to be nice?" The answer is … "Nothing!" It took me over 50 years to learn this simple lesson. It will help change your attitude and the attitude of those around you. This, in turn, will help ward off burn out.

Fear is not all bad; however, if you let it rule you, it can become an insurmountable obstacle to success for you and those you lead. Learn to conquer fear by:

- Controlling your emotions.
- Setting realistic expectations.
- Keeping things simple.
- Acknowledging loss as an inevitable part of things.
- Having a group of trusted advisors you can go to for assistance.

- Being humble enough to learn how to improve your leadership skills and style.
- Taking care of yourself both physically and mentally to avoid burn-out.

Chapter 14
What insights can we gain from leaders across different Specialties?

> **He who thinks he is leading and has no one following him is only taking a walk.**
>
> 
>
> **African Proverb**

Throughout this book we've been deliberate about offering different perspectives on leadership development. Traditional leadership books, as we discussed in the introduction, offer two varieties: one detailing the life and experiences of a "famous" person or, the other lists successful leadership traits a reader should follow. Leadership is all about learning and taking advice from those who have demonstrated success in their respective fields.

We interviewed leaders in many disciplines and professions to better understand how their journey from self-leadership to strategic leadership can inform the path for others. We did not have preconceived ideas but provided open-ended questions to elicit a direct response. As the interview data showed several common themes.

- **Theme 1: Trust** - Trust doesn't happen overnight, it builds gradually; however, can be lost instantly. Trust is learned and earned in tough times and maintained in good times. We have talked about the fact that leadership is about authenticity and genuine connection to people. This is making certain others know your words and actions are not contrived, letting them know you deserve their trust.

- **Theme 2: Creating and Communicating Vision to Team** - Comes from within … It's the ability to see the success of the future and the path to get there. Making vision a reality may be one of the toughest things a leader will ever do. To be a successful visionary there are several things you must do: Articulate and Communicate the vision; have a Strategy for vision realization; Develop a plan and prioritize resources; Monitor vision implementation because people do what gets checked.

- **Theme 3: The Power of Listening** - Listen more and talk less. Make certain people know their ideas are valued. You must earnestly listen to their ideas, ask their opinion, and realize their insights may be better than yours. When you, as the leader, put their thoughts and ideas into action you engage them. This is also a great form of recognition and respect.

- **Theme 4: Know that YOU don't know everything, trust in your team** - As the leader, you don't know everything! Many leaders fail to own this fact. However, you must embrace your vulnerabilities and find a way to mitigate and/or assuage them. There are many ways to do this: surround yourself with smart, capable people; educate yourself in the vulnerable areas; create experience, over time, by taking small steps outside your comfort zone.

- **Theme 5: Be available and on time** - Being available to your immediate subordinates is one of the single most important aspects of leadership. Since there are so many things pulling a leader away from being available, time management becomes essential. You must make time for those people reporting directly to you, if this doesn't happen then the cascading of the vision and the mission doesn't happen. In addition to being available, you must be on time. Time is one of the most valuable resources the leader and employees have. This is a show of respect to your subordinates and shows them they are valuable.

- **Theme 6: Lifelong Learning** - True leaders are Lifelong learners. Learning comes from those we interact with daily (small traits or characteristics of effective people). We learn by understanding our development areas and take active steps to improve via professional development (workshops, training, formal courses, etc.). You cannot lead or help others if you can't help yourself.

Each of these themes is discussed in detail in this book and reiterated / reinforced by these interviews.

AN INTERVIEW WITH GEORGE SIMMS

President and CEO of the Ohio Minority Supplier Development Council (OMSDC)

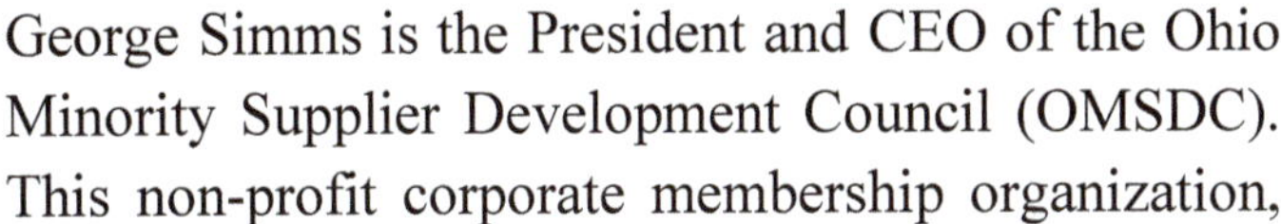

George Simms is the President and CEO of the Ohio Minority Supplier Development Council (OMSDC). This non-profit corporate membership organization, originally chartered in 1972, helps to advance business opportunities for minority business enterprises. The suppliers within the organization contributed nearly $16 billion annually.[113] He was born in New Orleans, Louisiana and grew up in the lower 20% of wealth distribution, which is the source of his scarcity mentality but, with an abundance outlook. Despite challenges early in life, George excelled academically, earning an Engineering degree from Southern University and later a Master's degree from Louisiana State University (LSU) in Petroleum Engineering. George was selected as a National Fellowship Scholar and worked as a NASA intern supporting the Space Shuttle's internal engines and solid rocket boosters. This experience opened a new world of opportunities and possibilities for his future.

He then worked for Exxon and Chemicals USA where he developed process management, people, and organizational skills. Additionally, George served as the Assistant Dean of the College of Engineering at Southern University and the Director of a Pre Engineering program that also managed and distributed the university's scholarships. Later, George spent 28 years with Proctor and Gamble (P&G) working in greater positions of responsibility eventually managing the company's global supply chain including several manufacturing facilities and plans.

[113] Ohio Minority Supplier Development Council © 2022. https://ohiomsdc.org/ - May 9th, 2024

These roles enabled him to apply his strategic leadership skills as the global supply chain lead for external supply operations Pampers, Always, and Sherman. After a long and distinguished career, George "retired" and then started his own business–Break the Solution–to help minority businesses grow profitably and become strategic suppliers for large corporations. He finally found his North Star–that guiding value, principle, or goal which helps drive people–of helping to eliminate economic injustice through operational excellence.

During our interview, George shared several insights and thoughts about self-development and how to think and lead strategically. For him, it starts with people. How to understand them, how to understand what motivates them, and what tools and resources people need to drive an organization. He explains the process includes an understanding of organizations, people, equipment, materials, methods, and the environment. The most important one is people–they drive how all those pieces of the process work and function effectively. As you gain a better understanding of your people, you can begin to "deploy" your *people resources* into the organization's technology and into the business operations.

Leadership is also about ownership of the good and bad. George recalled a time where one of the five manufacturing plants he managed needed to be shut down. In the preceding months before the shut down announcement, George and his team diligently worked to improve their production productivity and key performance indicators (KPIs). He mentored technicians to become managers and helped create a culture where people brought their best version to work. In a relatively short time, the plant became the top producing of the five. However, the plant's location was not aligned to the company's long-term goals and decided to shut down the plant. Rather than blame management for the shut down decision, George shared the shut down analysis with every employee to show transparency and honesty. Even though the employees would lose their job, they were given the respect of being included into the process.

With all the success and ability to work in a field that nourishes his North Star, George also relied upon mentors and sponsors. He began by defining each:

- Mentors challenge you to improve while considering what is best for you. This could mean stay and grow within the organization or pursue external opportunities.
- Sponsors see the potential in others while being mindful of the organization. Their top priority is the organization and how you best fit into the business.

We wrapped up the discussion with a unique way of thinking about leadership and how to inspire others. **Envision, energize, and enable.** A leader needs to be able to have a vision of the future, where they want the organization to go and clearly understand the future desired state.

In the end there are some guidelines for new leaders to follow:

- Connect your passion (what you love to do) to something that matters (North Star).
- Focus on building your technical skills and mastering them (self-development and self-leadership).
- Listen to your employees and ask what motivates them. Then help and develop them in positions where their motivations come to light.

AN INTERVIEW WITH GEORGE B. MCGILL
Mayor, City of Fort Smith Arkansas

George McGill was elected Mayor of Fort Smith in August of 2018. As the first African American to ever be elected as Fort Smith Mayor, McGill is a trailblazer who has used his dedication to public service to advance the common good at the federal, state, and local levels. Prior to serving as Mayor, McGill represented Fort Smith, his hometown, in the Arkansas House of Representatives for three terms.[114]

As a State Representative for District 78, McGill earned the respect of his legislative peers on both sides of the political aisle. He gave the closing argument for the separation of Robert E. Lee and Martin Luther King, Jr. Holidays in Arkansas.

He served as Deputy Speaker Pro-Tempore of the Arkansas House of Representatives.

His service in the House of Representatives also included Chair of the Aging, Children, Youth Legislative & Military Affairs Committee and Co-Chair of Policy-Making Subcommittee for the Legislative Governing Board of the Council of State Governments. These leadership positions allowed McGill the opportunity to focus on issues that he deeply cares for, such as hunger relief, higher education, the protection of the elderly, children and families, and veterans.

Mayor McGill's leadership experience as a United States Army Veteran, former small business owner, and community leader has been recognized through many awards including The National Guard Association of Arkansas Joseph T. Robinson Award, the Arkansas Municipal League Distinguished Legislator Award in 2013, 2015, and 2017, and the University Of Arkansas School Of Business Trailblazer Award.

Mayor McGill earned his Bachelor of Science in education and a Master of Business Administration from the University of Arkansas.

Commissioned as Second Lieutenant, United States Army Field Artillery, during the Vietnam War, McGill is the embodiment of Public Service.

---

[114]City of Fort Smith, Arkansas. About Mayor George McGill. https://www.fortsmithar.gov/government/leadership/mayor/about-mayor-george-b-mcgill - Jan 3rd, 2024

Mayor McGill graciously hosted us in his office for a sit-down face-to-face interview on January, 17th 2024. He shared with us his thoughts on leadership:

Leadership is influencing and guiding in a certain environment to accomplish predetermined goals or objectives. This could be an overall vision or a very definable goal needing specific skills coupled with being motivated and energized.

In order to move past day-to-day management and administration you must trust your knowledge of the subject matter and have the courage to allow others to perform using their expertise and knowledge. This means inspiring people to perform at their very best bringing all of the technical skills and knowledge to bear.

As a small business owner you must be able to work across Leadership, Management and Administration. With good management comes a knowledge of the subject matter. In this case, Financial Services. In these small groups you should get input from those you are leading, a key part of that is listening (Listening was a key thread for Mayor McGill) and allow people to be a part of the decision-making processes. What you find is when people find they have a "say" in the matter their energy level is higher when it is time to accomplish something. Making certain you select the best idea, or course of action, generates passion for accomplishment. Being the leader doesn't mean the best idea always comes from you. Oftentimes asking a simple question, "What do you think?" generates the best ideas.

In a small organization or small business, you are the decision maker. Decisions could be made very quickly; make an honest assessment and make the call right then. In the House of Representatives of the Arkansas General Assembly there are 100 members, all with an equal vote. Consequently, decision making requires more time and discussion. In this arena listening and understanding is the key to good leadership and finding common ground is a must to get things done. Listening remained the "driving force" when moving from the Arkansas General Assembly to being the Mayor. Listening allows understanding of problems “zeroing in” on the resources necessary to help people solve their own issues.

When choosing advisors and the members of the team closest to you, in this form of government, you must look at the person's “motive for serving”. There are many motives, the motive must be work focused on lifting every element of the community. One of the role models the Mayor looked to was a member of the opposite political party. A reminder that all elected officials represent their entire constituency, including those that did not vote for you or even voted against you. Ultimately, elected officials are public servants with their schedule, time and thoughts driven by the needs of the public.

Poor leadership is driven by people who are self-interested and / or motivated by self-advancement or motivated by special interest. Every leader has “shortcomings or flaws” that may not suit everyone. Leaders must recognize their own weakness and find ways to make sure they don’t negatively impact relationships or objective outcomes. “Staying calm” is one of the easiest and best ways to accomplish this.

Finding yourself in a leadership role is a “humbling” experience. It should be humbling to find people trusting you to be their voice and trusting you to show the way. Some of the best leaders have the ability to make each person feel special, even in groups.

Isolation is one of the most difficult parts of leadership. The old adage of “it’s lonely at the top” is appropriate here. The leader is the one who “carries the weight” of the organization or group and it takes its toll. To overcome this you need to find another voice you can turn to.

Some advice for new leaders would include:

- Listen.
- Doing and making honest assessments.
- Have courage to make tough decisions.

As a parting comment: “Once you accept the leadership role, operate with authority and knowledge in whatever organization you're in.”

AN INTERVIEW WITH CHRISTOPHER KANE[115]
Military to Corporate Leadership
Vice President at Capital One

Christopher Kane is a Transformation Lead for a major financial institution. He graduated from West Point in 2001, nearly three months before 9/11. Like the vast majority of those in uniform at that time, war was inevitable. At the time, Chris was stationed as a Field Artillery officer assigned to the First Armored Division, in Baumholder, Germany. He was also accompanied by his wife, a 2003 West Point graduate and Logistics officer. He deployed to Iraq in April 2003. His unit experienced an increasingly dangerous insurgency which extended his deployment to 15 months. After re-deploying, he and his wife decided to experience life in the civilian sector.

After his five-year service commitment, Chris left the military to experience the world from a different lens. He transitioned from the Army into corporate business development roles while living in the Middle East. This allowed Chris and his wife to better understand the region from a people, culture, and religious perspective. Next, Chris eventually got into banking, focusing on transformation and process improvement. He credits his military leadership training and experiences for providing him the confidence to lead and manage civilian organizations. Military officers typically spend 2-3 years in one role before having to transfer to an entirely different location and organization. They become the new leader in a new space but learn how to quickly assess and understand an organization. These transferable skills translate into nearly every other sector–they all still need effective leaders to drive change and organizational transformation.

The Leader needs to establish a vision and effectively communicate that to the organization and its employees. Even if a clear vision is communicated, how does a Leader bring those resources and people

---

[115] Linkedin. Christopher Kane, Vice President at Capital One. Copyright 2024. https://www.linkedin.com/in/kanece/ - July 1st, 2024

together? Having an understanding of employee strengths and how to apply those strengths is how a leader begins to make an impact. This understanding allows the leader to then think about how to get the most out of people. Chris applies the "Hierarchy of Needs" concept. Have I met the basic needs of my employees? This need for physiological safety is critical in establishing employee trust and a perceived confidence that the leader is operating in the best interests of both the organization and their employees. This nuanced concept is the safety blanket an employee will reference when thinking about their level of confidence that an organization (and the Leader) is looking out for them.

In recent years, cynicism, distrust and self-interests in the motives of leaders have exploded. Organizations have devolved into places where collaboration and teamwork for the greater good (or company objectives) are replaced by individual achievement and exposure. When contrasting against the military, the typical civilian employee lacks many of those psychological concerns such as: Will I have a job next year due to changing business needs or market conditions? Is my compensation on par with my colleagues? What about work-life balance?

To change the dynamic, leaders take the initiative by replacing self-interests with a change in how the organization thinks about a shared identity, starting with how we communicate. Using simple terms like "we" and "us" instead of "I" or "me". Additionally, getting employee buy-in or the "why we are doing this" overcomes much resistance to change. They are now part of the problem and have been empowered to be part of the solution–in a psychologically safe environment.

Then what is a good leader? Finally, the leader must deliver results. Delving deeper than delivering results, it is ***how*** the leader delivers results. **Influential leadership** is the method Chris uses to deliver those results. The leader must show others they are able to be influenced. The goal is not to convince or persuade but to develop another type of psychological safety that conveys, "I'm here to enable and support your needs". You show an ability and capability to be a follower. In a sense, the leader is giving up a portion of their "power" to others but, in reality, they are establishing a foundation of trust and mutual support.

A common blunder among unsuccessful corporate leaders is taking charge before understanding the organization, how their people operate, and what opportunities exist to improve. This "Lone Wolf" mentality does not message that one is willing to follow or open to being influenced. They disproportionally rely upon their past experiences without understanding the uniqueness of their current environment. Adding to the "isolated leader" concept, some leaders also lack self-awareness of the difference between confidence and arrogance (see Chapter 4 - Self Leadership "If you can't lead yourself, how can you lead others?").

Chris summarized how he deals with issues brought to him by his leadership team or employees. Is this a *head, heart or hands* problem? This simplified way of receiving problems or information also speeds up how a leader can help and support. "Hands on problems" are those where resources, people or systems may be needed for resolution. The solution often requires more bodies. "Head problems" focus on influencing others to agree on a course of action or path. When looking at the team internally, head problems can be how the team thinks about a problem. The Leader can help reframe the problem–after actively listening to and understanding the employees position and justification. The Heart problem implies a lack of motivation or desire to understand and resolve problems or tasks.

AN INTERVIEW WITH RYAN GEHRIG
President, Mercy Arkansas Communities

Ryan Gehrig was named president of Mercy Arkansas Communities in June 2022 and leads all hospitals across the state, including the two largest hospitals in Fort Smith and Rogers. Gehrig first came to Mercy as the president of Mercy Hospital Fort Smith in April 2012. Before Mercy, Gehrig served as vice president of enterprise systems and chief administrative officer for Moore Medical Center in the Norman Regional Health System in Oklahoma. He previously served as chief operating officer of Wesley Medical Center in Hattiesburg, Mississippi, as CEO and chief operating officer of Bristow Medical Center in Bristow, Oklahoma, and as chief operating officer of Cushing Regional Hospital in Cushing, Oklahoma.[116]

Mr. Gehrig graduated from Texas A&M University with a bachelor's degree in biomedical science. He received his Master's in Healthcare Administration from Trinity University in San Antonio, Texas. He completed an administrative residency at Hillcrest Healthcare System in Tulsa, Oklahoma.

Mr. Gehrig kindly provided us with his time in a sit-down face-to-face interview on January, 16th 2024. What follows are his insights and perspectives.

Leadership is ensuring you have built a team culturally aligned with, and emotionally connected to, the vision you have established for your organization and inspiring them to meet the vision.

Teams do not achieve the vision without necessary resources. That often includes team building. This means making certain the collective members of the team possess all the necessary attributes for the vision. It also includes making time for progress checks.

He noted over the last 25 years of leadership from small groups to leading leaders he is "less reactive" and dictatorial, becoming more "process focused". Time management was a common thread and today the need for thought and reflection, asking good socratic questions of his team leaders and ensuring the right perspective of the situation are necessary in larger organizations.

As you grow to leading larger organizations you have to grow a circle of trust. Again, make certain those trusted team members have what they need, including time, to get things done and providing periodic feedback

[116] Mercy. Ryan Gehrig. Copyright 2024. https://www.mercy.net/about/leadership/arkansas-region-leadership/ryan-gehrig/ - Jan 4th, 2024

along the way. Simultaneously, the leader needs to understand the processes people are working with and trust those processes to help achieve closure. As a leader of a small group you can be "person" focused; however, as your scope of responsibility increases, shifting more to process is necessary.

Choosing those team members closest to you requires some assessment. You must look for a certain level of experience and, in many cases, a technical background. In large organizations, like this one, the use of an agency to do some screening allows for time management. Evaluation of potential team members often entails looking for and at value systems, finding people able to articulate the vision and lead others to it. You must consider their authenticity coupled with the ability and willingness to respectfully challenge leadership. Do you have a team with a diverse range of ideas?

For new leaders, having a more senior leader with patience and the willingness to teach will help foster skills for the future. You need to understand leadership is a "full contact" sport; this includes understanding people and being able to roll your sleeves up when necessary.

Most leaders want better oratory skills. There are those leaders throughout history who are able to inspire with their speaking ability. There are things you can do to make this work and one is the power of storytelling to get your point across. Those people who possess both "authenticity" and oration skills have "next level stuff."

Being visible and available to your subordinate leaders is one of the single most important aspects of leadership. There are so many things pulling a leader away from being available, time management here again becomes essential. You must make time for those people reporting directly to you, if this doesn't happen then the cascading of the vision and the mission doesn't happen.

The poorest leaders are all about "self-preservation." These people are not willing to "buck the system" or tell the boss something is not working or are unwilling to take action. Along with this, attempting to lead with "intimidation" rarely has long term positive effects.

In the end there are some guidelines for new leaders to follow:

- Always listen to the person closest to the work. Learn from them and they will become your biggest advocate.
- Roll your sleeves up and be out with your team. If they know you have their back they will carry the ball for you.
- Learn from experiences, not sitting in your office.
- Slow down and spend time reflecting and "ruminating" on what does and doesn't work. You will remember things you may not have realized or picked up on in the moment.
- Build trust and have humility.

We appreciate these valuable lessons from more than 25 years of leadership experience from small teams to a large complex organization.

AN INTERVIEW WITH DR. PATTI CONARD
Endowed Professor for the College of Health, Education, and Human Sciences.
University of Arkansas Fort Smith

Texas Woman's University: Nursing Science Doctor of Philosophy (PhD), Nursing Science, 2009 - 2013
Texas A&M University: MSN, Nursing Leadership, 2008 - 2009

Dr. Conard lived a life many would dream of. She spent six years overseas living in Japan and Okinawa, traveling the world providing nursing care, continuing her education to earn a bachelor, master, and doctorate, and finding solace in assisting the men and women – and their families – who have served this nation. Dr. Conard has been published

26 times across a wide array of topics. She also teaches leadership in the University of Arkansas Fort Smith Nursing program.[117]
Dr. Conard's husband became a military psychiatrist, and she became one of the first 300 nurses to earn a Ph.D. from the first Ph.D. nursing program at Texas Women's University. Saying she is proud of her accomplishments, "I got to do different types of nursing. I got different types of education. I fulfilled every degree I could get in nursing, and it has been a wonderful experience."

In conjunction with her husband's military work, Conard connected with servicemen and -women. Through these relationships, Dr. Conard found a personal passion that continues today.

Leadership is working with a person or group and inspiring them to attain their goals or their shared goal(s). It is impossible to achieve true success unless you can inspire others to follow. In order to be effective, the leader must be able to guide people to adapt to changing environments, problem solve and think critically.

Four decades of experience have permitted the latitude to work across disciplines. It has also fostered the opportunity for creativity and shown the need to balance work / life over time (sometimes this requires the making of a schedule).
Good leaders have compassion, are approachable, care for those they lead and are flexible to the situation. Good leaders are able to positively influence others even through adversity. Most importantly, they look to cultivate the best in others and this truly inspires others. These attributes teach, through example, the ability to focus on a vision, promote active listening, ensure integrity and promote cultural competence taking into consideration other points of view.

Learning from other cultures helps broaden communication skills and facilitate the true understanding of other thoughts and ideas. This deeper understanding also boosts enjoyment.

---

[117] University of Arkansas Fort Smith. Dr. Patti Conard. https://uafs.edu/news/2023/fv-patti-conard.php - January 25th, 2024

The weakest of leaders lack integrity, and a lack of integrity can become contagious. These poor leaders always focus on and seek out the worst in people and situations. This approach breeds the need for micro management because there is no inspiration for success and it takes the breath out of enthusiasm. You must be able to delegate, and poor leaders lose that ability.

Not everyone with a title is a leader. Ascension to leadership should be merit based, a derivative of a solid work ethic and the ability to collaborate. These leaders will have a vision and begin setting goals. Real leaders realize they don't know it all. This makes them committed Lifelong learners, pushes them to seek out mentors and ensures they have a command of the foundational competencies in their area of expertise.

One of the most difficult aspects of leadership is dealing with personnel and personal problems or confrontation. There is the need for difficult conversations; however, these situations routinely generate some level of "negativity". Using Lifelong learning and available educational opportunities to gain skills in confrontation resolution is worth the time.

Advice to the leader beginning a career would include:

- Create a healthy environment.
- Always advocate for others.
- Maintain a positive attitude.
- Always look for what inspires others.
- Seek out the best quality in each member of your team and match it to the situation.

Leading both students and faculty in this environment leaves little time for "management". You must trust the people who perform in their areas of management. It permits the leader to remain focused on the people–teaching the students and leading the faculty teams in their research for presentation and publishing.

We are grateful for these insightful comments from a seasoned student, practitioner and teacher of leadership.

AN INTERVIEW WITH BEAU SPARKMAN
Entrepreneur and Small Business Owner

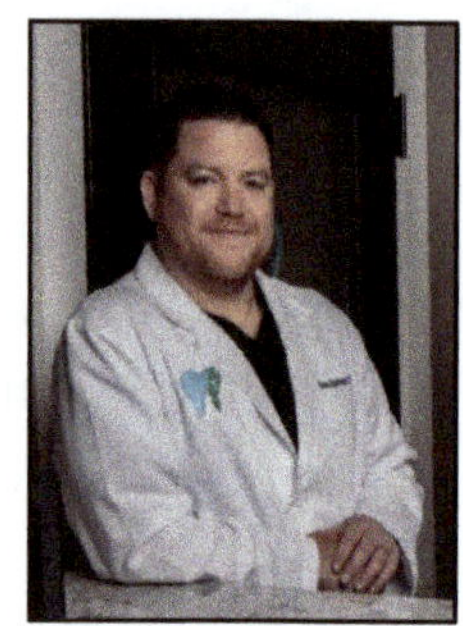

Dr. Beau Sparkman earned his Bachelor of Science with an emphasis in Pre-Medicine from Sterling College. He graduated from the University of Oklahoma's College of Dentistry in 2011 and immediately returned to his home in the Arkansas River Valley area to begin practicing dentistry. He has grown a small business with three distinct dentistry locations in less than 15 years and is still growing providing services across a wide array of needs.

In addition to practicing general dentistry for children and adults, he also provides orthodontic (Braces, Invisalign & Myobrace) services and sleep apnea services. He is a member of the American Dental Association, the Arkansas State Dental Association, the Oklahoma Dental Association, the Fort Smith Dental Association, the American Orthodontic Society, the American Academy of Dental Sleep Medicine, and the Academy of General Dentistry.[118]

Leadership is a way of guiding people to a desired outcome, influencing them to move to an endpoint or a goal the leader has set the vision for.

The vision for a small business can be short (1 year) and can stretch out 5 to 10 years. There is no restriction on vision. When the organization is in the execution of the vision there are "blindspots" found requiring agility. Some of this is being a "Lifelong learner" and determining how to discover the blindspots. If the leader learns early, they can more easily navigate the obstacles or blindspots.

In the beginning of leadership, being passive and submissive is the norm because of title, or position. With leadership maturity and experience

---

[118] Valley Family Dental. Dr. Beau Sparkman. https://valleyfamilydentalpractice.com/about/doctors/dr-beau-sparkman/ - January 13th, 2024

comes awareness of the environment and understanding of team member capabilities and limitations. Also with time comes emotional growth as a leader. This growth and understanding allows the leader to expand their vision by navigating strong personalities. Some leaders see team members with strong personalities as a roadblock; however, a mature leader can redirect this into an advantage. This is done through positive communication; particularly, making certain dominant personalities feel heard. For some leaders this is difficult because it requires earnest "listening" not simply "hearing".

A leader must understand their strengths and weaknesses. In doing so, it allows the leader to surround themself with team members complementing them. An example might be a visionary leader who will need people to execute and see a project or vision through to completion. Small business, particularly in the medical field, requires people with "attention to detail." This is a screening criterion used for hiring. There are several methods to determine if an applicant possesses attention to detail: Asking an unusual question on the job application like, "What is your favorite flavor of ice cream?" This forces the applicant to read through the entire application; being interviewed by peers or potential co-workers and watching body language, including facial expressions (nonverbal communication); being articulate or succinct in verbal communication skills; wearing an unforced smile. All of these can be and are indications of attention to detail.

Once in the organization, promotion is a component of several areas: excelling in the current position, is the person leading from the current position, and positive peer and stakeholder evaluations.

One way to move from management and administration is to let direct reports do the hiring. This authority makes certain they have buy-in to the success of the organization. Also, encouraging the Lifelong learning of subordinate leaders loosens the grip of management and administration on a leader's time. Leaders must be "consumers of knowledge." Employment and the application of knowledge becomes the power of leadership. Time management of the leader in smaller organizations is a must and should be a habit.

In order to expand the organization requires the leader to "train and develop" the next level leaders, to "train and develop" the next level of leaders below them. The ability to do this lifts the growth cap of a small business. Some refer to this as the "ceiling of complexity."

Good / ideal leaders ask good questions. Good leaders listen more than they speak. Good leaders realize they are not perfect and help those they lead understand mistakes are going to happen.

Poor leaders fail to understand the culture of the organization. Failed leaders are passive in the face of obstacles. Poor leaders overlook weakness and permit gossip, leading to a toxic environment.

Key aspects of successful leadership include:

- Conflict resolution. Navigating around conflict brings a level of consciousness to members of an organization promoting growth. This also helps grow the emotional intelligence of the organization and its members. Additionally, navigating conflict can stop an organization from slowly spiraling out of control.

- Guiding change and embodying the vision of the organization. People don't really mind change; however, they often don't like the method of change. Leaders' understanding of their organization will help facilitate change in a positive way.

- Effective communication. This is a leader's responsibility, to ensure understanding of the message / vision / task / expectations.

- Accountability. Leaders at all levels must take responsibility. You can delegate tasks; however, the leader must have a system of checks, a repetitive cadence of accountability.

- Storytelling. This can be a very effective method of sharing the vision of the organization. When used correctly it can create imagery of the vision and how it will help both the organization and the individual.

- Being Present: with next level leaders and helping them to understand how to cultivate their leaders.

In the end, Dr Sparkman provided advice for leaders, regardless of the situation or size of the organization they lead:

- Be a Lifelong learner. Information and content is available everywhere so there is no excuse.
- Put information into practice. Implementation of information is one of the true powers of the best leaders.
- Execution through human capital. Understand the strengths and weaknesses of your team members and take advantage of the strengths while ensuring team makeup compensates for any weakness.

We appreciate the valuable insights from more than 15 years of leadership experience and entrepreneurship.

Chapter 15
Summary & Takeaways

> **The consummate leader cultivates the moral law, and strictly adheres to method and discipline; thus it is in his power to control success.**
>
> **- Sun Tzu**

See the future = vision
Engage and Develop Others = Produce and mentor Leaders (Phase 4)
Reinvent Continuously = AARs and make changes for the future
Value Results and Relationships = Celebrate success
Embody Values = Moral Courage

We are all going to lead, even if it is leading only yourself. If we think we're smarter than the people we are leading, if we don't respect the people we're leading, or if we are threatened by the people we are leading, we are headed for trouble.

Definitions		
Leadership	**Management**	**Administration**
Leadership is the ability to foster an environment in which people motivate themselves to achieve beyond their own perceived capabilities, and face problems for which there appear to be no simple solutions.	**Management** is bringing the right resources together at the right place and time to achieve the leaders and organizations goals and objectives.	**Administration** is applying stream-lined functions / processes to an organization which facilitate the accomplishment of the leaders and organizations goals and objectives.

- ***Table 3 (Definitions): Refined definitions of Leadership, Management and Administration***

All three are required for the success and health of an organization; however, they are all distinct
(Chapter 2 - Overview of the Leadership, Management, Administration (LMA) Model).

- ➢ Leadership is about People.
- ➢ Management is about Stuff (Resources).
- ➢ Administration is about Process / Function.

The Leader is the point of "Responsibility" for everything that happens or fails to happen good, bad or indifferent. The "Authority" and decision making of others is a derivative of the Responsibility provided by the Leader (Chapter 3 - Responsibility vs Authority).

Responsibility & Authority Defined		
Responsibility is the acceptance of blame for all things good, bad or indifferent in the organization.	For the entire organization: It doesn't matter if you were present. It doesn't matter if you knew it was happening. It doesn't matter whether you are awake or asleep.	Final **responsibility** can only be held by one person. The leader!
Authority is being empowered with the ability to make decisions based on the responsibility held by the overall leader!	This is for a subset of a larger organization. Think of this as specialized sets of an organization (examples may include: Logistics / Human Resources / Communications)	Authority can only be delegated or granted by the overall leader.

- ***Table 4 (Definitions): Refined definitions of Responsibility and Authority***

There are 4 phases of leadership that we progress through.

- ***Graphic 3 (Diagram): The Phases of Growing Leaders and Leadership.***

Phase One is **Self-Leadership** (Chapter 4 - Self Leadership "If you can't lead yourself, how can you lead others?"). In this organization of one, you are responsible for ***everything***, Leading, Managing and Administering. This requires individual personal discipline and the desire to succeed. You are responsible for you. No one else is going to be looking over your shoulder to hold you to a standard. You must hold yourself to the standard you have set. To reach Phase Two, Tactical Leadership, and lead others, you must first develop the capability to successfully lead yourself. You will find this phase is continuous and even though you may reach a higher phase you will always need to lead yourself to some degree.

Phase Two is **Tactical Leadership** - leading others (Chapter 7 - Leading Others - When is the First Time We Lead Someone Other than Ourselves?). The keys to this phase of leadership are being present, effective one-on-one communication and receiving and implementing vision and guidance from the higher-level leaders. If you are a Tactical Leader, you are in routine direct contact with those you lead. This phase builds upon the skills acquired and developed from Phase One. Moving on to Phase Three, Operational Leadership, means you have "mastered" the ideas of Tactical Leadership.

Phase Three is **Operational Leadership** - leading leaders at scale (Chapter 7 - Leading Others - When is the First Time We Lead Someone Other Than Ourselves?). This requires vision and the identification and establishment of long-term goals and objectives. In this phase you must be able to match teams to goals, objectives and strategies for the long-term effectiveness of the organization. You should be able to identify subordinate leaders to whom you can delegate and have a high assurance for success. You are providing guidance and direction to subordinate leaders and teams. You must be able to effectively employ multiple forms of communication (see Chapter 5 - Communication "Do leaders really communicate or just tell people what to do?" - Learning to communicate with others). Operational Leaders are responsible for obtaining and maintaining organizational results. At this level of leadership, you are looking at the systems used by your organization and making certain they are the most effective and efficient for success.

Phase Four is **Strategic Leadership** - mentoring leaders (Chapter 8 - "Influential Leadership ... It Doesn't Need a Title [Phase 4]). At this point, your decisions touch every level of your organization with the potential to impact beyond the confines of your own group. You are not thinking about tomorrow, next week, next month or even next year. Your attention and focus is 5 to 10 years down the road. You need a panoptic view of your organization and understand its relationship with other groups. You mentor others to grow to the challenge of strategic leadership. At this phase of leadership your vision predicts and drives the need for change.

The most effective leaders are:

<u>On Time and Present</u> (This is a common theme throughout this book): Being on time is the most personally and professionally respectful thing anyone can do! Being on time should be the norm. Others should expect it from you and YOU should expect it from YOURSELF as a matter of habit. Once you are present physically, it is imperative you are also present mentally and emotionally. Those you lead expect and deserve nothing less. You can't be an effective leader if your head and heart are somewhere else.

<u>Good Communicators</u> (Chapter 5 - Communication "Do leaders really communicate or just tell people what to do?" - Learning to communicate

with others.): The ability to utilize multiple forms of communication and employ technology to get the message out allows leaders to spread their influence into the far reaches of an organization. A key derivative of good communication is trust (Chapter 6 - How to Build Trust and to Trust in Others.). Consistency of message and follow up will help provide the leader with the leverage to make every member of the organization feel a connection. Remember, communication is a two-way street. The most valuable form of communication is "listening" and that is not simply hearing it is also the ability to comprehend the incoming message.

TRUST	
Merriam Webster Dictionary	Reliance on the character, ability, strength, or truth of someone or something.
Cambridge Dictionary	To believe that someone is good and honest and will not harm you, or that something is safe and reliable.
Britannica Dictionary	Belief that someone or something is reliable, good, honest, effective.
Synonyms	Confidence, Expectation, Faith, Hope, Assurance, Certainty, Certitude, Conviction, Credence, Credit, Dependence, Positiveness, Reliance, Stock, Store, Sureness
Antonyms	Disbelief, Distrust, Doubt, Uncertainty

- ***Table 6 (Trust): Definitions / Synonyms / Antonyms.***

<u>Visionary</u> (This is a common theme throughout this book): The leader's ability to focus the organization's direction and effectively communicate a vision sets them apart from the Manager and the Administrator. Having a vision is the difference between a JOB and a Profession.

Treating people professionally and sharing your vision is motivating. Otherwise, the monotony of 9 to 5 eventually stifles initiative.

Trustworthy and Leading with Humility (Chapter 6 - How to Build Trust and to Trust in Others.):

Trust is a derivative of many things. Look at the common terms in the definitions of "trust" in the Table above: Truth, Honesty, Good, Reliance, and Character. These are qualities proven out over time. They can't be fully demonstrated overnight or in a single event. So how do we earn trust? In a word: *consistency*. Building trust requires consistent truth, consistent honesty, consistent good, consistent reliability, and consistent character.

Humility is about Confidence. There is a difference between someone who is boastful or a braggart, and someone who speaks with confidence. Everyone knows the person … They can't help but show everyone how good they are. However, the truth is, if the person were really that good, why do you need to tell everyone - I believe that at one point or another we're all guilty. If the leader is practicing humility they act with confidence and never actually need to talk about themself.

"Do not boast about tomorrow, for you do not know what a day may bring." Proverbs 27:1 ESV.

Lifelong Learners (This is a common theme throughout this book): During all phases of leadership you should continue to proactively be a *Lifelong learner*. Educate yourself, look for ways to improve your skills and assuage your weaknesses, we all have them. This includes taking advantage of formalized training generated by the organization and community. This includes practicing "Moral Courage." Even if no one is watching, you are doing the right thing and you are doing those things right!

We have provided you with a Start-point! Our definition of Leadership is transferable to any situation and any size organization. If you want to be a "Producer of Leadership" and not remain a "Consumer of

Leadership" this book empowers you with the tools for long term success.

"But among you it will be different. Whoever wants to be great among you must be your servant." Matthew 20:26 ESV

Acknowledgements

We would like to express our deepest gratitude to our families for their unwavering support throughout this journey. They endured late nights and countless revisions with a smile.

We would also like to thank the many great leaders we encountered in our own journeys to leadership. We have intentionally not mentioned any names for fear of leaving someone out. There are so many, it would be a real possibility. These great leaders are the ones who recognized something early on and were willing to coach, teach and mentor us to grow to our full potential.

A special thanks to those leaders who lent their time and leadership insights to our work through the interviews you find in the book. These wonderful people practice leadership every day and set the example for many.

Our appreciation goes to our editors for their generous support, time and insightful feedback to shaping this work.

This book would not be the same without the exceptional advice from our publisher who helped a team of first-time authors with all the details we would not have discovered on our own.

Finally, to the readers! We hope you do indeed feel like "Better Leaders."

Bibliography

Definitions

Source	Leadership	Management	Administration
https://www.merriam-webster.com/ July 24, 2023	1: the office or position of a leader 2: capacity to lead 3: the act or an instance of leading	1: the act or art of managing: the conducting or supervising of something (such as a business) 2: judicious use of means to accomplish an end 3: the collective body of those who manage or direct an enterprise	1: performance of executive duties: 2: the act or process of administering something 3: the execution of public affairs as distinguished from policymaking 4a: a body of persons who administer 4b: often capitalized: a group constituting the political executive in a presidential government 4c: a governmental agency or board 5: the term of office of an administrative officer or body
https://www.britannica.com/dic	1a: a position as a leader of	1a: the act or skill of controlling and	1a: the activities that relate to

tionary July 24, 2023	a group, organization, etc. 1b: the time when a person holds the position of leader 2: the power or ability to lead other people 3: the leaders of a group, organization, or country	making decisions about a business, department, sports team, etc. She's planning a career in (business) management. 1b: the people who make decisions about a business, department, sports team, etc. 2: the act or process of deciding how to use something 3: the act or process of controlling and dealing with something	running a company, school, or other organization 1b: a group of people who manage the way a company, school, or other organization functions 2a: a government or part of a government that is identified with its leader (such as a U.S. president or British prime minister) 2b: a U.S. government department 3: the act or process of providing or administering something
Military definitions:	What Is Military Leadership? Military leadership involves making critical decisions,	Until recently, leadership and management have often been considered synonyms, used interchangeably in discussions as though they were	Military administration identifies both military departments, agencies, and technologies and systems used by the

	often in high-pressure situations with consequential risks. Effective military leaders ask the right questions and think strategically in making well-informed conclusions upon which they can act. Military leaders also build and motivate teams. https://online.norwich.edu/academic-programs/resources/what-is-military-leadership#:~:text=Military%20leadership%20involves%20making%20critical,also%20build%20and%20motivate%20teams. July 24, 3023	one and the same. The simplest way to separate the two is by stating that leadership is the ability to influence others to go somewhere or do something, whereas management provides the administrative tools and supervision used to get there or do the task. https://cove.army.gov.au/article/management-and-leadership#:~:text=The%20simplest%20way%20to%20separate,there%20or%20do%20the%20task. July 24, 2023	military that are involved in the management of the armed forces. It describes the processes that take place within military organizations outside of combat, particularly in the management of military personnel, their training and services provided as part of their service. Military administration, in many ways, serves the same role as civil society administration and is often cited as the root of bureaucracy throughout government. Due to its broad scope, military administration is often limited by specific areas of application within the military, such as

			logistics management, doctrine development management, and military reform management. https://academic-accelerator.com/encyclopedia/military-administration July 24, 2023
Biblical definitions:	In Matthew 20:25-28, Jesus tells His disciples that leaders should not exercise authority over people. Instead, whoever wants to become great must lower himself to be a servant. Leaders realize that serving others is the only way to lead with a pure heart, free of pride and arrogance. Proverbs,	Management Luke 14:28 ESV - For which of you, desiring to build a tower, does not first sit down and count the cost, whether he has enough to complete it? 1 Corinthians 14:40 ESV - But all things should be done decently and in order. Luke 16:11 ESV - If then you have not been faithful in the unrighteous wealth, who will entrust to you the true riches? Proverbs 21:20	Ephesians Chapter 3 begins in a different vein, with Paul explaining his mission in light of God's cosmic work. After noting that he is a prisoner (literally) because of his ministry to the Gentiles (3:1), Paul writes: "Surely you have heard about the administration of God's grace that was given to me for you..." The Greek word translated here as

	Chapter 16: 10 The king speaks with divine wisdom; he must never judge unfairly. 11 The Lord demands accurate scales and balances; He sets the standards for fairness. 12 A king detests wrongdoing, for his rule is built on justice. 13 The king is pleased with words from righteous lips; He loves those who speak honestly. 14 The anger of the king is a deadly threat; the wise will	ESV - Precious treasure and oil are in a wise man's dwelling, but a foolish man devours it. Proverbs 11:14 ESV - Where there is no guidance, a people falls, but in an abundance of counselors there is safety. Colossians 3:23 ESV / 19 helpful votes Whatever you do, work heartily, as for the Lord and not for men, Proverbs 16:9 ESV - The heart of man plans his way, but the Lord establishes his steps. Proverbs 21:5 ESV - The plans of the diligent lead surely to abundance, but everyone who is hasty comes only to poverty.	"administration" is oikonomia, which means "management, arrangement, or stewardship." It is closely related to the word oikonomos, which referred to one who managed a household or property belonging to a master. Paul sees himself as one to whom God has entrusted his grace, and who is responsible for administering this grace faithfully. God endowed Paul with a very specific element of grace, namely, the gospel of Jesus Christ and its implications. Paul's particular administration meant delivering this good news to the Gentiles.

	try to appease it. 15 When the king smiles, there is life; his favor refreshes like a spring rain. 16 How much better to get wisdom than gold, and good judgment than silver! 17 The path of the virtuous leads away from evil; whoever follows that path is safe. 18 Pride goes before destruction, and haughtiness before a fall. 19 Better to live humbly with the poor than to share plunder with the proud. 20 Those who		https://www.theologyofwork.org/the-high-calling/daily-reflection/are-you-administrator-grace#:~:text=After%20noting%20that%20he%20is,%22management%2C%20arrangement%2C%20or%20stewardship July 24, 2023

	listen to instruction will prosper; those who trust the Lord will be joyful.		
	Situational Leadership This is the ability to understand when and how to apply LMA tools in different leadership settings		
https://www.techtarget.com/searchcio/definition/leadership?Offer=abt_pubpro_AI-Insider July 24, 2023	**What is leadership?** Leadership is the ability of an individual or a group of people to influence and guide followers or members of an organization, society or team. Leadership often is an attribute tied to a person's title, seniority or ranking in a hierarchy.		
https://www.indeed.com/career-advice/career-development/what-is-management July 24, 2023	**What is management?** Management is the coordination and administration of tasks to achieve a goal. Such administration activities include setting the organization's strategy and coordinating the efforts of staff to accomplish these objectives through the application of available resources. Management can also refer to the seniority structure of staff members within an organization.		
6 Common Examples of Administrative Tasks (With Resume Tips) | Indeed.com Australia. July 24, 2023	**What are administrative tasks?** Administrative tasks are duties and responsibilities performed by an administrative professional who provides office support for an organization or business. Common administrative tasks include answering and transferring phone calls, managing email enquiries, processing and transferring data, scheduling appointments and many other responsibilities that help maintain a productive office workplace.		
Synonyms	Management.	administration.	government

https://www.merriam-webster.com/thesaurus/ July 24, 2023	Governance. Government. Administration. Direction. Stewardship. Control. Running. Lead. Steering. Generalship. Policing.	operation. control. handling. supervision. stewardship. oversight. governance.	governance rule regime jurisdiction reign régimebregimen authority leadership sovereignty power dictatorship
Traits	Many lists – with good arguments for all of these traits / qualities.	Again, many lists… Take care to NOT make them synonymous with Leadership.	Again, many lists… Take care to NOT make them synonymous with Leadership and / or Management.

Source	**Responsibility**	**Authority**
https://dictionary.cambridge.org/us/dictionary/english November 9, 2023	Something that it is your job or duty to deal with.	The moral or legal right or ability to control.
https://www.merriam-webster.com/di	Moral, legal, or mental accountability.	Power to influence or command thought, opinion, or behavior.

ctionary November 9, 2023		
https://www.britannica.com/dictionary November 9, 2023	The state of being the person who caused something to happen.	The power to give orders or make decisions : the power or right to direct or control someone or something.
Synonyms https://www.thesaurus.com/ November 9, 2023	Duty power importance restraint authority liability guilt burden obligation trust	force government jurisdiction rule

Responsibility (A duty to deal with or take care of somebody/something, so that you may be blamed if something goes wrong [https://www.oxfordlearnersdictionaries.com/us/definition/english/responsibility - July 24, 2023]) vs Authority (The power to give orders to people [https://www.oxfordlearnersdictionaries.com/us/definition/english/authority?q=Authority –])

	**President Kennedy Picture:** https://www.google.com/url?sa=i&url=https%3A%2F%2Fm.youtube.com%2Fwatch%3Fv%3DVaFTVR-hZqg&psig=AOvVaw0A0FAoiSrAhz1H7sn2pSdI&ust=1696538225447000&source=images&cd=vfe&opi=89978449&ved=0CBAQjRxqFwoTCLiMocSf3YEDFQAAAAAdAAAAABAE – October 4, 2023
	**Apollo 11 Picture:** https://www.nasa.gov/mission/apollo-11/ - October 4, 2023 Apollo Space Program: NASA Staff. The Apollo Program. NASA. May 12th, 2024. https://www.nasa.gov/the-apollo-program/ - May 22, 2024 15 Things Veterans Want You to know: https://www.va.gov/HEALTHPARTNERSHIPS/docs/PsychArmor_15ThingsCourseNotes.pdf – November 27, 2023
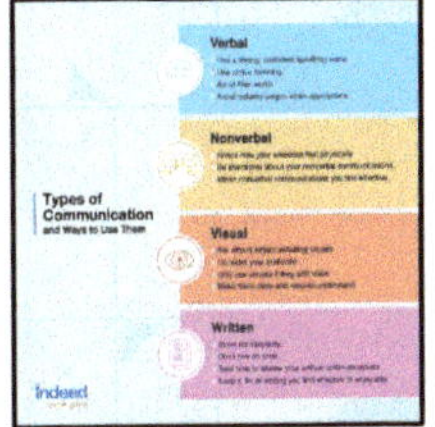	**Communications** 8 Toxic Communication Traps to Avoid: https://www.ramseysolutions.com/business/8-toxic-communication-traps - January 5, 2024 Forms of communication https://www.indeed.com/career-advice/career-development/types-of-communication - January 5, 2024 The Impacts of Positive Communication: https://www.tangramins.com/news-insights/the-impacts-of-positive-communication/ - January 26, 2024

	consequences of ineffective workplace communication: https://www.axioshq.com/insights/5-consequences-of-ineffective-workplace-communication#
	**Gossip** https://villagevoicenews.com/2023/04/19/gossip-the-ugly-side/ - January 29, 2024.
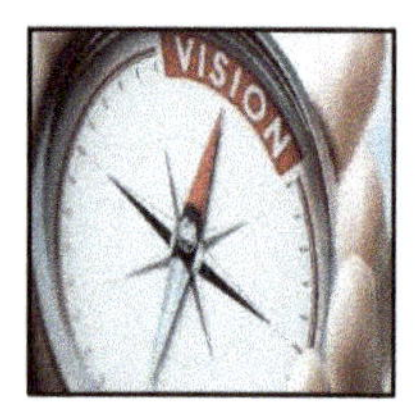	**Vision** https://verticalperformance.us/whats-your-leaders-intent/ - January 29, 2024
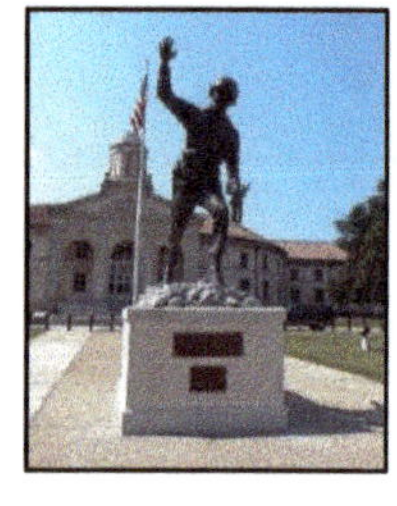	**Iron Mike, U.S. Army Infantry School** https://www.allnineyards.com/2012/05/meet-the-real-iron-mike-this-memorial-day/ - January 10, 2024
	Phases of Leadership https://leading-resources.com// - January 17, 2024 https://studentaffairs.lehigh.edu/content/three-phases-leadership-lehigh - January 17, 2024 https://www.inc.com/joe-procopio/the-three-phases-of-leadership.html

	- January 17, 2024 https://maryalbright.com/4-stages-leadership/ - January 17, 2024 https://bloch.umkc.edu/posts/2019/april/first-rule-of-leadership-everything-is-your-fault.-hopper,-a-bugs-life.html#:~:text=The%20first%20true%20step%20of,of%20personal%20reflection%20and%20growth. - January 19, 2024 https://hbr.org/2004/01/understanding-leadership - January 19, 2024 https://hbr.org/2018/11/ego-is-the-enemy-of-good-leadership - January 22, 20204 https://www.dameleadership.com/research-and-insights/how-a-growth-mindset-shapes-leadership-skills/# - March 16, 2024
	Apprentice, Journeyman, Master Craftsman. https://www.bls.gov/careeroutlook/2017/article/apprenticeships_occupations-and-outlook.htm - January 20, 2024. https://www.indeed.com/career-advice/career-development/what-is-a-journeyman#:~:text=A%20journeyman%20is%20a%20professional,work%20on%20job%20sites%20independently. - January 20, 2024.
	Army Education System usgovcloudapi.net - January 22, 2024. https://www.armywarcollege.edu/programs/mel_1.cfm

	- January 22, 2024. Senior Executive Service: https://www.opm.gov/faq/ses/whats-the-difference-between-ses-st-and-sl-positions-2. - January 25, 2024. The 10,000 Hour Rule: https://www.ncbi.nlm.nih.gov/pmc/articles/PMC4662388/ - January 25, 2024
	DEEP ATTACK 'Deep Attack showcases major MLRS investment' - Article - December 5, 2002 - The Lawton Constitution. https://www.swoknews.com/news/deep-attack-showcases-major-mlrs-investment/article_fb1cdb68-96bc-501d-b162-bbab28487f14.html
	Fort Sill bids farewell to 400 more soldiers - Article - February 8, 2003 - The Lawton Constitution. https://www.swoknews.com/news/fort-sill-bids-farewell-to-400-more-soldiers/article_fc951b6e-a366-55b0-97cf-3035b0ee5a0a.html https://www.americasmarketingmotivator.com/we-need-more-fearless-leaders/quote-about-fear-and-leadership-nelson-mandela/ - February 6, 2024
	Dwight D. Eisenhower https://www.si.edu/object/dwight-d-eisenhower%3Anpg_NPG.94.45 - February 7, 2024.

	**Brené Brown:** Vulnerability in leadership https://www.cultureamp.com/blog/brene-brown-vulnerability-in-leadership - February 12, 2024.
	https://survivingchurch.org/2020/08/10/the-peter-principle-incompetence-and-the-church/ - February 24, 2024
	**Anna Ella Carroll** https://time.com/4382031/this-woman-may-have-helped-win-the-union-win-the-civil-war/ - February 16, 2024
	**Frederick Douglass** https://www.history.com/topics/black-history/frederick-douglass - February 16, 2024
	**President Abraham Lincoln** https://www.whitehouse.gov/about-the-white-house/presidents/abraham-lincoln/ - February 16, 2024.
	**President George W. Bush** https://www.britannica.com/biography/George-W-Bush - February 17, 2024.
	**Billy Graham** https://www.britannica.com/biography/Billy-Graham - February 18, 2024.

	**Sammy Lee Davis, Medal of Honor** https://www.cmohs.org/recipients/sammy-l-davis - January 23, 2024
	**Pastor Craig Groeschel** https://www.craiggroeschel.com/about - February 19, 2024 Craig Groeschel's Top 25 Leadership Quotes: https://globalleadership.org/news-and-updates/craig-groeschels-top-25-leadership-quotes-gls21-faculty-spotlight/ - January 25, 2024.
	**Dave Ramsey** https://www.ramseysolutions.com/dave-ramsey?snid=personalities.ramsey-personalities.dave-ramsey - February 19, 2024
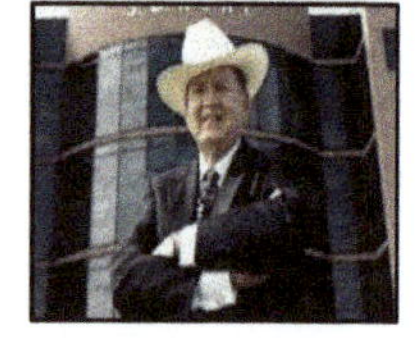	**Johnnie Bryan "J. B." Hunt** https://encyclopediaofarkansas.net/entries/johnnie-bryan-j-b-hunt-4531/ - February 19, 2024.
	**Steve Jobs** https://www.britannica.com/biography/Steve-Jobs - February 19, 2024

	**Colin Powell** https://www.britannica.com/biography/Colin-Powell - February 19, 2024
	**John Emerich Edward Dalberg Acton, 1st Baron Acton** https://www.britannica.com/biography/John-Emerich-Edward-Dalberg-Acton-1st-Baron-Acton - February 19, 2024.
	**Jack Welch** https://www.investopedia.com/terms/j/jack-welch.asp - February 19, 2024.
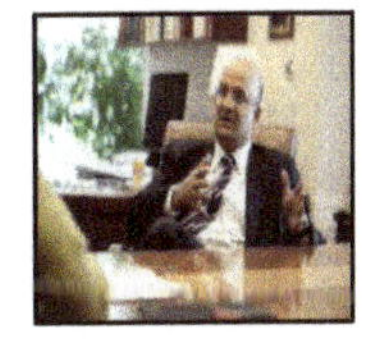	**Dean Nitin Nohria** https://www.hbs.edu/about/history/dean-nitin-nohria - February 19, 2024.an Nitin Nohria
	**George S. Patton** https://www.britannica.com/biography/George-Smith-Patton - February 19, 2024

	**Warren Buffett** https://www.forbes.com/profile/warren-buffett/?sh=1faf91fb4639 - February 19, 2024
	**Harold S Geneen** https://www.encyclopedia.com/humanities/encyclopedias- almanacs-transcripts-and-maps/geneen-harold-sydney –February 19,2024.
	**President Harry S. Truman** https://www.whitehouse.gov/about-the-white-house/presidents/harry-s-truman/ - February 19, 2024.
 	Herschel Walker https://www.georgiaencyclopedia.org/articles/sports-outdoor-recreation/herschel-walker-b-1962/ February 29, 2024
	**Pastor Andy Stanley** https://andystanley.com/ - March 1, 2024
	**Robert Gould Shaw** https://www.battlefields.org/learn/biographies/robert-gould-shaw - March 1, 2024

	Mohandas Gandhi https://www.history.com/topics/asian-history/mahatma-gandhi - March 1, 2024
	President Franklin D. Roosevelt https://www.whitehouse.gov/about-the-white-house/presidents/franklin-d-roosevelt/ - March 1, 2024
	President George Washington https://www.whitehouse.gov/about-the-white-house/presidents/george-washington/ - March 2, 2024
	Lao Tzu https://www.worldhistory.org/Lao-Tzu/ - March 3, 2024.
	Sun Tzu https://www.worldhistory.org/Sun-Tzu/ - May 3, 2024
	Ernest Hemingway https://www.britannica.com/biography/Ernest-Hemingway - May 9, 2024
	Michael McKinney https://servetolead.com/michael-mckinney-authentic-service/ - May 29, 2024

	**William S. Burroughs** https://www.britannica.com/biography/William-S-Burroughs - May 16, 2024
	**Thomas Alva Edison** https://www.loc.gov/collections/edison-company-motion-pictures-and-sound-recordings/articles-and-essays/biography/life-of-thomas-alva-edison - May 18, 2024

BOOKS

- The Holy Bible, English Standard Version (ESV), Containing the Old and New Testaments, Copyright 2001 by Crossway, a publishing ministry of Good News Publishers.

- Blanchard, Ken; Hodges, Phil; Hendry, Phyllis. Lead Like Jesus Revisited. Nashville, Tennessee: W Publishing, 2016.

- The Arbinger Institute. Leadership and Self-Deception (getting out of the box). San Francisco, California: Berrett-Koehler Publishers, Inc, 2010.

- Cordeiro, Wayne. Leading on Empty (Refilling your Tank and Renewing your Passion). Minneapolis, Minnesota: Bethany House, 2009.

- Lt. Gen.(R) Moore, Harold G; Galloway, Joseph L. We Were Soldiers Once… and Young. New York, New York: Random House, 1992.

- Army Regulation 600 - 8 - 10, Leaves and Passes, Headquarters Department of the Army, Washington, DC. 3 June 2020

- Price Jr., Jeffrey. The ENS and Outs of Leadership. Columbus, OH: Independently published (link), 2023.

Dictionaries

Merriam Webster Dictionary:

https://www.merriam-webster.com/ - January 30, 2024

Cambridge Dictionary:

https://dictionary.cambridge.org/us/ - January 30, 2024

The Britannica Dictionary:

https://www.britannica.com/dictionary - January 30, 2024

Trust

- https://www.mindtools.com/ai9794o/how-to-preserve-your-integrity
  - March 28, 2024

- https://www.indeed.com/career-advice/career-development/how-to-build-trust-on-your-team
  - March 28, 2024

- https://hbr.org/2020/05/begin-with-trust
  - March 28, 2024

- Indeed Career Guide
  https://www.indeed.com/career-advice/career-development/building-trust
  - February 17, 2024

- Why are we afraid to lead?
  https://leaddiff.com/fear-of-leading/
  - February 16, 2024)

www.ingramcontent.com/pod-product-compliance
Ingram Content Group UK Ltd.
Pitfield, Milton Keynes, MK11 3LW, UK
UKHW050140280726
14058UKWH00006B/756